CONTENTS

ISBN 0 85147 336 9
First Edition 1972

Printed and bound in Brighton England for Autopress Ltd by G Beard & Son Ltd

VOLVO 160 SERIES 1968-72 AUTOBOOK

Workshop Manual for
Volvo 164 1968-72
Volvo 164E 1971-72

by

Kenneth Ball G I Mech E

and the

Autopress team of Technical Writers

AUTOPRESS LTD GOLDEN LANE BRIGHTON BN1 2QJ ENGLAND

The AUTOBOOK series of Workshop Manuals covers the majority of British and Continental motor cars.

For a full list see the back of this manual.

ACKNOWLEDGEMENT

My thanks are due to Volvo Concessionaires Ltd for their unstinted co-operation and also for supplying data and illustrations.

I am also grateful to a considerable number of owners who have discussed their cars at length and many of whose suggestions have been included in this manual.

Kenneth Ball G I Mech E
Associate Member Guild of Motoring Writers
Ditchling Sussex England.

INTRODUCTION

This do-it-yourself Workshop Manual has been specially written for the owner who wishes to maintain his car in first class condition and to carry out his own servicing and repairs. Considerable savings on garage charges can be made, and one can drive in safety and confidence knowing the work has been done properly.

Comprehensive step-by-step instructions and illustrations are given on all dismantling, overhauling and assembling operations. Certain assemblies require the use of expensive special tools, the purchase of which would be unjustified. In these cases information is included but the reader is recommended to hand the unit to the agent for attention.

Throughout the Manual hints and tips are included which will be found invaluable, and there is an easy to follow fault diagnosis at the end of each chapter.

Whilst every care has been taken to ensure correctness of information it is obviously not possible to guarantee complete freedom from errors or to accept liability arising from such errors or omissions.

Instructions may refer to the righthand or lefthand sides of the vehicle or the components. These are the same as the righthand or lefthand of an observer standing behind the car and looking forward.

CHAPTER 1

THE ENGINE

1 :1 Description

The power unit, designated the B.30 series is an in-line six-cylinder, watercooled overhead unit. It is fitted either with two horizontal-draught Zenith-Stromberg carburetters, designed, in conjunction with a modified induction manifold and the introduction of an exhaust emission control system, to reduce the contents of carbon monoxide and hydrocarbons in the exhaust gases or with electronic fuel injection. The engine is also fitted with an air preheater and a totally enclosed crankcase ventilation system. The fan is of the slip-coupling type and the seven bearing crankshaft has a flywheel damper mounted on its front end (see **FIG 1 :1**).

The single unit cylinder block and crankcase is made of special cast iron, the cylinder bores are machined directly into the block and are surrounded by watercooled jackets. Drillings in the block channel the oil from the pump to the crankshaft, camshaft and overhead rocker gear. The steel crankshaft has ground, case-hardened bearing journals, of which, the rear bearing flange also functions as an axial pilot for the clutch shaft. Oil seals are fitted at the front and rear ends and oilways are drilled through the journals and webs for lubrication of the main and big-end bearings. A gear mounted on the front of the crankshaft is in constant mesh with a similar but larger gear on the camshaft, which it drives at half-speed. The crankshaft end projecting through the gear carries a flywheel damper and also a pulley which drives a V-belt around similar pulleys mounted on the alternator and water pump and fan. The main and big-end bearing liners, which are renewable, consist of a steel saddle the concave section of which is coated with an indium and lead/bronze material.

The connecting rods are of drop-forged steel fitted with renewable small-end bushes, the gudgeon pins are fully floating. The pistons are made of light alloy and have two compression rings and one oil scraper ring. The top compression ring is chromed to reduce cylinder wear.

The camshaft, made of special alloy cast iron, is carried in four uniform diameter bearings, end thrust is taken up by a bronze axial washer located at the front end of the camshaft. The tappets are actuated directly by the cams and transfer movement to the valves by means of push-rods and rocker arms.

The camshaft, through an integral skew gear, drives the distributor and oil pump. The oil pump is of the gear type and is fitted under the crankshaft in the sump, a spring-loaded relief valve is incorporated in the body of the pump

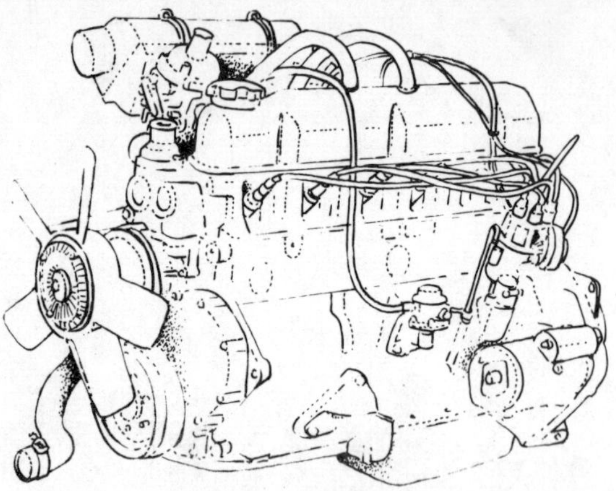

FIG 1 : 1 The B 30 A engine viewed from the left

to allow surplus oil to drain back into the crankcase sump. A fullflow oil filter is screwed into the cylinder block, it is manufactured as a single unit and is only renewable as such. The oil passes through the filter directly from the pump, the filter element is made of special paper. In the event of a blockage in the element, due to infrequent changes of oil, a bypass valve allows unfiltered oil to circulate through the system.

A cut-away illustration of the working parts of the engine is shown in **FIG 1 : 2**.

With a new or reconditioned engine the oil should be changed after the first 1500 miles (2500 km) with subsequent changes at every 6000 miles (10,000 km). It should be drained immediately after the car has been driven, whilst the engine is still warm, from the drain plug at the bottom of the sump. Allow the oil to drain fully before replacing the plug and fill up the sump through the filter cap orifice in the rocker gear cover. Refer to **Technical Data** at the back of this manual for information regarding the different oil grades to use depending on the prevailing weather conditions and environment in which the car is driven. The quantity of oil required to fill to the correct level is 9.15 pints (10.97 US pints) or 5.2 litres. If the oil filter is changed at the same time, fill up with 10.56 pints (12.66 US pints) or 6 litres.

1 : 2 Removing and refitting the engine

To remove the engine from the frame will also necessitate the removal of the gearbox, although the gearbox can be removed separately for the purpose of dismantling as described in **Chapter 6**. A hoist and lifting attachment will be required and safety stands to support the front of the car whilst working underneath. A ramp set or a pit would also be suitable.

1 Disconnect the positive lead from the battery. Set the heater control lever inside the car to maximum heat, open the drain cock at the cylinder block and disconnect the lower hose at the radiator. This will drain off the coolant.

2 Remove the bonnet from the car, disconnecting it at the hinge point. Remove the upper radiator hose, disconnect and remove the expansion tank from the side of the radiator. Remove the bolts from the radiator

Key to Fig 1 : 2 1 Valve guide 2 Valve spring 3 Air preheating flap 4 Valve guide seal 5 Valve collet 6 Intake valve 7 By-pass valve 8 Temperature compensator 9 Exhaust valve 10 Secondary throttle 11 Front carburetter 12 Air cleaner 13 Manifold pipe 14 Bracket 15 Hose for fresh air supply 16 Nipple 17 Fuel hose 18 Carburetter control 19 Flame protector 20 Rear carburetter 21 Cylinder head gasket 22 Hose for crankcase gases 23 Vacuum hose for ignition/distributor 24 Rocker arm shaft 25 Spring 26 Adjusting device 27 Rocker arm 28 Bearing bracket 29 Thrust rod 30 Cable terminal 31 Rubber seal 32 Rubber seal 33 Choke wire 34 Vacuum hose for negative vacuum adjustment 35 Rocker arm casing 36 Ignition cable to ignition coil 37 Cylinder head 38 Distributor 39 Oil dipstick 40 Vacuum governor 41 Valve tappet 42 Retainer 43 Cylinder block 44 Gear heel 45 Bush 46 Rubber lip seal 47 Flywheel 48 Sealing flange 49 Main bearing bolt 50 Delivery pipe 51 Coverplate 52 Oil pump 53 Sump 54 Cap 55 Connecting rod 56 Splash plate 57 Main bearing 58 Bush 59 Gudgeon pin 60 Circlip 61 Camshaft 62 Piston 63 Piston rings 64 Crankshaft 65 Thrust washer 66 Spacer ring 67 Camshaft rear 68 Nut 69 Seal 70 Crankshaft gear 71 Rubber lip seal 72 Polygon hub 73 Washer 74 Pulley 76 Flywheel damper 78 Coolant pipe 79 Fan blade 80 Pulley 81 Flange 82 Washer 83 Centre bolt 84 Fan coupling 85 Water pump 86 Alternator 87 Tensioner 88 Water distributor pipe 89 Thermostat

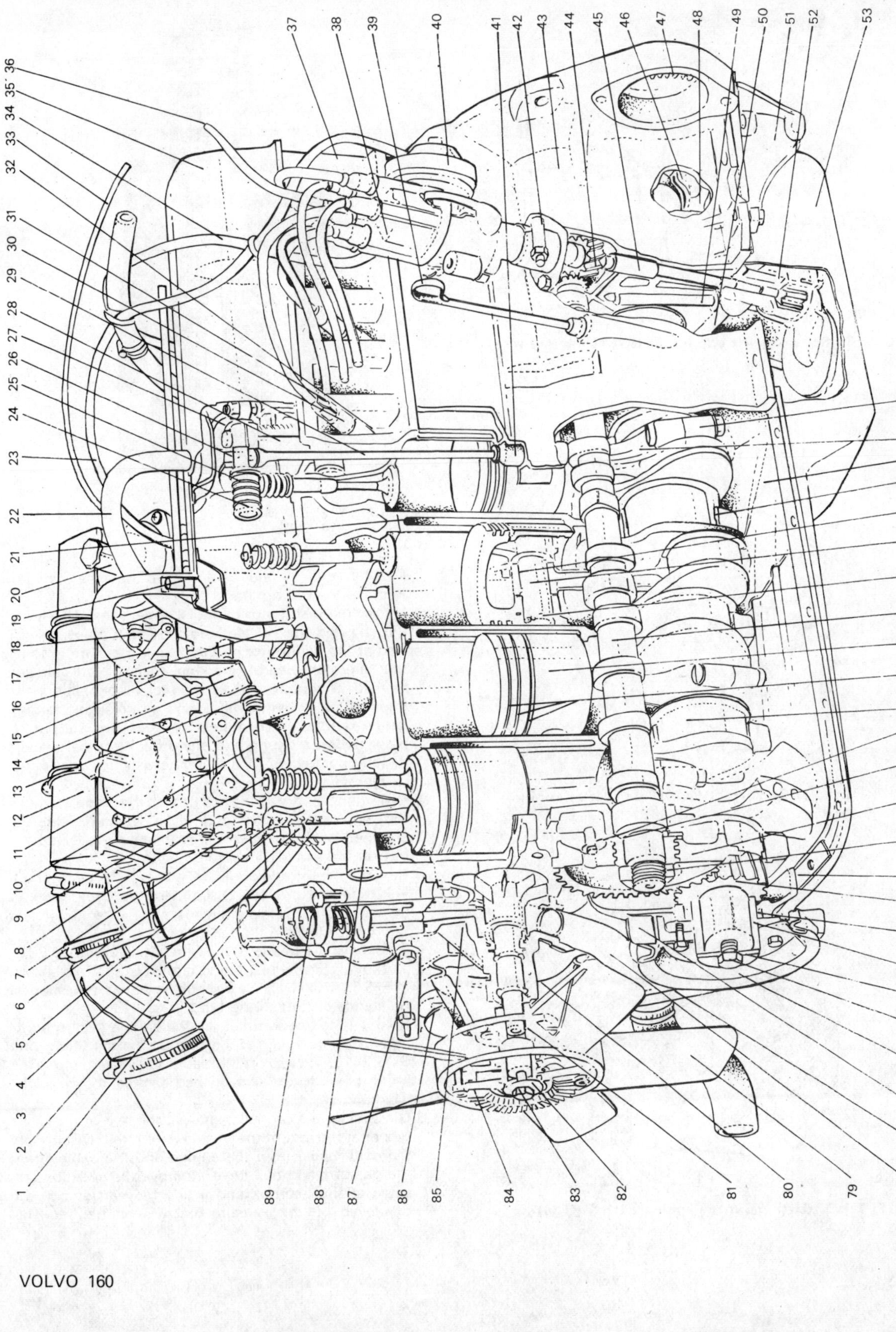

FIG 1:2 Part section view of B 30 A engine

FIG 1:3 Showing lifting lug SVO 2811 on front of engine

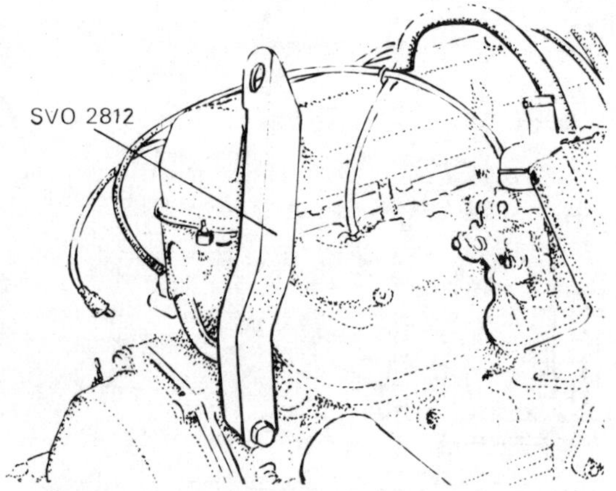

FIG 1:4 Lifting arm SVO 2812 on rear of engine

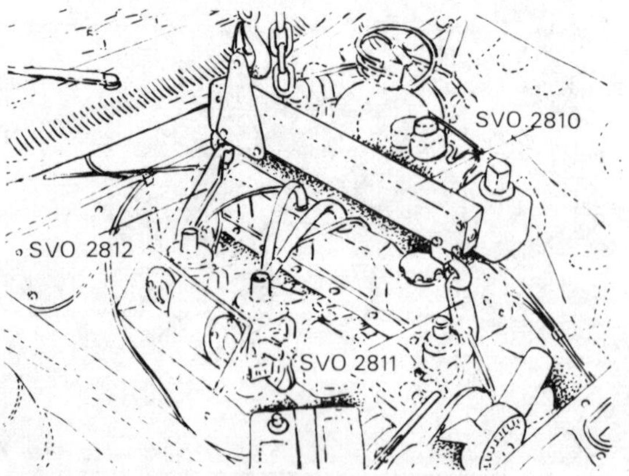

FIG 1:5 Lifting out the engine with SVO 2810

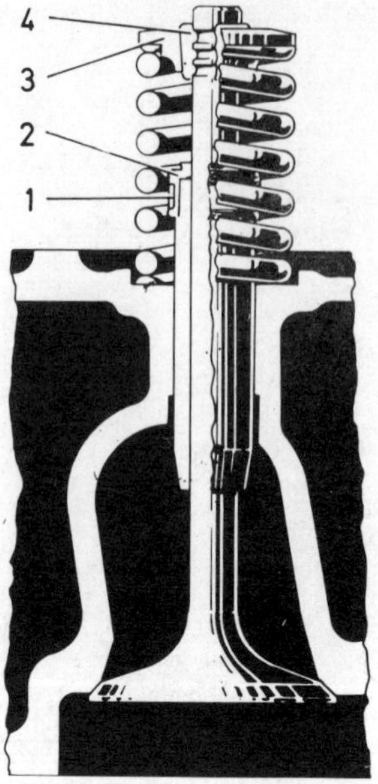

FIG 1:6 A valve assembly

Key to Fig 1:6 1 Metal ring 2 Rubber seal 3 Spring retainer 4 Split collet

and fan casing and carefully lift out the radiator. Remove the bottom hose.

3 Unclip the distributor cap, disconnect the HT lead to the coil and the HT leads to the spark plugs, the LT lead at the distributor, the cables at the starter motor, the alternator leads, marking them if not already marked or foolproofed for correct reconnection, the transducers for temperature and oil pressure warning lamps and/or transmitters where the output is presented at a gauge and any other electrical circuits directly connected to the engine which would affect its removal.

4 Disconnect and plug the fuel hose to the pump. Remove the air cleaner cover and lift it forward with the attached hose. Remove the preheating plate and the nuts at the exhaust manifold flange.

5 Remove the throttle control shaft from the pedal shaft, link rods and bracket. Disconnect the choke wire at the carburetter, the vacuum hoses to the servo unit and the water hoses to the heater unit.

6 Refer to **FIG 1:3** and fit the front lifting arm SVO.2811 as shown. Fit the rear lifting arm SVO.2812 as shown in **FIG 1:4**. Jack up the front of the vehicle and support on stands or firm strong blocks.

7 Remove the lower nuts from the engine front mountings. Refer to **FIG 1:5** and fit the engine lifting unit SVO.2810, slacken off the clamp screws and move the lifting block to the rear of the beam as shown in the illustration.

8 Disconnect the propeller shaft at the rear of the gearbox or at the rear of the overdrive, if fitted. Disconnect the earth cable from the engine and the cables from the gearbox and overdrive. Remove the speedometer cable at the gearbox and inside the car remove the gearlever, but first ensure that it is in neutral. This

instruction does not apply to automatic transmissions but the selector controls should be disconnected at the control shaft and at the reinforcing bracket under the oil pan. Remove also the dipstick and the filler pipe clamp.

9 Uncouple the exhaust pipe clamp from its bracket. Remove the gearbox support member and the rubber block and bracket from the gearbox.

10 Remove the pin from the fork and the clutch release lever and disconnect the wire sleeve from the clutch housing.

11 Hoist the engine with the lifting unit and by adjusting the block on the lifting beam, lower the rear end of the engine. Pull the engine forward across the front member, raising it at the same time. Level out the engine and gearbox and pull the entire unit forwards.

Refitting:

Refit the engine into the car by following the removal operations in reverse sequence but noting the following points:

1 When pushing the engine forward make sure the oil filter does not foul the exhaust.

2 Fit the rubber block and bracket to the gearbox, but do not tighten the bolts fully until the support member has been fitted, the propeller shaft reconnected, the front support is secured and the exhaust manifold and pipe clamps are reconnected.

3 Adjust the clutch as described in **Chapter 5**.

4 Fill with coolant and engine oil.

1:3 Dismantling the engine

Many of the operations which the owner/driver will wish to do for himself will not require the removal or the total dismantling of the engine, but as these may be part of a general overhaul it will be convenient to describe the order in which the various components should be dismantled. Instructions concerning the individual components will be given under their respective headings.

Having removed the engine from the car, transfer it to a suitable stand and drain the oil from the sump.

Remove the starter motor and the reinforcing plate on the lower front edge of the flywheel housing. Unbolt the flywheel housing and remove it together with the gearbox. Remove the clutch and flywheel, not forgetting to mark them to ensure later reinstallation in the same positions.

Remove the alternator, water pump, distributor, rocker cover and the rocker gear. Remove the two carburetters with the manifolds and then take off the cylinder head.

Remove the timing gear cover and the timing gears, then take out the camshaft and the oil nozzle.

Turn the engine over and remove the oil sump, rear sealing flange and the oil pump with strainer. Unbolt and withdraw the connecting rod and piston assemblies, being careful to replace each big-end cap and bearing shell correctly on its own connecting rod.

With the engine upside down, unbolt the main bearing caps and remove the crankshaft, replacing the caps correctly in their respective positions.

Wash all parts thoroughly, being careful not to use any caustic solutions when dealing with light-alloy castings such as pistons or bearing shells. Clean out all oilways and blow dry with compressed air.

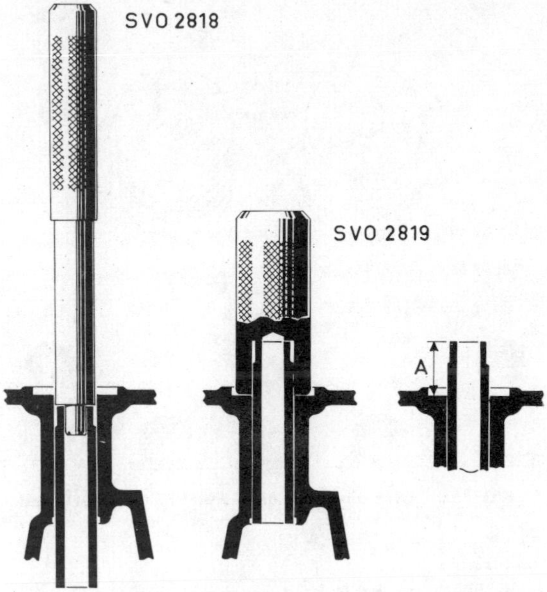

FIG 1:7 Replacing valve guides A=.689 inch (17.5 mm)

1:4 Servicing the cylinder head and valves

Drain off the cooling system, then remove the choke wire and all the hoses from the intake manifold, carburetter and air cleaner casing. Remove the throttle control shaft from the pedal shaft, the link rods and bracket.

Remove the heat control valve hose from the engine and also the upper radiator hose.

Take the ignition leads off the sparking plugs and the electric lead from the temperature transmitter. Unscrew the preheating plate from the exhaust manifold and then securing nuts from the exhaust manifold flange.

Remove the tensioning plate for the alternator from the cylinder head.

Remove the valve cover and then unbolt and remove the rocker shaft assembly. Lift out the pushrods and either mark them or store them so as to ensure replacement in their original positions.

Remove the cylinder head bolts and lift off the head and the joint gasket and clean off all traces of oil and dirt.

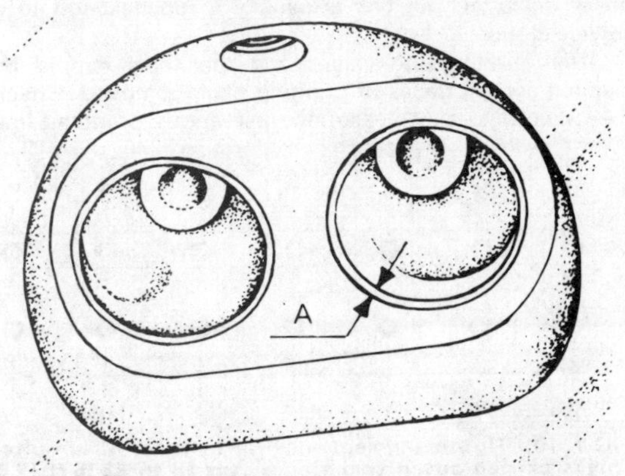

FIG 1:8 Checking a valve seat A=.08 inch (2 mm)

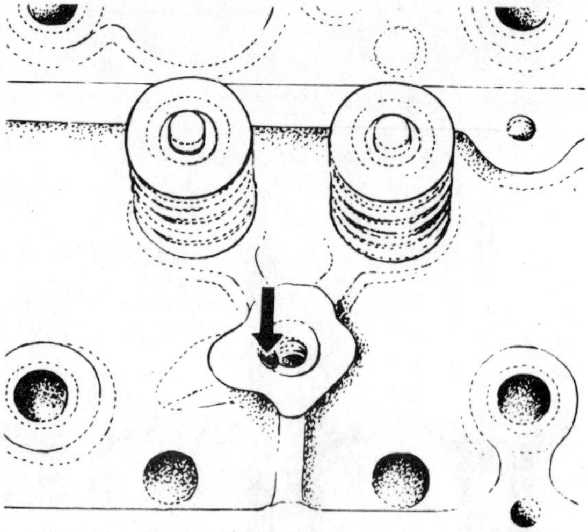

FIG 1:9 Oil hole for rocker shaft in cylinder head

Valves:

Place the head face downwards on a clean bench and by means of a suitable spring compressing tool remove each valve and spring assembly, again noting the position each one occupied. The valves are secured in position by an arrangement of cup washer and split collets as shown in **FIG 1:6**. Do not forget the rubber oil seal.

Remove all carbon deposits from the valves, combustion chambers and ports, then measure the clearance between the valve stem and the guide. This should not exceed .006 inch (.15 mm), and the maximum permissible wear on a valve stem is .0008 inch (.02 mm).

Worn valve guides should be pressed out using tool SVO.2818 and new guides pressed in with tool SVO.2819 which also gives the correct depth as shown in **FIG 1:7**.

Grind the valves on to their seats using a medium grade carborundum paste and finishing with a fine grade. A suction cup tool is used for this operation with a rotary movement and occasionally lifting the valve off its seat. When finished the seats on both head and valve should have a smooth matt grey finish at an angle of 45 deg. and a width of .08 inch (2 mm) (see **FIG 1:8**). If either surface is badly pitted it may be necessary to cut them with a miller or cutter, but this is usually a job best left to a service station.

After grinding the valves and the seats should be cleaned and all traces of grinding paste removed. Check the valve springs by measuring their length. Standing free

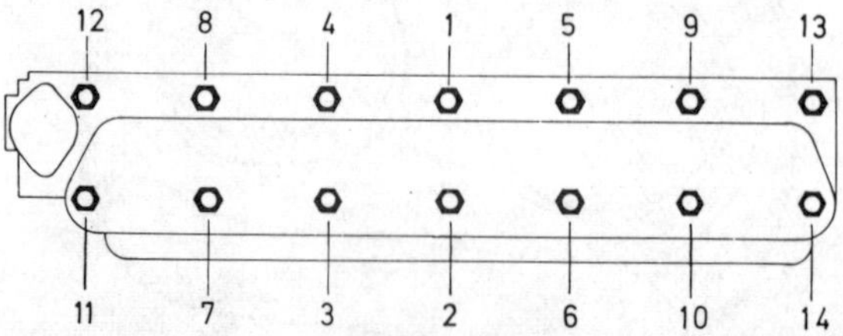

FIG 1:10 Tightening sequence for cylinder head bolts. This is carried out in two stages: 1st 18 to 22 lb ft (2.5 to 3 kgm), 2nd 61 to 69 lb ft (8.5 to 9.5 kgm)

this should be 1.77 inch (45 mm), while with a loading of 56 lb the length should be 1.54 inch (39 mm).

Reassemble all the valves in the head and refit the head as follows:

Refitting the cylinder head:

This is a reversal of the removal procedure after checking that the head, block, pistons and bores are all clean and in good condition.

Check that the oilway for the rocker shaft mechanism is clean (see **FIG 1:9**). Mount the manifold on to the cylinder head, place a new gasket in position and fit the cylinder head. Fit the cylinder head bolts and tighten them in two stages as detailed in **FIG 1:10**. When lowering the cylinder head into position it will be helpful if guide pins SVO.2435 are first inserted into two of the holes.

Replace the pushrods, fit the rocker shaft assembly and adjust the valve clearances. These are the same for both inlet and exhaust valves and it should be noted that the clearance is the same whether the engine is hot or cold.

A simple way to adjust the clearances, which is done by means of the conventional adjusting screw on the end of the rocker arm, is to turn the engine until No. 1 piston (front) is at TDC on the compression stroke. In this position valves 1, 2, 3, 6, 7, and 10 (counted from the front) are adjusted, then turn the engine until No. 6 piston is at TDC and adjust valves 4, 5, 8, 9, 11 and 12. The correct clearance is .020 to .022 inch (.50 to .55 mm).

Fit the remaining components and fill the cooling system. Start up the engine and run it while checking that everything is functioning correctly.

Stop the engine and check the tightness of the cylinder head bolts, noting that if these have to be moved it may be necessary to readjust the valve clearances.

1:5 The cylinder block

After removing the head, clean and examine the top surface for any signs of cracking or distortion.

Remove the carbon ridge at the upper ends of the cylinder bores and polish. Examine the bores for signs of scoring or corrosion and then, with a special dial indicator, measure the bores at top, centre and bottom.

Should the bores show that the differences between the diameters measured at 90 deg. (ovality), or between the bores at top, centre and bottom of the cylinders exceed .010 inch, a rebore will be required. This is a specialist job necessitating equipment not normally available to an owner/mechanic. It must therefore, be placed out with an approved Volvo agent who will also supply the oversize pistons and rings necessitated by reboring.

Note that in production there is always a slight difference in the original bore diameters caused by wear in the hones during the final lapping operations. The six cylinders are lapped simultaneously in a special machine and the wear on the hones is not always identical. As a result, after honing, pistons are matched with the bores and each bears a classification letter stamped on the piston head and adjacent to the bore on the block (see **FIG 1:11**).

Check that all oilways in the cylinder block are clear and unobstructed and, if clearing has to be carried out, flush through the oilways in turn with a high pressure oil jet to clear out any gritty deposits.

Clean all gasket faces, particularly those round the manifold ports and water joint flanges, and check for flatness.

1 :6 Crankshaft and flywheel

Clean the crankshalt and examine the bearing surfaces, checking each in turn with a micrometer to ensure that it is perfectly round. Out of roundness on the main bearings must not exceed .002 inch or on the big-end bearings .003 inch. If these values are exceeded, the crankshaft must be reground, again a specialist task which must be passed to a Volvo agent with the necessary equipment and skills. Regrinding necessitates the fitting of oversize bearing shells and these will be supplied by the agent with the reground crankshaft. In each case fit the shells to the bearing indicated by the agent.

Examine the flywheel for three things, smooth, unscored clutch bearing face, undamaged starter ring gear and pilot bearing for the gearbox input shaft. A lightly worn clutch bearing face may be cleaned up by hand honing but excessive scoring necessitates a regrind. The amount of metal removed is limited, otherwise clutch operation can be impaired, so regrinding of the flywheel face should be passed to a Volvo agent when it is necessary.

The ring gear is a shrink fit on the flywheel. If the ring gear is damaged or the teeth are worn or broken, drill through the root of the gear teeth at diametrically opposite points and fracture the ring by applying a cold chisel at the two points. Do not drill into the metal of the flywheel itself. Take the new ring (the renewal will not be undertaken until the replacement ring has been obtained, of course), check that it will not fit over the flywheel and then place in an oven set to 220°C and allow to soak. Do not heat by a flame as the ring is surface hardened and if the temperature is raised much above 220°C locally, the casing will be softened and the ultimate wear will be rapid.

Clean the seating on the flywheel and, if possible, place in a refrigerator for an hour or so. Remove both ring and flywheel and quickly seat the ring in position holding it in place with clamps until both ring and flywheel are down to ambient temperature. After fitting, both flywheel and crankshaft, as an assembly, must be rebalanced.

To remove the pilot bearing, two methods are possible. In the first, the bearing can be extracted by means of a special puller such as Volvo tool SVO.4090. Alternatively, obtain a circular drift, which will just fit inside the bearing ring, fill the ring and cavity behind with a thick grease, insert the drift in the hole and give it a sharp blow with a hammer. The grease behind the bearing will expel the bearing from its seating. After cleaning and inspection repack the race with a heat-resistant grease and reinstall driving home by means of a hollow drift bearing on the outer ring of the race.

Replacing the crankshaft rear oil seal:

If this operation is necessary without a complete strip down, the gearbox, clutch and flywheel must first be removed from the engine and the two bolts for the oil sump in the sealing flange. It is also advisable to slacken one of the two bolts on each side so that oil sump pressure on the sealing flange will be reduced. Remove the sealing flange.

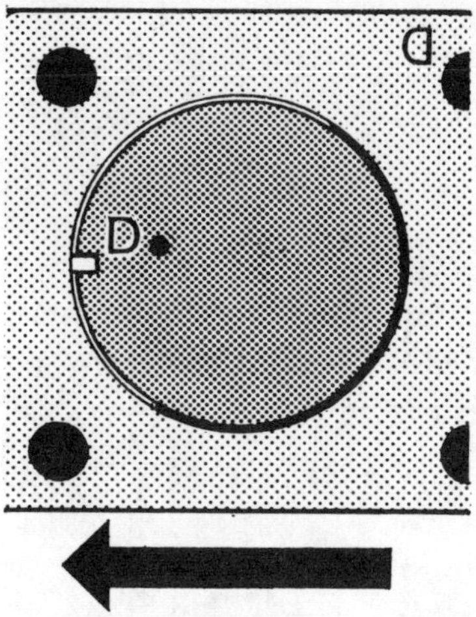

FIG 1:11 Markings on piston and cylinder block. Arrow indicates front of engine.

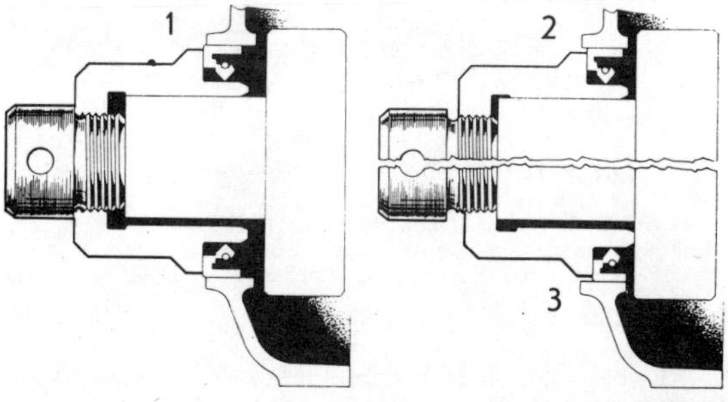

FIG 1:12 Pressing in new sealing ring with tool SVO 2817

Key to Fig 1:12 1 Key screwed fully in 2 Key screwed out two turns 3 Key screwed fully out

FIG 1:13 Rear end of engine showing position of sealing flange and rings

Key to Fig 1:13 1 Dowel pin 2 Core plug 3 Sealing flange 4 Circlip 5 Pilot bearing 6 Sealing ring 7 Crankshaft 8 Plug 9 Dowel pin

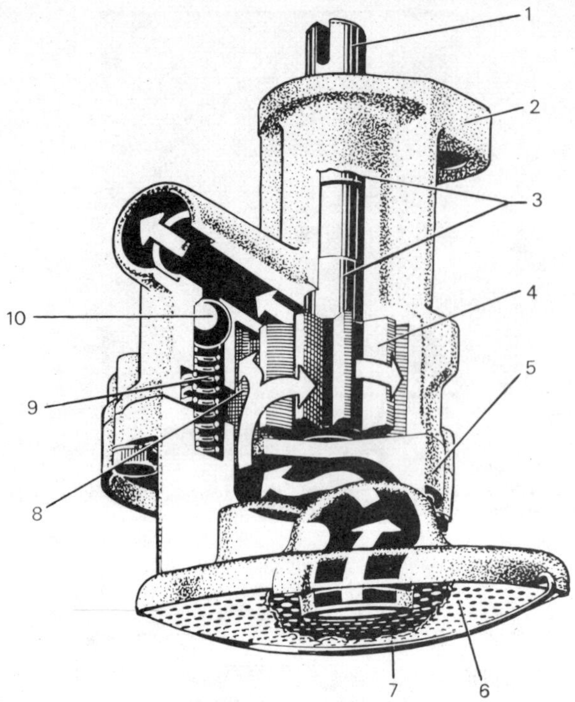

FIG 1:14 Part sectional view of oil pump

Key to Fig 1:14 1 Drive shaft 2 Pump body 3 Bushes 4 Driving gear 5 Cover 6 Strainer 7 Retainer clip 8 Driven gear 9 Spring for relief valve 10 Valve ball

The old seal may be pressed out using the drift for tool SVO.2817 which is also used for pressing in the new sealing ring as shown in **FIG 1:12**, which also shows the three positions possible. With a new crankshaft the seal should be fitted in its outer position (centre bolt fully screwed in), but with a worn crankshaft it should be fitted with the centre bolt screwed out a couple of turns or completely.

Fit the sealing flange, having first cleaned it thoroughly and a new gasket. The sealing ring should be well oiled and when the flange is mounted the fingers should be used to fit on the sealing lip (see **FIG 1:13**).

1:7 Servicing pistons and rings

Clean and check each piston assembly for signs of wear arising out of the skirt bearing on the sides of the cylinder bores. Examine the rings fo fit in the piston grooves and check that none are broken. Should it be necessary to replace a ring, first check that it is properly gapped by inserting it in the cylinder bore and checking that the gap between the ends is between .016 to .022 inch with a feeler gauge.

Next, check that the clearance in the groove is between .002 and .003 inch on the two upper compression rings and .002 inch on the scraper ring. Fit the rings into position using a proper ring insertion tool and arrange the gaps so that they are displaced 120 deg. apart round the circumference.

Clean and polish the heads of the pistons and then turn attention to the gudgeon pin and connecting rod. The gudgeon pin is fully floating in both the little-end of the connecting rod and in the piston, being centred by circlips inserted in the piston bores.

To remove the gudgeon pin, extract the circlips and extract the gudgeon pin. Before final separation, make sure that the piston is identified with the connecting rod so that it cannot be replaced 180 deg. out. Separate the connecting rod from the piston and examine it for straightness and tendency to twist. Use a special gauge or any other method which will give comparable results. The little-end bush is a press-fit in the connecting rod and, should it be worn, drive the old one out and replace the new one in a press, making sure that the replacement bush oil hole is correctly aligned with that in the little-end.

If the gudgeon pin is a tight fit in the new bush, carefully ream it out with a special reamer. Refit the connecting rod to the piston, the right way round, and reinsert the circlips. Examine the big-end shell bearings for scoring or wear and replace as necessary. Do not attempt to scrape the bearing surfaces of shells and never file the bearing caps to obtain a tighter fit of worn shells. Check the clearance between the big-end and crankshaft bearings by means of Plastigage if necessary as a means of determining the suitability of the shells for each position.

1:8 Oil pump and strainer

The oil pump is a conventional gear pair meshed within a housing, the oil flowing through from the inlet side, around the outer peripheries of each gear, to the outlet side within the close fitting figure-of-eight cavity in the housing. The driving gear is coupled by a dog on the end of the shaft to the distributor shaft both of which are driven by skew gears from the camshalt. A bypass relief valve between inlet and outlet channels opens to circulate the oil within the pump should the outlet become blocked (see **FIG 1:14**).

The perforated foot strainer is secured in the pump cover by a wire clip and removal of the strainer gives access to the four cross-head screws securing the cover to the pump body. Removal of the cover gives access to the pump gears and relief valve and no special instructions are needed for the cleaning and reassembly. The pump is secured to the underside of the cylinder block and crankcase by a single bolt.

After the pump has been dismantled and cleared, check that all the parts are in good condition. The relief valve spring should have a free length of 1.54 inch (39.0 mm), or .83 inch (21.0 mm) when loaded with 15.4 lb $\pm$1.7 lb.

Check the tooth flank clearance as shown in **FIG 1:15**. This should be between .006 and .014 inch (.15 to .35 mm). End float should be between .0008 and .0040 inch (.02 to .10 mm).

Any wear beyond these limits should be rectified by fitting new parts.

The sealing rings at the ends of the delivery pipe are specially made for this application and it is important that only the official parts be used. The delivery pipe must be clamped in its correct position first in the oil pump and then the oil pump and pipe together clamped against the block. The pump connecting flange should be flush against the block before being tightened (see **FIG 1:16**).

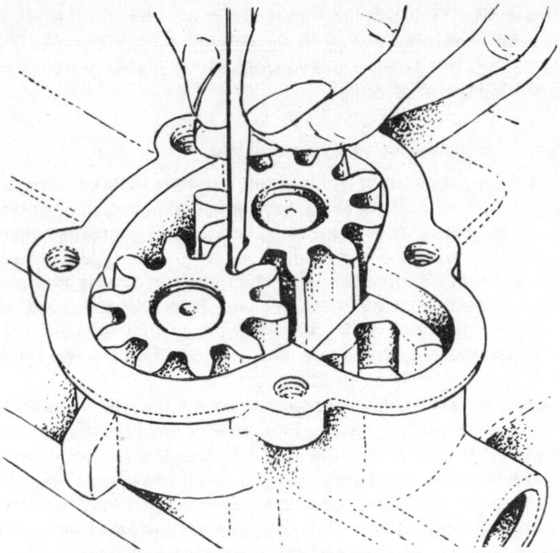

FIG 1:15 Measuring tooth flank clearance

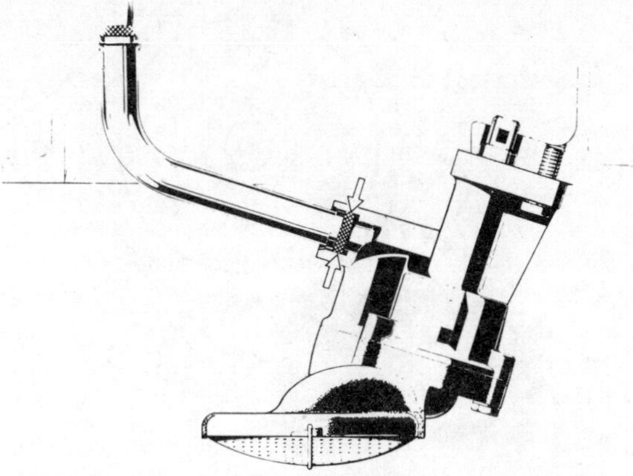

FIG 1:16 Oil pump delivery pipe sealing rings

Refitting the oil pump:

Turn the engine until No. 1 piston is at TDC when the drive shalt will appear as in **FIG 1:17** which is the correct position when refitting the distributor and oil pump.

Make sure that the drive shaft drops completely into its slot in the pump shaft.

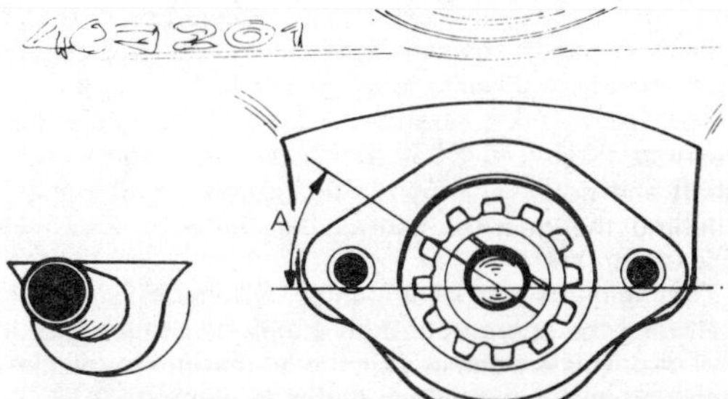

FIG 1:17 Fitting position of oil pump and distributor drive shaft A=35°

1:9 Oil filter

The oil filter, shown in section in **FIG 1:18** is a fullflow type manufactured as a single unit and screwed directly into the cylinder block. The filter element is made of specially prepared paper and if this should become blocked to the extent that oil flow is seriously limited there is a bypass valve which passes on the oil unfiltered and so prevents a complete breakdown in the engine lubrication.

Every 6000 miles the oil filter should be unscrewed, discarded and a new one screwed in firmly by hand.

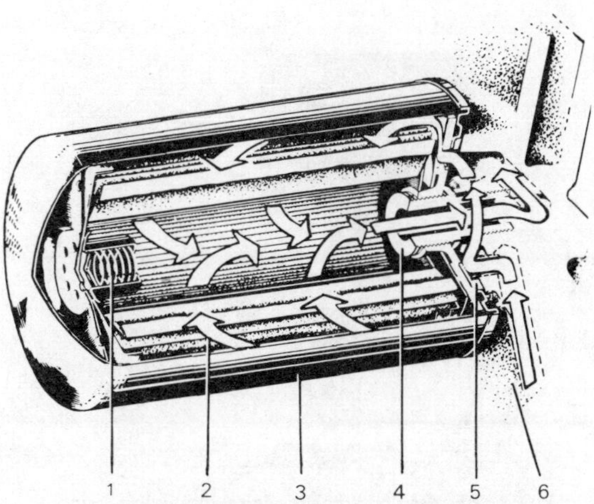

FIG 1:18 Section through oil filter

Key to Fig 1:18 1 Overflow valve 2 Element 3 Body 4 Nipple 5 Gasket 6 Cylinder block

1:10 The timing gear

If access to the timing gears and camshaft is required other than as part of a complete stripdown, empty the cooling system and remove the radiator and radiator grille remove the fan belt and fan. Unscrew the bolts and remove the pulley and flywheel damper.

Remove the centre bolt and take off the polygon hub with tool SVO.2814. Remove the securing bolts and lift off the timing gear casing taking care not to damage the sump gasket. This will disclose the timing gears as in **FIG 1:19**. It may be noted here than when the timing gear marks are opposite each other No. 6 piston is at TDC in the firing position.

Remove the camshaft nut and pull off the gear using tool SVO.2250. Pull off the crankshaft gear with tool SVO.2822. Unscrew the oil nozzle and see that it is clean before refitting as the two gear wheels receive their lubrication from it.

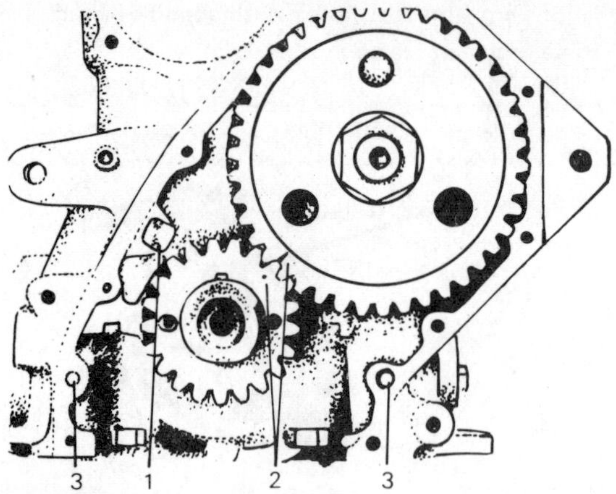

FIG 1:19 Showing timing marks on crankshaft and camshaft gear wheels

Key to Fig 1:19 1 Oil nozzle 2 Markings 3 Dowel pin

Refitting is a reversal of the above procedure, but take care not to press the camshaft backwards so that the sealing washer at the rear end is loosened. The camshaft nut should be tightened to 94 to 108 lb ft.

The tooth flank clearance on the two gears should be between .0016 and .0032 inch (.04 to .08 mm) and the camshalt end float, which is determined by the spacing ring behind the gear, should be .0008 to .0024 inch (.02 to .06 mm).

The timing gear cover is located by two dowel pins, and before fitting the polygon hub it may be desirable to fit a new oil seal. This is done in a similar manner to the crankshaft rear oil seal described earlier in **Section 1:6**.

Before fitting the sliding surfaces of the polygon hub they should be well greased and note the centre punch marks on the crankshaft end and the polygon hub. The centre bolt is tightened to 50 to 57 lb ft.

The flywheel damper and pulley can only be fitted in one position as the bolt holes are not symmetrical.

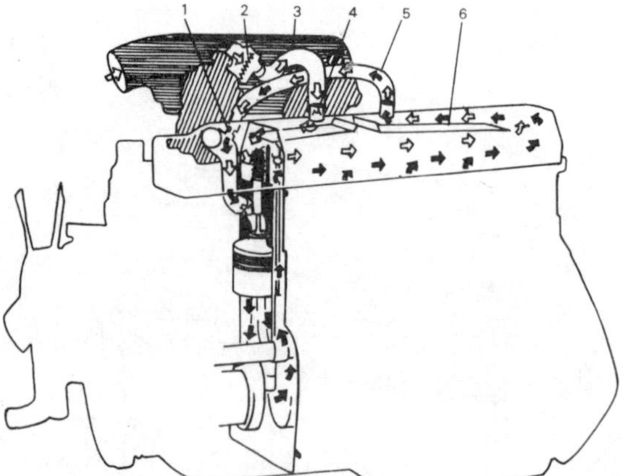

FIG 1:20 Positive crankcase ventilation system

Key to Fig 1:20 1 Nipple 2 Air cleaner 3 Hose for fresh air supply 4 Flame arrestor 5 Hose for crankcase gases 6 Plate

Fit the fan belt and tension it so that the friction torque of the fan pulley in the direction of rotation is 8.7 to 12.3 lb ft. Use a torque wrench with suitable graduation on the alternator pulley nut.

1:11 Reassemgling the engine

When reassembling the engine, follow the instructions given for the individual components earlier in this chapter.

First install the crankshalt, checking that the main bearings, which are marked from 1 to 7, are positioned correctly in accordance with the numbers on the bearing caps. Check that all the parts are clean and lubricate all sliding parts well with oil before assembly. Always use new gaskets, splitpins and lockwashers. Tighten the bolts to a torque of 87 to 94 lb ft.

The pistons and connecting rods are inserted into their bores from above, having first taken off the bearing caps and shells. Note that the small slot in the piston crown faces forward and use a clamp to hold the piston rings in place during the operation as failure to do so may result in a broken ring. Ensure that the ring gaps are not adjacent to each other but spaced out around the piston.

Insert the bearing shells and fit the big-end caps which are numbered 1 to 6 in their correct positions and tighten the bolts to a torque of 38 to 42 lb lt. Check that the crankshaft assembly rotates smoothly as this operation proceeds so that a tight bearing may be spotted before it is too late to identify.

Fit the oil pump, camshaft and crankshaft gears as previously described. Fit the flywheel, tightening the securing bolts to a torque of 36 to 40 lb ft.

Use a new gasket and fit the cylinder head, observing the correct tightening sequence in two stages. Insert the pushrods and fit the rocker gear, not forgetting to check that the oil feed hole is clear. Adjust the valve clearances as described in **Section 1:4**.

Continue assembly in the reverse order of dismantling and reinstall the engine as described in **Section 1:2**.

1:12 Positive crankcase ventilation

In order to reduce air pollution by escaping crankcase gases, arrangements are made to have them inhaled into the engine through the intake manifold and take part in the combustion process. The installation is shown in **FIG 1:20**.

The hose 5 is connected between the valve cover and the inlet manifold, being coupled to the latter through a calibrated nipple 1. Also connected to the valve cover and linking it with the air cleaner is the hose 3, which provides a fresh air supply to the engine. This hose includes a flame trap 4 consisting of a metal filter element.

The depression in the inlet manifold sucks in the crankcase gases through the hose 5 while fresh air is admitted through the hose 3 after being filtered and circulated by the action of the plates 6.

At full load or when a large air flow is required, the direction of flow in the hose 3 is reversed and both hoses are used to extract the fumes.

Maintenance required is restricted to unscrewing the nipple 1 and cleaning it at intervals of about 25,000 miles (40,000 km). At the same time the condition of the hoses should be checked and any found to be faulty should be renewed.

1:13 Fault diagnosis

(a) Engine will not start

1 Flat battery
2 Loose or corroded battery terminals
3 Faulty starter switch
4 Faulty starter motor
5 Faulty earth connection to the engine or battery
6 Disconnected HT lead from distributor to coil
7 Broken HT pencil in distributor cap
8 Broken make-and-break spring
9 Dirty make-and-break contacts
10 Faulty ignition coil
11 Faulty capacitor
12 Ignition timing slipped
13 Crossed over HT leads to plugs
14 Dirty sparking plugs
15 Choked fuel line or carburetter jets
16 Faulty fuel pump or filter
17 Empty fuel tank
18 Air lock in fuel line
19 Water in carburetter
20 Open circuit in starter solenoid
21 Condensation on leads, plugs or in distributor cap

(b) Engine fires, then stalls

1 Idling jet out of adjustment
2 Choke not in use
3 Slow-running adjustment too fine
4 Dirty or over-gapped plugs

(c) Engine runs but without power

1 Ignition timing slipped
2 Automatic advance systems inoperative
3 Valve springs weak
4 Worn distributor cam
5 Vacuum advance line disconnected or punctured
6 Tappet clearance slipped
7 Valve faced burned

(d) Engine runs but fades with speed or load

1 Fuel starvation through faulty pump
2 Fuel starvation through faulty needle setting
3 Fuel starvation through choked filters
4 Fuel starvation through blockage in fuel line

(e) Engine fires erratically on idling

1 Wrong idling jet fitted
2 Faulty plug
3 Weak valve spring on one cylinder
4 Incorrect tappet adjustment on one cylinder

(f) Engine 'spits'

1 Water in carburetter
2 Leaking head gasket

(g) Engine 'Pinks'

1 Wrong octane fuel
2 Engine timing too far advanced

(h) Engine overheats

1 Low water in radiator
2 Slipping fan belt
3 Ignition too far retarded
4 Blocked tubes in radiator
5 Faulty thermostat
6 Blown head gasket

(i) Engine spits back into carburetter

1 Weak inlet valve spring
2 No clearance on inlet valve tappet
3 Sticking inlet valve stem
4 Transposed plug connections

CHAPTER 2

THE FUEL SYSTEM

The fuel system employed on these cars can be either a twin carburetter layout as on the B.30.A engine or an electronic injection system used on B.30.E and B.30.F power units. It will be convenient to deal entirely with the carburetter system first and to leave a description of the highly automated injection system until the end of this Chapter.

2:1 The fuel pump

This is mounted low down on the lefthand side of the cylinder block and is driven by a cam on the camshaft. It is of conventional design with the diaphragm being operated by a rocker arm and is shown in part section in **FIG 2:1**.

No maintenance is required other than an occasional inspection and cleaning of the filter element 10 which is withdrawn after unscrewing the plug 12.

The pump is removed by unscrewing the two securing bolts after disconnecting the two fuel pipes and lifting it away from the engine.

Dismantling the pump

Refer to the exploded view in **FIG 2:2**. Screw out the plug 3 and the fuel strainer, then make line-up marks on the upper and lower body sections for later assembly. Take out the six retaining screws and separate the two halves.

Remove the circlrp 13 from the lever pivot pin 12 and press out the pin. Withdraw the lever 14 and its return spring 16.

Lift out the diaphragm assembly 7 and spring 8, guide and rubber seal 10. Prise the rubber seal over the nylon washer and remove the spring.

The outlet valve is not removable, but the inlet valve 4 and stop arm 5 are removed by unscrewing the screw 6.

Check all parts for damage or excessive wear, particularly the diaphragm and seals, and replace any which are faulty.

Assembly:

Fit the inlet valve in position with the stop arm, tightening the screw just sufficiently to hold the spring well against the pump body.

Fit the spring 8 and guide 9, then prise on the rubber seal 10 with the flange facing inwards towards the guide.

The diaphragm unit is fitted into the upper section of the pump and should be pressed downwards so that the rubber seal comes into its correct position. While pressing downwards move the lever 14 inwards into location with the diaphragm rod, then fit the pin 12, circlip 13, retainer 15 and spring 16.

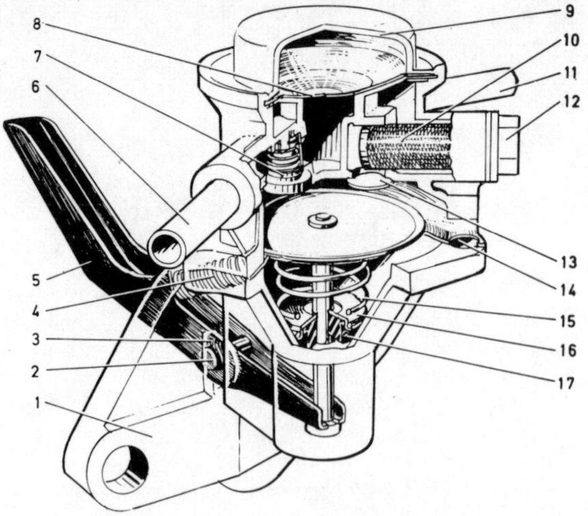

FIG 2:1 Section through the fuel pump

Key to Fig 2:1 1 Lower pump housing 2 Pin 3 Circlip 4 Return spring 5 Lever 6 Outlet pipe 7 Outlet valve 8 Diaphragm 9 Cap 10 Strainer 11 Inlet pipe 12 Plug 13 Inlet valve 14 Diaphragm 15 Diaphragm spring 16 Guide 17 Rubber seal

Line up the upper and lower half casings and fix the six securing bolts. Fit the strainer and plug.

When installing the pump, make sure that the operating lever locates correctly above its cam.

2:3 Carburetters, Zenith-Stromberg 175CD.2SE

Two horizontal draught carburetters of the above type are fitted to these engines and a view of the complete installation is given in **FIG 2:3**, while exploded views may be seen in **FIGS 2:4** and **2:5**.

These carburetters, and the entire fuel system, have been designed with air pollution very much in mind and the owner is discouraged from carrying out any adjustments unless they are absolutely necessary and then the use of a CO meter is recommended. Since such a meter is not always available a few hints on possible routine maintenance and adjustments may be of assistance.

A fixed jet is used, pressed into the carburetter housing, and the fuel flow orifice is varied by means of a tapered needle whose position is determined by the rising and falling of the air valve into which the needle is fitted. The needle is spring-loaded in its mounting so that it is always pressing slightly against the same side of the jet and so ensures continued accuracy in metering the fuel.

Both carburetters are fitted with a temperature compensator which is in fact an air valve regulated by the carburetter temperature and maintains a constant air/fuel mixture irrespective of temperature.

The front carburetter is provided with a throttle bypass valve, the purpose of which is to allow a regulated flow of air/fuel mixture past the butterfly when this is closed at high speeds. By this means a combustible mixture is admitted to the cylinders on the overrun and greatly reduces the volume of noxious gas usually produced at this time.

Also included in the system is an arrangement for the carburetters to inhale any gas fumes generated in the fuel tank and also a device for improving starting under very hot conditions.

Cold start device:

A different system from the conventional choke plate is used and may be seen in diagrammatic form in **FIG 2:6**.

The cold start device consists of a valve disc 3, provided with four calibrated holes and an elongated opening and also a channelled disc 4 mounted on a spindle operated by the choke control. On the same spindle but outside the housing 5 there is a cam which opens the throttle through the fast-idle stop screw and gives a fast, rich mixture, tick-over during the warming up period.

When the choke control knob is pulled out the valve disc turns and links up the channel 1 from the float chamber via one of more holes to the channel behind the disc, through channel 2 to the venturi. Thus a rich mixture is provided for starting and as mentioned previously, the throttle butterfly is opened accordingly at the same time.

2:4 Servicing the carburetters

Removal:

Disconnect the valve control for the hot start valve and remove the air cleaner. Remove the link rod ball joints from the carburetters. Disconnect the fuel pipes, vacuum hose and the choke control wire.

Remove the nuts from the carburetter securing studs and lift off the two carburetters. Remove the protection plates and gaskets. Cover the intake holes to prevent the entry of any dirt.

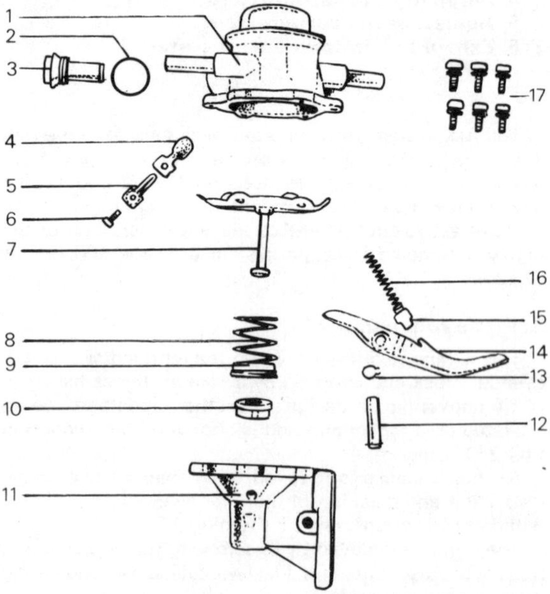

FIG 2:2 Components of fuel pump

Key to Fig 2:2 1 Upper pump housing 2 Sealing washer 3 Plug with strainer 4 Inlet valve 5 Stop arm 6 Screw 7 Diaphragm 8 Spring 9 Spring guide 10 Rubber seal 11 Lower pump housing 12 Lever pin 13 Circlip 14 Lever 15 Spring retainer 16 Return spring 17 Screw

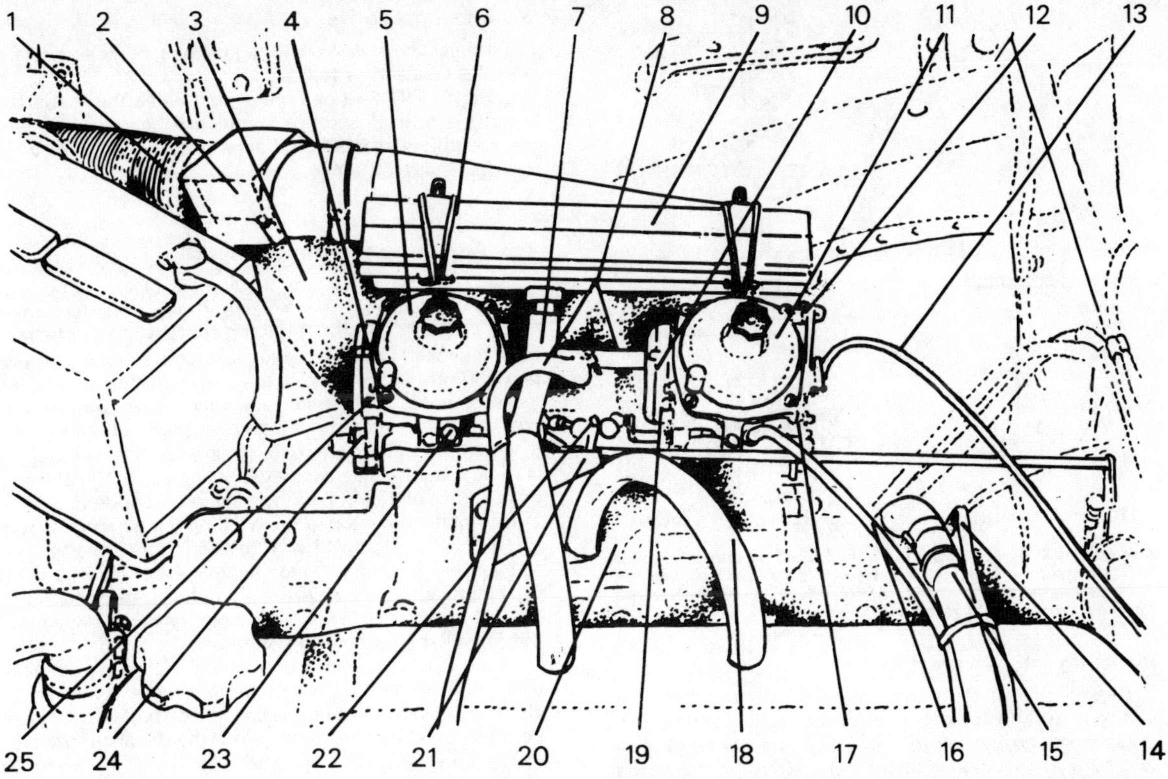

FIG 2:3 Twin carburetter installation

Key to Fig. 2:3 1 Cold-air hose 2 Constant temperature device flap 3 Warm-air hose 4 Temperature compensator 5 Front carburetter 6 Clamp for air cleaner cover 7 Hot air hose for crankcase gases 8 Fuel hoses 9 Air cleaner 10 Temperature compensator 11 Rear carburetter 12 Hot start valve 13 Choke wire 14 Vacuum hose for distributor (negative vacuum setting) 15 Vacuum hose for brake servo 16 Vacuum hose for distributor (positive vacuum setting) 17 Throttle stop screw 18 Hose for crankcase gases 19 Idle trimming screw 20 Manifold with preheating chamber 21 Bracket 22 Throttle control 23 Plug (connection for vacuum hose on cars with venting filter) 24 Throttle by-pass valve 25 Idle trimming screw

Float level:

The float chamber is removed by unscrewing the plug 5 in **FIG 2:5** and also the screws 1. Note that when replacing the float chamber a new rubber ring 4 and a new gasket 3 should be used.

Invert the assembly and refer to **FIG 2:7**. At the correct level the highest point on the float should be between .59 and .67 inch above the sealing surface and the rear edge .35 to .51 inch. If these dimensions are not obtained, adjust by bending the tag at the float valve. Do **not** bend the arm between the float and the pin.

Diaphragm:

Unscrew the damper piston. Make alignment marks on the suction cover, then remove the seal plug, release the screws and lift off the cover and spring.

Pull up the air valve and release the diaphragm by taking out the four screws. Clean the air valve and take care that the needle is not disturbed or bent.

When fitting the new diaphragm see that the rubber register fits into the valve groove, then push the air valve down and ensure that the tabs locate correctly in their recesses.

Fit the suction cover and refill the damper with oil (ATF, Type A). Replace the plug-seal.

Bypass valve and temperature compensator:

In the event of trouble with either of these components a new part must be fitted complete as part replacement is not possible. Note that the bypass valve is identified by the letter Y, and the compensator is marked 60 on a mounting lug. Adjustment details are given in **Section 2:5**.

Pedal adjustment:

The length of the long vertical link for the accelerator pedal is adjusted so that there is a clearance of .04 inch (1 mm) between the throttle lever lug and the full throttle stop on the carburetters when the pedal is fully depressed. By this means the force of the drivers foot at full throttle is taken by the floor board instead of the throttle control linkage.

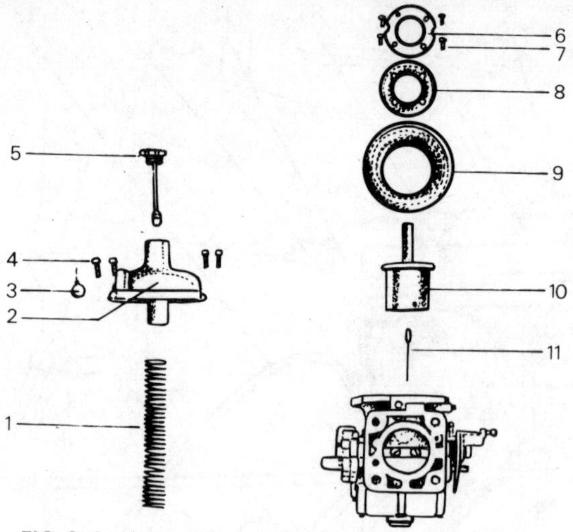

FIG 2:4 Components of carburetter upper section

Key to Fig 2:4 1 Spring 2 Suction chamber cover 3 Sealing plug 4 Screw 5 Hydraulic damper 6 Washer 7 Screw for diaphragm 8 Washer 9 Diaphragm 10 Air valve 11 Metering needle

Refitting the carburetters:

Carefully clean the mating surfaces, then fit the protection plates and new gasket before fitting the carburetters.

Connect up the ball joints, hoses and choke control wire, ensuring its correct attachment relative to the choke control on the instrument panel. This is done by pushing the knob fully in and then securing the pull wire in the clamping screw of the fast-idle cam. Then clip on the outer sleeve of the control wire.

Fit the air cleaner and connect the hose for the crankcase ventilation. Fit the control for the hot start valve. Adjust the carburetters as described in **Section 2:5**.

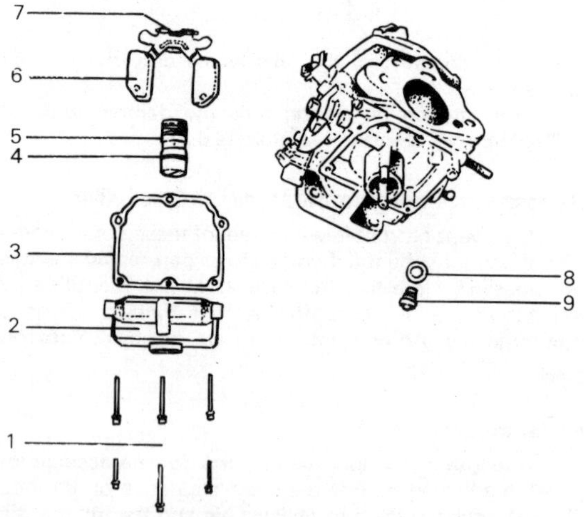

FIG 2:5 The float chamber dismantled

Key to Fig 2:5 1 Screw for float chamber 2 Float chamber 3 Gasket 4 Rubber ring 5 Float chamber plug 6 Float 7 Float pin 8 Washer 9 Float valve

Secondary throttles:

To check the operation and adjustment of the secondary throttles proceed as follows:

Refer to **FIG 2:8** and check that when the secondary throttle is fully closed, the distance **A** between the lever pin and the inlet manifold flange is between .11 and .17 inch (2.7 and 4.3 mm).

2:5 Adjusting the carburetters

Before carrying out any adjustment to the carburetter settings because of unsatisfactory engine performance, make sure that all other possible sources of trouble have been checked. Valve clearance, plugs, contact breaker gap and ignition timing. Check also that there are no air leaks to upset carburation and that the air cleaner and constant air temperature unit are in good condition.

As stated earlier, the best setting for the carburetters is to be obtained by using a CO meter, but in the absence of this, the following method should be adopted.

Bring the engine up to full working temperature. Check that the damper is filled with the correct grade of oil.

By using the throttle stop screws 2 in **FIG 2:9** bring the engine speed to 800 rev./min in the case of cars with manual gearboxes. When automatic transmission is fitted this speed should be 700 rev/min.

Make this adjustment by moving the screw on each carburetter by the same amount and make sure that the lift of the air valve is the same on each carburetter. This can be done by checking visually that the distance between the carburetter bridge and the air valve is the same on each. A more accurate synchronization is not needed.

Using the idle trimming screws 7 in **FIG 2:10** equally from their basic setting, which in two turns screwed out from fully in, obtain the smoothest idling speed. If this should increase the engine speed above that specified, reset the throttle stop screws.

Adjust the link rods. With the control against its stop on the manifold bracket, these should be so adjusted that there is a clearance of .004 inch (.1 mm) between the lever and the primary throttle spindle flange (see **FIG 2:11**).

Adjust the valve control of the hot start valve so that it is against the throttle lever when the valve piston is in its upper position and the throttle control is at idle. Lightly lubricate the contact surfaces with a grease such as Molycote and check that the engine returns to idle after blipping the throttle a few times (see **FIG 2:12**).

Setting the fast-idle:

Refer to **FIG 2:13**. Pull out the choke control by about 1 inch (23 to 25 mm) so that the line scribed on the fast-idle cam comes opposite the centre line of the fast-idle screw.

Adjust the fast-idle screw to give an engine speed of between 1100 and 1300 rev/min.

Temperature compensator:

This component is shown broken open in **FIG 2:14** and its operation may be suspect if the idling deteriorates after a long idling period, particularly in hot weather. Its function may be checked by removing the plastic cover

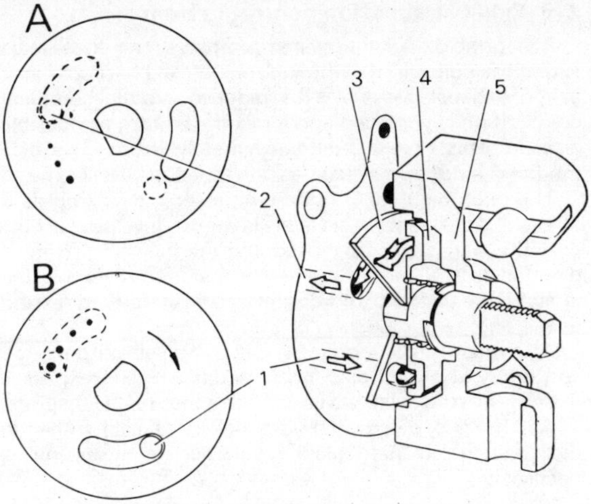

FIG 2:6 The cold start device

Key to Fig 2:6 **A** Disengaged **B** Engaged 1 From float chamber 2 To venturi 3 Choke lever 4 Channel disc 5 Housing

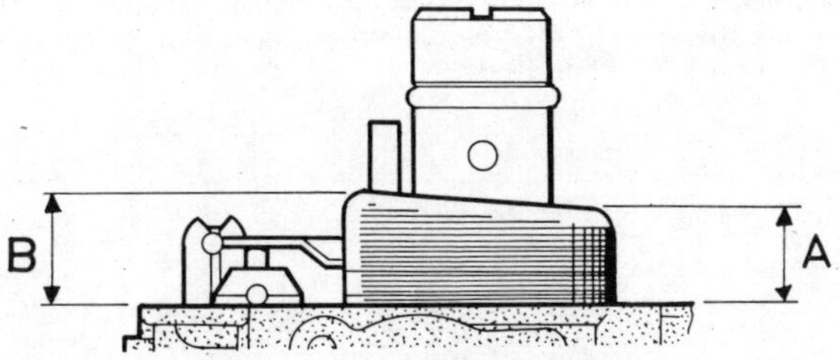

FIG 2:7 Setting the float level

Key to Fig 2:7 **A**=.35 to .51 inch (9 to 13 mm) **B**=.59 to .67 inch (15 to 17 mm)

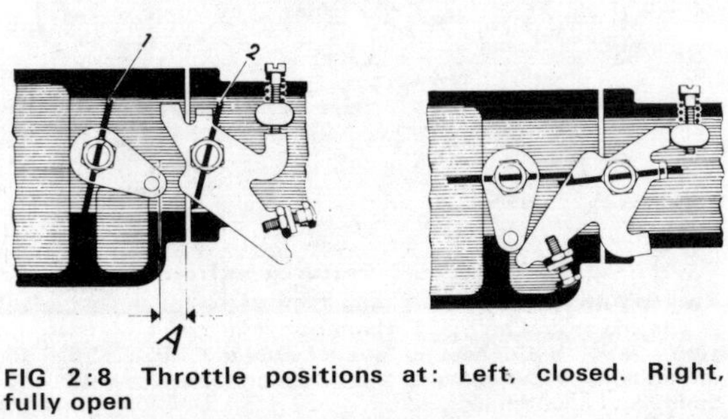

FIG 2:8 Throttle positions at: Left, closed. Right, fully open

Key to Fig 2:8 1 Secondary throttle 2 Primary throttle **A**=.11 to .17 inch (2.7 to 4.3 mm)

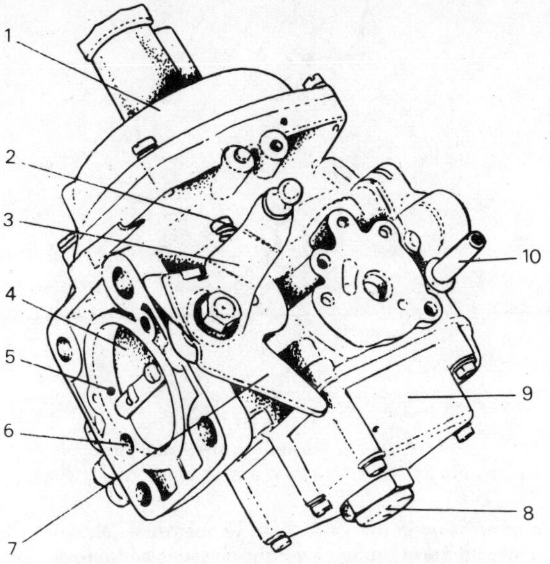

FIG 2:9 Front carburetter seen from the left

Key to Fig 2:9 1 Suction chamber 2 Throttle stop screw 3 Lever 4 Primary throttle 5 Drilling to vacuum side of bypass valve 6 Drilling for fuel-air mixture from bypass valve 7 Throttle spindle cam (for regulating secondary throttle) 8 Float chamber plug 9 Float chamber 10 Fuel inlet

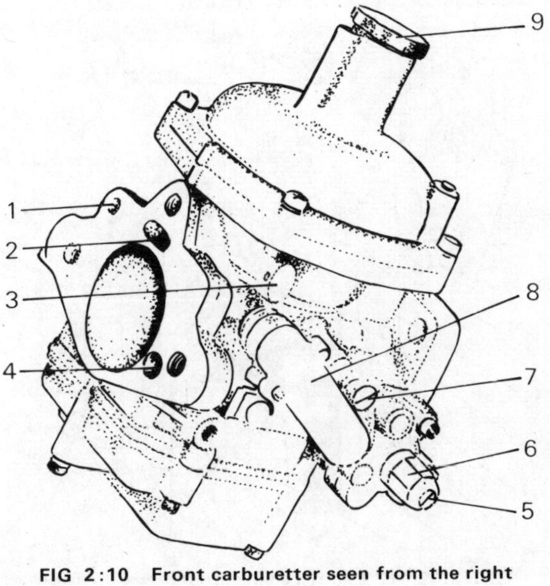

FIG 2:10 Front carburetter seen from the right

Key to Fig 2:10 1 Venting channel from float chamber 2 Drilling for air supply under diaphragm 3 Sealed plug 4 Drilling for air supply to temp. comp. and idle trimming screw 5 Stop screw for bypass valve 6 Bypass valve 7 Idle trimming screw 8 Temperature compensator 9 Hydraulic damper

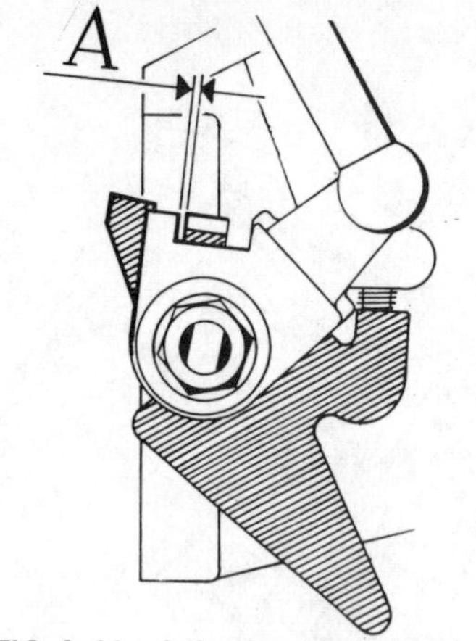

FIG 2:11 Adjusting the link rods

Key to Fig 2:11 A=.004 inch (.1 mm)

and pressing in the valve 3 At temperatures above 80°F it should move under very light pressure and return to its position quite freely.

The valve should start opening at 70 to 77°F and if it does not do so the bi-metal spring can be adjusted to obtain this performance, preferably after removing the complete unit and storing it at the indicated temperature, by turning the nut 9.

If the valve is not moving freely it may require centring by slackening off the cross-slotted screw 8 and moving as necessary.

FIG 2:12 Hot start valve showing idle position

Key to Fig 2:12 1 Throttle lever 2 Valve control 3 Screw for valve control 4 Locknut 5 Control rod 6 Hot start valve 7 Outlet to air cleaner 8 Hose to float chamber 9 Rivet 10 Air cleaner housing 12 Outlet to atmosphere or venting filter 13 Rubber rings 14 Piston 15 Thrust spring 16 Control rod 17 Rubber seal

2:6 Exhaust emission control system

The principle of the system employed on these cars is that the content of carbon monoxide and hydrocarbons in the exhaust gases will be reduced if more complete combustion is achieved and a mixture as lean as possible is used. This object is attained mainly by the use of a modified induction system as illustrated in **FIG 2:15**.

The inlet manifold is fitted with a secondary throttle 3 at each carburetter. In normal driving at low power outputs these throttles are closed and the fuel/air mixture is directed to the central preheating chamber 6 where the intake is heated and thoroughly mixed before admission to the engine combustion chambers.

At wider throttle openings and higher outputs the secondary throttles also open and the mixture passes directly into the cylinders as shown in the smaller diagram.

As the two carburetters are linked to each other in this system no particularly accurate synchronizing is necessary.

2:7 Gas evaporite control system

For certain markets, notably the USA, these cars are equipped with a system designed to prevent fuel fumes generated in the fuel tank from being released into the atmosphere (see **FIG 2:16**).

Fumes from the fuel tank 1 are led to an expansion tank 2 and thence to the venting filter 3 where the gases are absorbed by active carbon. The expansion tank is mounted behind the wall board lining of the luggage compartment, while the venting filter is located in the engine compartment on the lefthand side.

FIG 2:13 Rear carburetter seen from the left

Key to Fig 2:13 1 Attaching sleeve for choke control 2 Throttle stop screw 3 Throttle spindle cam 4 Fast-idle stop screw 5 Connection for choke control 6 Cam disc for fast-idle 7 Float chamber 8 Drilling for air supply to temp. comp. and idle trimming screw 9 Cold start device 10 Drilling for air supply under diaphragm 11 Venting channel from float chamber 12 Hot start valve control 13 Suction chamber

Fuel fumes from the carburetter float chambers are led via the hot-start valve 4 to the venting filter when the throttle is closed, but when the throttle is opened the valve 5 closes so that the fumes are directed to the air cleaner.

All the time the engine is running suction is applied to the venting filter by means of the pipe 6 connected to the carburetter, the extent of which will depend upon the engine load. Fuel fumes which have been absorbed in the carbon are picked up by the resulting air flow, as shown in the diagram, and conveyed to the carburetter and the engine where they take part in the normal process of combustion.

The hot-start valve is fitted to all cars in this series, but in the case of those cars not fitted with a gas evaporite system there is no hose to the venting filter and the fumes exhaust directly into the atmosphere instead under low throttle conditions or when switched off.

Hot-start valve:

When the engine is hot considerable quantities of fuel fumes develop in the float chamber and these are normally vented back to the carburetter intake giving a somewhat richer fuel mixture, so much so that starting may be badly affected. This is counteracted by the hot-start valve.

When the throttle is at its idling position the lever 1 in **FIG 2:12** presses against the valve control 2, lifts the piston to its upper position, closes the passage to the air cleaner and carburetter, and so directs the fuel fumes to the venting filter or to atmosphere.

When the accelerator pedal is depressed the piston returns to its lower position, closes the outlet port and the fumes are led into the air cleaner.

Adjustment of this device was described in **Section 2:5**.

2:8 Air cleaners and preheater

The air cleaner, which functions both as a cleaner and intake silencer, has a replaceable paper element. This must not be washed or lubricated, but every 25,000 miles (40,000 km) should be removed and a new element fitted. If the vehicle is being operated in unusually dusty areas replacement will be required more often.

On some cars the air cleaner is coupled to a preheater as shown in **FIG 2:17**. This consists of a body 5 which incorporates a hose 6 for cold air, a hose 7 for hot air and a heater plate 8 which is secured to the exhaust pipe. A thermostat 2 regulates the flap 4 through the control rod 3 and so controls the air intake through the two intake hoses and supplies air to the carburetters at a constant and predetermined temperature.

The flap should be closed for cold air at 70 to 77°F and for warm air at 95 to 105°F, and its function can be observed from the position of a small tab outside the

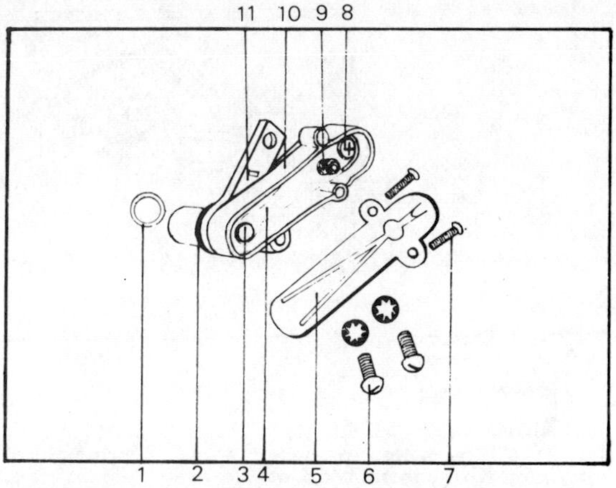

FIG 2:14 Components of temperature compensator

Key to Fig 2:14 1 Rubber seal 2 Rubber seal 3 Valve 4 Bi-metal spring 5 Cover 6 Screw for temperature compensator 7 Screw for cover 8 Cross-slotted screw 9 Adjusting nut 10 Housing 11 Marking

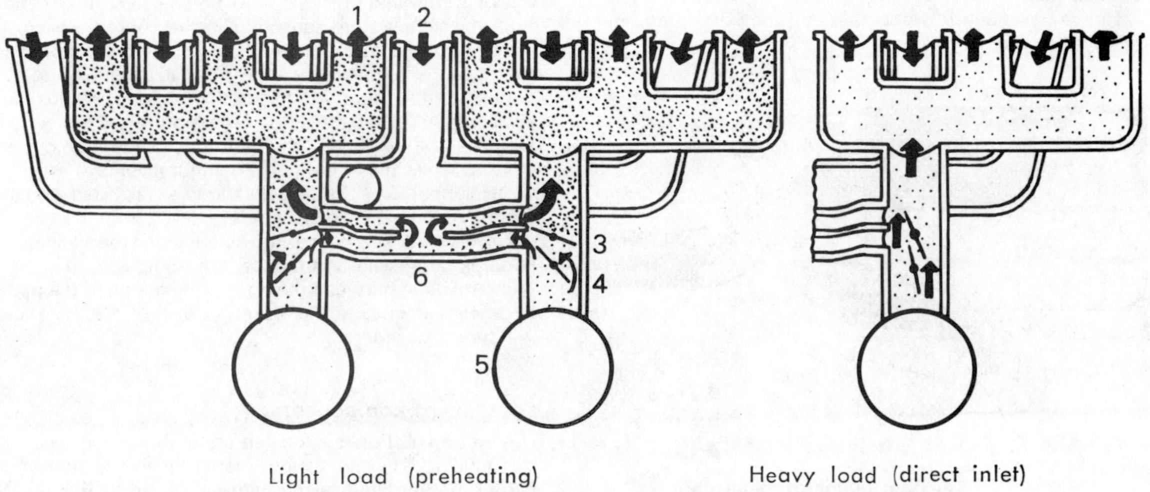

FIG 2:15 Exhaust emission control system showing principle of operation

Key to Fig 2:15 1 Intake manifold 2 Exhaust manifold 3 Secondary throttle 4 Primary throttle 5 Carburetter 6 Preheating chamber

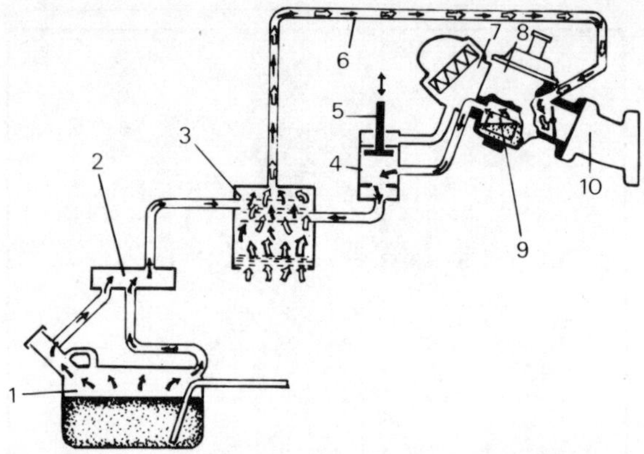

FIG 2:16 Gas evaporite system showing principle of operation with control rod 5 at idle

Key to Fig 2:16 1 Fuel tank 2 Expansion tank 3 Venting filter 4 Valve (hot start valve) 5 Control rod (connected to throttle) 6 Vacuum line (connected to carburetter) 7 Air cleaner 8 Carburetter 9 Float chamber 10 Intake manifold

housing which corresponds to the position of the flap inside.

If necessary, the thermostat can be removed and its operation checked in water heated to the required temperature. If correct operation is not obtained it will be necessary to renew the flap housing and thermostat complete.

When fitting the flap housing make sure that the thermostat is located in the centre of the air flow and the securing screw for the hose clamp is on the upper side.

Venting filter:

The foam plastic filtering element which is contained inside the metal canister should be changed every 25,000 miles (40,000 km). This is done by loosening the bracket screws, lifting up the filter assembly and withdrawing the foam element.

The new element is dropped in and the unit refitted in the reverse order.

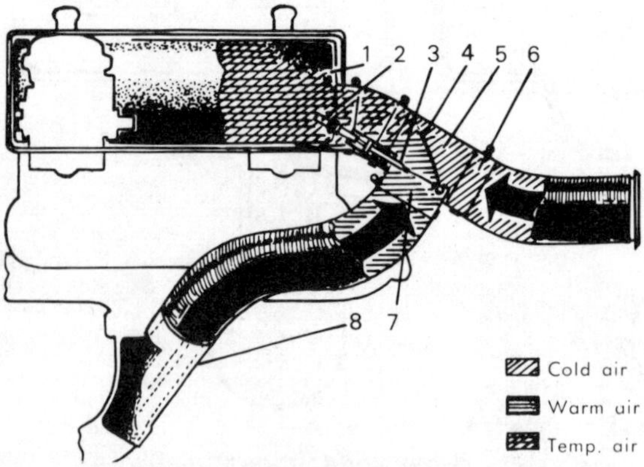

FIG 2:17 Constant temperature air unit

Key to Fig 2:17 1 Air cleaner 2 Thermostat 3 Flap control 4 Flap 5 Flap housing 6 Cold-air intake 7 Warm-air intake 8 Heater plate

2:9 The fuel injection system

Towards the end of 1971 the Bosch system of electronically controlled fuel injection was added to the equipment available on the Volvo 160 series. It must be stressed at the outset that fault finding and rectification on this system requires very highly specialized instruments without which very little by way of maintenance can be done. Even when faults have been located at the service station, the remedy is usually by substitution rather than adjustment or repair of the faulty component.

A short description of the system will be given here, but the owner is advised strongly against interfering with it himself and to entrust any maintenance to his Volvo agent.

Refer to **FIG 2:18**. The fuel, stored in the tank 9, is drawn by the electric fuel pump 12 through the filter 10 and then passed through the discharge side filter 11 to the injectors at a pressure, limited by the pressure regulator 14, of 28 lb/sq inch. From the regulator excess fuel flows back to the tank by way of a return pipe.

The duration of each injection (fuel quantity) is governed basically by engine speed and engine load. The triggering contacts 13 in the distributor provide the control unit 7 with the information about engine speed, while the pressure sensor 5 is affected by the pressure in the inlet duct and passes this in the form of electrical impulses to be computerized by the control unit. Since this pressure is proportional to the engine load, the control unit is supplied in this way with the necessary information on this point. Having received the two sets of data, the control unit processes them and determines how long the injectors shall remain open to provide the correct amount of fuel for the current running conditions.

In addition to the basic fuel supply, extra fuel must be provided when starting, warming up and during acceleration.

For a cold start, extra fuel is supplied through the cold start valve 4 on the inlet duct. The opening of this valve, which reduces as the engine warms up, is regulated by a thermal timing device.

While warming up, the control unit receives information from the temperature sensor 17 in the cooling system at the front of the cylinder head and allows the injectors to stay open a little longer than normal according to the coolant temperature. Alongside this sensor is an auxiliary air regulator 18 which is also temperature controlled and supplies the extra air required to provide the correct mixture while the extra fuel is being delivered.

Additional fuel for acceleration is provided by the control unit according to signals received from the throttle valve switch 2. This comes into action when the accelerator pedal is depressed and results in a number of injections being made in between the normal injections. If the pedal is depressed quickly, the duration of the injections also will be increased.

Location of components:

The control unit is located under the drivers seat and is connected to the various components by means of cables incorporated in the harness shown in **FIG 2:19**. The connections are of the 'Amp' plug type which provide good electrical contact as well as rapid fitting and removal. They are provided with grommets to ensure proper

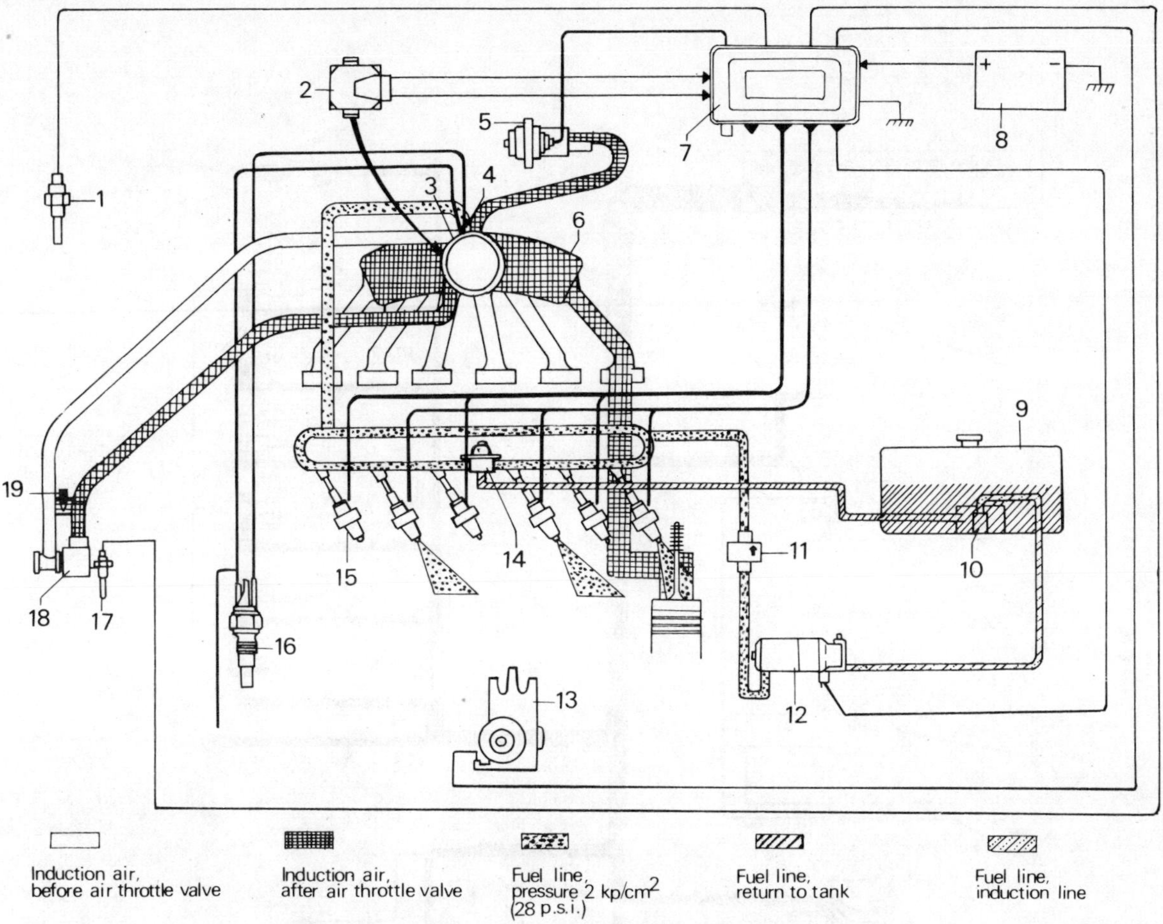

FIG 2:18 Schematic diagram of the fuel injection system

Key to Fig 2:18 1 Temperature sensor for induction air 2 Throttle valve switch 3 Throttle valve 4 Cold start valve 5 Pressure sensor 6 Inlet duct 7 Control unit 8 Battery 9 Fuel tank 10 Fuel filter, inlet side 11 Fuel filter, discharge side 12 Fuel pump 13 Distributor with triggering contacts 14 Pressure regulator 15 Injectors 16 Thermal timer 17 Temperature sensor, coolant 18 Auxiliary air regulator 19 Idle adjustment screw

installation and covered with rubber protectors which also serve as locking devices.

The fuel pump is mounted under the car at the righthand side of the fuel tank and includes its own relief valve which opens if for any reason the pressure should exceed 64 lb/sq in. The pump and motor are sealed and cannot be serviced. It runs for 1 or 2 seconds when the ignition is switched on and then operates only when the starter engages or the engine is running.

The pressure regulator is connected in the distribution pipe servicing the six injectors above the cylinder head and opens as soon as pressure exceeds 28 lb/sq inch, returning excess fuel to the tank.

The injectors are mounted in holders which sit in the cylinder head and operate in two groups of three. Numbers 1, 5 and 3 inject together and then 6, 2 and 4 inject at the same time. Any fuel injected into a port while the valve is closed is stored in the inlet port until the valve opens.

The injector, seen sectioned in **FIG 2:20,** consists of a housing containing a sealing needle, magnetic winding and return spring. When the magnetic winding is not in circuit the needle is pressed on its seat by the spring and no fuel passes. On receiving current from the control unit, the needle is lifted about .02 inch from its seat and fuel is allowed to pass, and since the needle and the aperture in the seat are accurately calibrated and the fuel pressure is constant, only the valve opening period (2 to 10 milliseconds) determines the amount of fuel injected.

The cold start valve is fitted in the induction pipe after the throttle to provide extra fuel for cold starting. As previously mentioned the injection time is regulated by a thermal timer and at —4°F (—20°C) or lower provides extra fuel for up to 12 seconds. At 95°F (35°C) the valve stops giving extra fuel for starting. The valve injects only while the starter motor is running.

The throttle valve switch is fitted in the induction pipe and connected to the throttle shaft. It has two functions: first to call for extra fuel during acceleration, and secondly to prevent the control unit from receiving impulses for fuel when the throttle is closed.

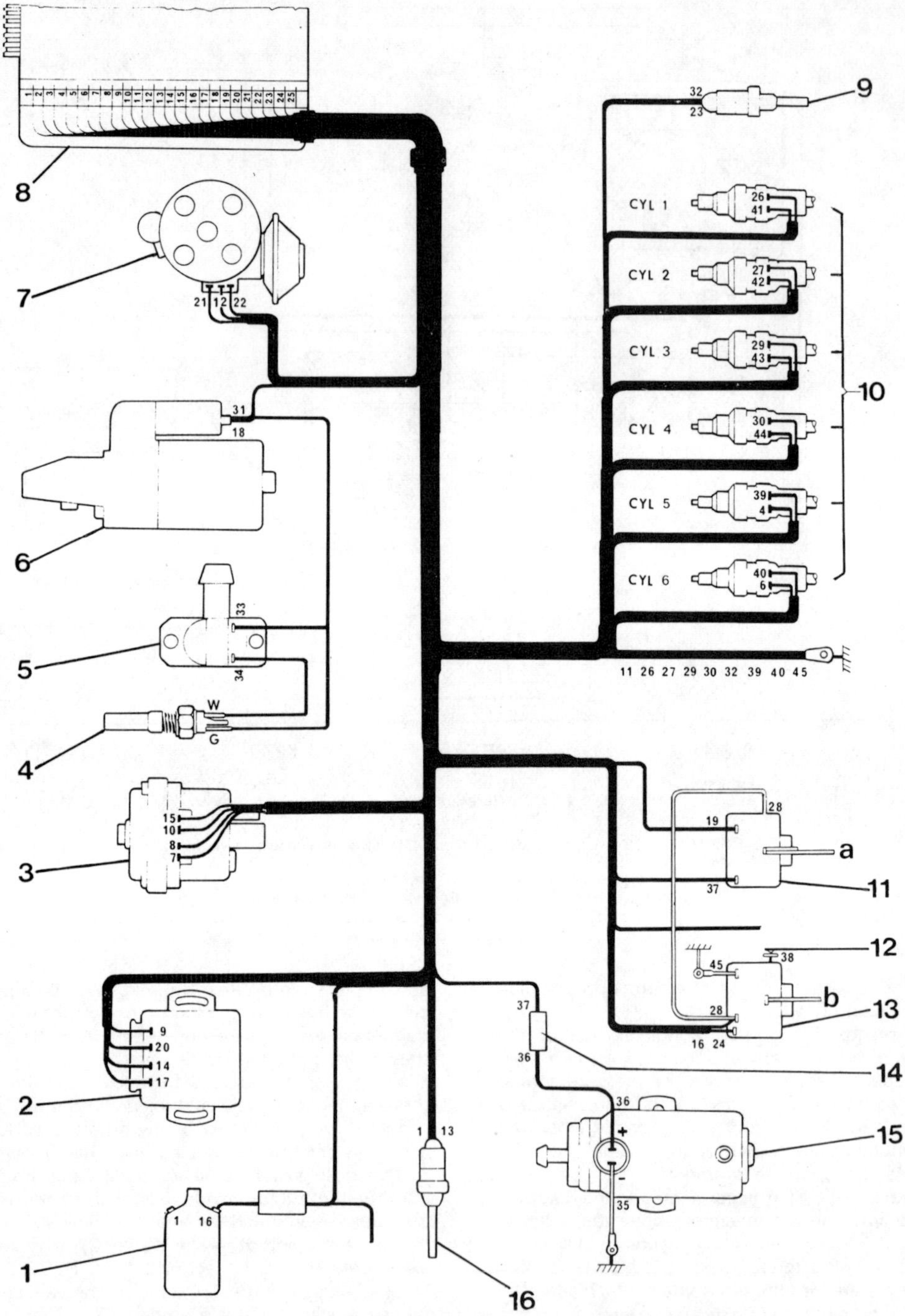

FIG 2:19 Diagram of cable harness and connections

Key to Fig 2:19 1 Ignition coil (term. 16) 2 Throttle valve switch 3 Pressure sensor 4 Thermal timer 5 Cold start valve 6 Starter motor (term. 50) 7 Distributor (triggering contacts) 8 Control unit 9 Temperature sensor for coolant 10 Injectors 11 Pump relay 12 Diode (located in relay) 13 Main relay 14 Connector 15 Fuel pump 16 Temperature sensor for induction air **a** To fuse 1 (small fusebox) **b** To battery, B+

The pressure sensor is located on the right wheel housing and connected to the inlet duct by means of a hose. It operates on the principle of an aneroid moving an armature over a series of contacts which inform the control unit of the fuel quantity demanded by operating conditions at any moment.

The auxiliary air regulator, connected with the cooling system at the front end of the cylinder head, has an operating range of from —13°F (—25°C), fully open, to 140°F (60°C) fully closed.

For a cold start the regulator opens to an extent dictated by the coolant temperature and admits extra air into the manifold, and as the engine warms up progressively closes the auxiliary air pipe and so ensuring the correct mixture with the additional fuel demanded by the temperature sensor.

There are **two temperature sensors,** one for coolant and one for intake air. The coolant sensor arranges for the injection period to be adapted according to radiator temperature while the intake air sensor, located just in front of the battery, arranges for increased injections at low intake air temperatures. This compensation ceases when the intake air temperature is higher than 86°F (30°C).

The air cleaner is mounted above the inlet duct and is of the paper type. The element should be renewed at least every 24,000 miles (40,000 km) by disconnecting the hoses and releasing the clamp.

FIG 2:21 shows the complete installation in the car.

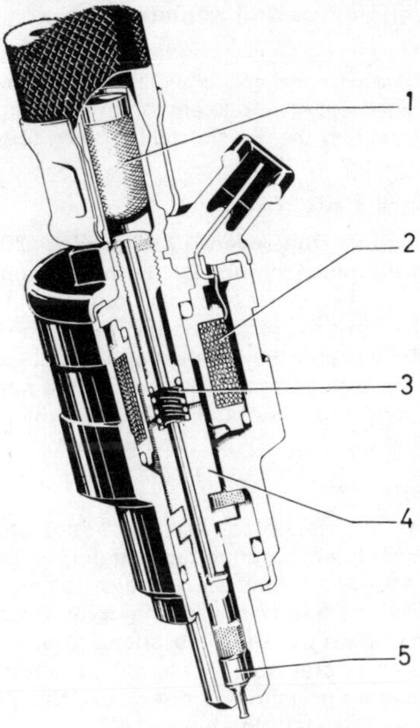

FIG 2:20 Section through an injector

Key to Fig 2:20 1 Filter 2 Magnetic winding 3 Return spring 4 Magnetic armature 5 Sealing needle

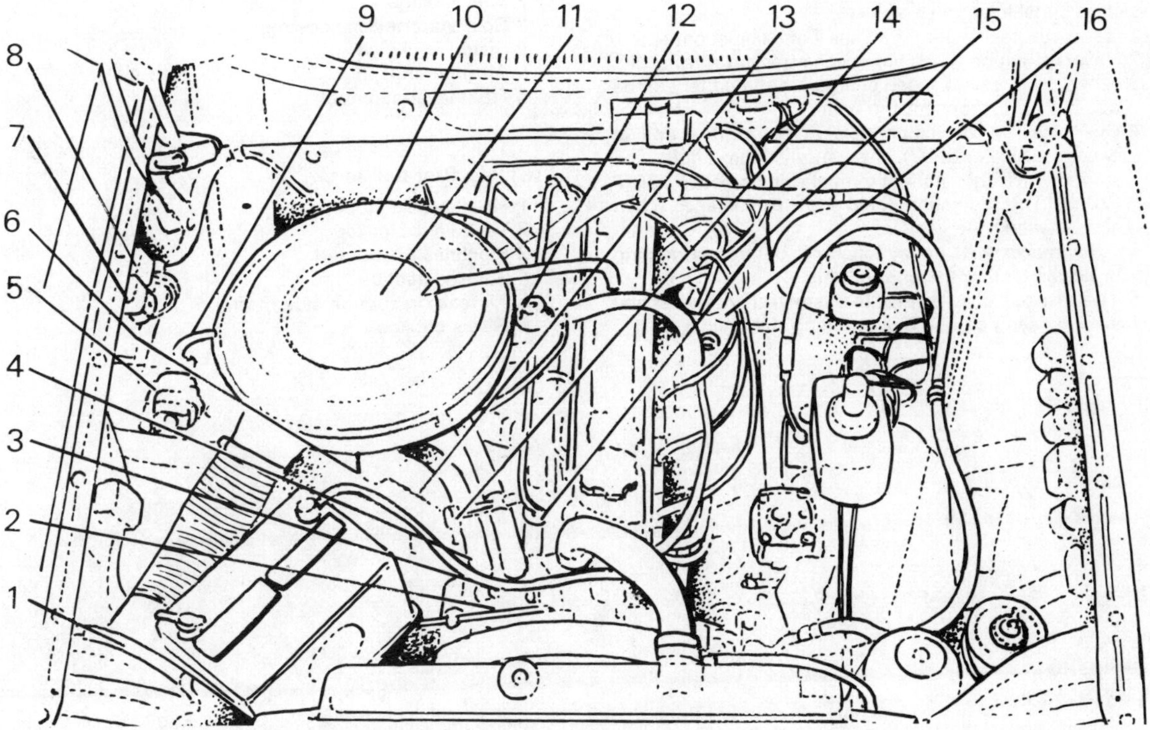

FIG 2:21 Fuel injection system installed

Key to Fig 2:21 1 Temperature sensor, induction air 2 Thermal timer 3 Auxiliary air regulator 4 Temperature sensor, coolant 5 Pressure sensor 6 Throttle switch 7 Pump relay 8 Main relay 9 Cold start valve 10 Stop screw for throttle valve 11 Air cleaner 12 Pressure regulator 13 Inlet duct 14 Screw for adjusting idling 15 Injector 16 Triggering contacts

2:10 Maintenance and adjustment

As mentioned previously, the testing and adjustment of the Bosch system requires specialist equipment which only accredited agents are likely to have and in the event of any malfunction the car should be taken to the service station.

Renewing the fuel filter:

This should be done every 12,000 miles (20,000 km).

Remove the plug contact for the fuel pump and take down the bracket on which the pump and filter are mounted. Remove the plastic clamp around the hoses and clean carefully round the connections.

Slacken the hose clamps and remove the filter.

When fitting the new filter make sure that the arrow is pointing in the direction of the fuel flow.

Idle adjustment:

Bring the engine up to working temperature and if possible connect an accurate tachometer.

Check that the auxiliary air regulator is fully closed by pulling off the hose between the inlet duct and the regulator and then covering the opening with a hand. If there is any appreciable variation in engine speed, provided the engine is fully warmed up, the auxiliary air regulator is faulty. Refit the hose.

Adjust the idling speed to 900 rev/min with synchromesh, 800 rev/min with automatic transmission by means of the throttle stop screw.

Special instructions when working on cars with electronic fuel injection

1 Never run the engine with the battery disconnected.
2 Never use a high speed battery charger as a starting aid.
3 When using a high speed charger on the battery in the car, always disconnect the battery.
4 Do not allow the temperature of the control unit to exceed 185°F (85°C), nor should the engine be started when the ambient temperature is above 158°F (70°C). This restriction could apply for instance when stove-heating the vehicle.
5 The ignition must be switched off before connecting or disconnecting the control unit.
6 **The utmost cleanliness is essential** whenever any work is being carried out involving the fuel lines.

2:11 Fault diagnosis (carburetter systems)

(a) Engine will not start

1 Low fuel in tank
2 Fuel pump faulty
3 Choked filter
4 Fuel pipes blocked
5 Sticking float or needle valve
6 Air leak in induction system
7 Fuel vaporizing in pipes due to heat
8 Dirt in carburetter

(b) Engine stalls

1 Throttle stop set too low
2 Under or overchoking
3 Tank air vent blocked
4 Faulty pump
5 Induction air leaks

(c) Poor acceleration

1 Air valve sticking
2 Air filter choked

(d) Excessive fuel consumption

1 Carburetters need adjusting
2 Fuel leakage
3 Cold start device sticking
4 Piston sticking
5 Air filter choked
6 Float level incorrect

(e) No fuel delivery

1 Float needle stuck
2 Tank vent blocked
3 Pipelines obstructed
4 Pump defective
5 Air leak on suction side of pump
6 Filters choked

CHAPTER 3

THE IGNITION SYSTEM

3:1 Description

The ignition system employed on these cars is of the battery ignition type and consists of the following main parts. Ignition coil with advance engaging resistance, distributor with both centrifugal and vacuum advance mechanisms and the sparking plugs.

The ignition coil is fitted on the engine bulkhead and is coupled to an advance engaging resistance which serves two purposes. It protects the coil from damage by overheating if the ignition should be left on when the engine is not running and also enables the voltage applied to the coil at the moment of starting to be increased. Reference to the wiring diagram in the **Appendix** will show how at all normal times the battery voltage to the coil is reduced by the resistance but for starting, the coil is actuated by the full battery voltage via a terminal on the starter motor.

The distributor is mounted on the lefthand side of the engine and is driven from the camshaft on an extension of the oil pump drive shaft (see **FIG 3:1**). A centrifugal governor is fitted under the contact breaker plate to control the ignition timing relative to the engine speed, and a double acting vacuum regulator controls the timing point relative to the engine load.

The vacuum regulator, shown in section in **FIG 3:2**, has two diaphragms and two vacuum chambers connected to the carburetters and to the inlet manifold. Under conditions of idling or overrun the throttles are closed and there is no vacuum in the connection from the carburetters 5 and the spring 6 presses back the primary diaphragm 7, against the stop 8. The pullrod 2, which is attached to the diaphragm, transmits this movement to the contact breaker plate and so retards the ignition. Similarly if the vacuum in the connection from the inlet manifold 3 is of sufficient magnitude it will pull the secondary diaphragm 4 to the left and again retard the ignition timing.

Under conditions of open throttle running the primary diaphragm is influenced by the greater vacuum in the carburetters, overrides the effect on the secondary diaphragm and advances the ignition accordingly.

3:2 The distributor

Removal (see FIG 3:3):

Release the two clips 8 and lift off the distributor cap 1.

Remove the lead from the primary terminal. Remove the two vacuum hoses from the regulator, being particularly careful of the bakelite tubes.

Slacken off the bolt on the securing clamp and lift out the distributor, carefully marking its position for later replacement.

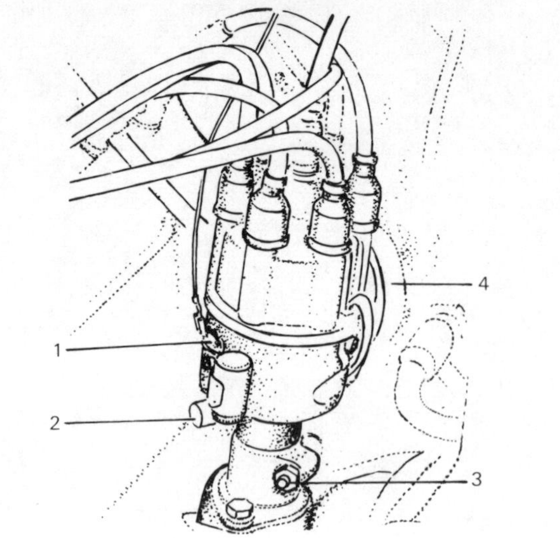

FIG 3:1 Showing distributor mounted on the engine

Key to Fig 3:1 1 Primary connection and capacitor 2 Lubricator 3 Attachment clamp bolt 4 Vacuum regulator

Dismantling:

Pull off the rotor arm 2. Remove the circlip for the pullrod from the vacuum regulator and then take out two securing screws to release the regulator. Note the attachment of the two clips for the cap and remove them.

Disconnect the lead from the contact breaker, remove the primary terminal connector and lift out the contact breaker plate.

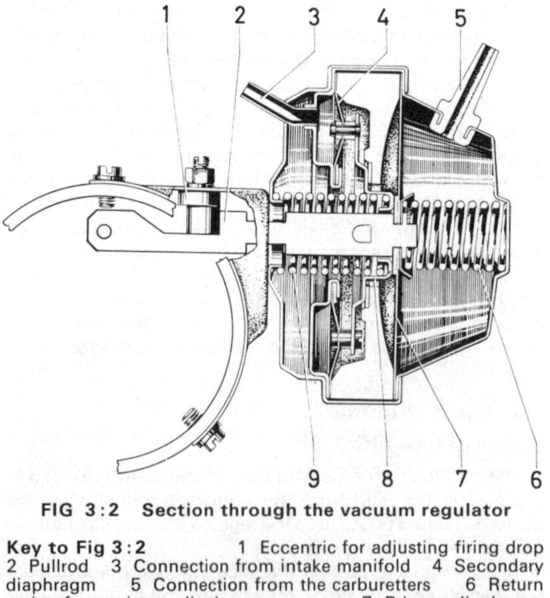

FIG 3:2 Section through the vacuum regulator

Key to Fig 3:2 1 Eccentric for adjusting firing drop 2 Pullrod 3 Connection from intake manifold 4 Secondary diaphragm 5 Connection from the carburetters 6 Return spring from primary diaphragm 7 Primary diaphragm 8 Register 9 Return spring for secondary diaphragm

Disconnect the springs for the centrifugal governor and make alignment marks for the breaker cam relative to the distributor shaft. Hold the breaker cam in a soft jawed vice and tap carefully on the distributor housing with a mallet until the circlip 22 is released.

Remove the spring ring 13 and make alignment marks on the driving collar 14 and the distributor shaft. Tap out the lockpin 12, lift off the driving collar and pull up the distributor shaft taking care not to lose any washers.

Remove the lock springs for the centrifugal weights and lift them away.

Examination:

Inspect all parts for corrosion or wear, not forgetting the holes in the two weights. Examine the condition of the contact breaker points which should be flat and smooth. Slight wear or discoloration can be cleaned up with a fine stone, but if they are badly pitted or worn the complete assembly should be renewed.

The play between the distributor shaft and the breaker camshaft must not exceed .004 inch (.1 mm).

Check the springs for the centrifugal weights that they are not deformed or weakened, and replace if in any doubt.

The clearance between the distributor housing and the shaft should not exceed .008 inch (.2 mm). If it does, new bushes should be fitted and if this does not prove sufficient the shaft also will have to be renewed.

Assembly:

First lubricate the various pieces as shown in **FIG 3:4**. Fit the two centrifugal weights and their lock springs. Place the breaker camshaft on to the distributor shaft and hook on the springs for the centrifugal governor. Fit the washer and circlip for the breaker camshaft. The use of a suitable sleeve will facilitate the correct location of the latter. Insert the lubricating felt pad.

Fit the distributor shaft into the housing and position the driving collar on to the shaft, making sure that the fibre washers come against the housing. Insert the pin through the collar and check the axial clearance on the distributor shaft. This should be between .004 and .010 inch (.1 to .25 mm) and any adjustment made by adjusting the number of washers on the shaft. Fit the spring ring on to the driving collar.

Fit the contact breaker plate, the clips for the distributor cap. Fit the primary connection terminal and the lead from the contacts.

Fit the vacuum capsule and connect the pullrod to the contact breaker plate.

Check the mounting of the contact breaker points and see that they are correct horizontally and vertically. The gap should be .010 to .014 inch and any adjustment should be made by bending the fixed contact with a suitable tool such as Bosch EFAW.57.A (see **FIG 3:5**).

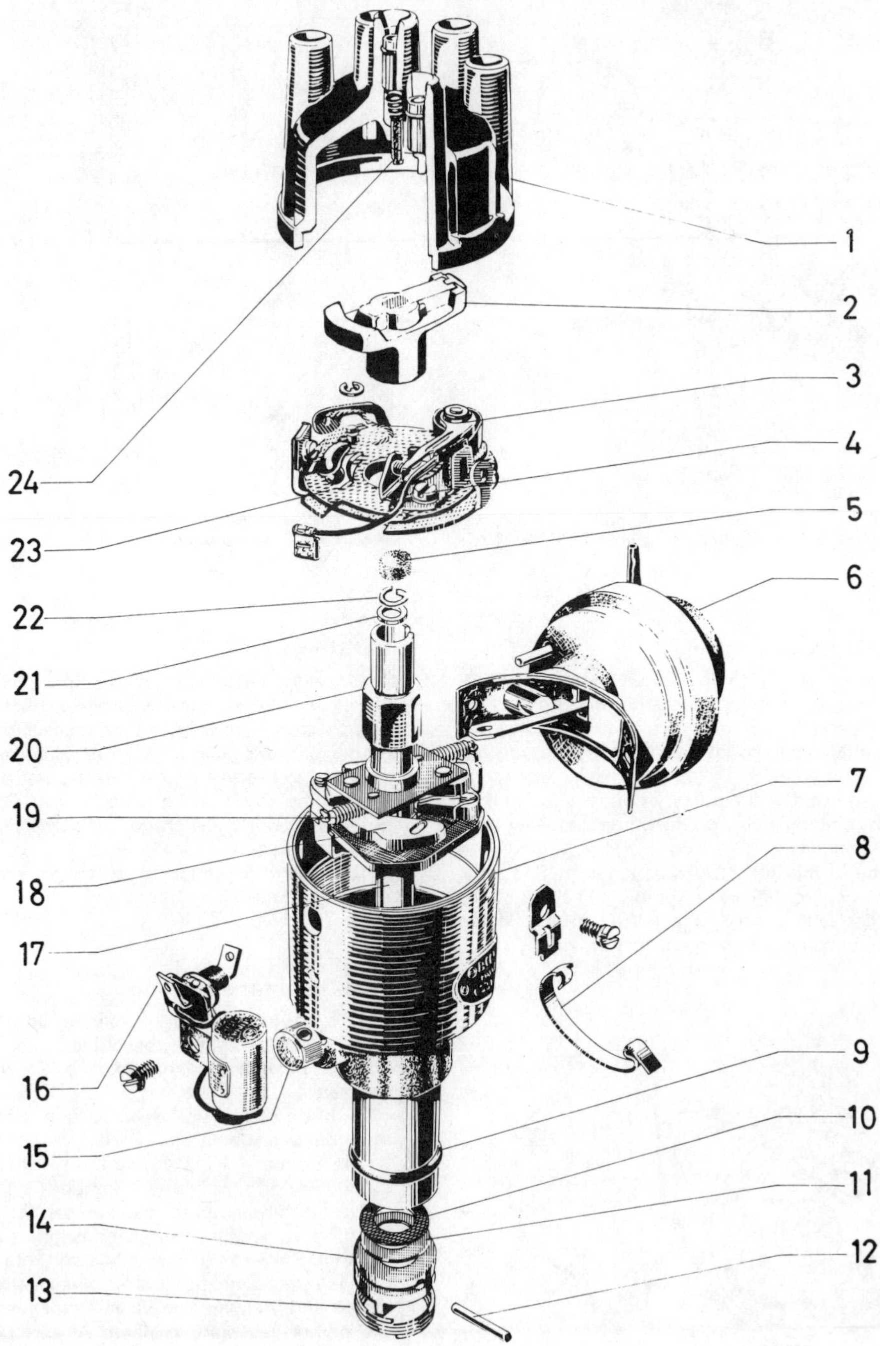

FIG 3:3 Components of the distributor

Key to Fig 3:3 1 Distributor cap 2 Distributor arm 3 Contact breaker 4 Lockscrew for breaker contacts 5 Lubricating felt 6 Vacuum regulator 7 Distributor housing 8 Cap clamp 9 Rubber seal 10 Fibre washer 11 Steel washer 12 Lockpin 13 Spring ring 14 Flange 15 Lubricator 16 Primary connection 17 Distributor shaft 18 Centrifugal weight 19 Centrifugal governor spring 20 Breaker cam 21 Washer 22 Circlip 23 Breaker plate 24 Rod brush (carbon)

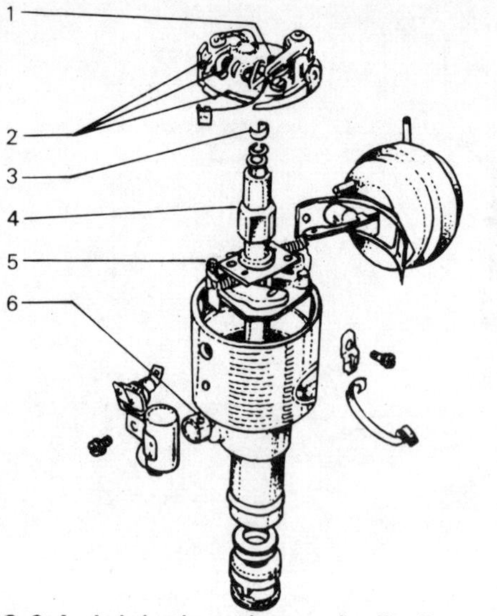

FIG 3:4 Lubricating points on the distributor

Key to Fig 3:4 1 Grease on contact lip 2 Grease 3 Oil on felt pad 4 Smear of grease 5 Grease 6 Fill with oil

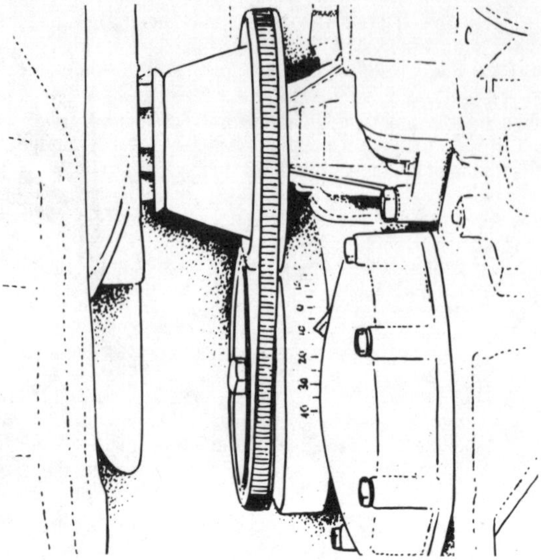

FIG 3:6 Flywheel damper with ignition graduation marks and timing case pointer

Contact breaker replacement:

Should it be necessary to fit a new contact breaker assembly without dismantling the distributor, proceed as follows:

Release the two clips and lift off the cap. Take out the rotor arm.

Disconnect the lead at the primary connection.

Remove the securing screw on the contact breaker and lift off the old contacts.

Lubricate the distributor in accordance with **FIG 3:4** and fit the new contact breaker assembly, checking carefully that it is correctly located. Check the gap and adjust if necessary by bending the fixed contact only.

FIG 3:5 Showing recess for adjusting contact breaker points. Gap=.010 to .014 inch (.25 to .35 mm)

Refitting:

Place the distributor in position and press it downwards while turning the rotor arm at the same time. When the distrbutor drops about $\frac{3}{16}$ inch (5 mm) and it is no longer possible to turn the rotor, the driving collar has engaged in the slot on the distributor drive shaft.

Turn the distributor housing into the same position as before removal and tighten the clamp bolt sufficiently to hold it in place.

Connect the primary lead and fit the cap. Start the engine and set the ignition.

3:3 Timing the ignition

This should always be carried out with the engine running and using a stroboscopic timing lamp, but in the absence of such an instrument the following method may be used.

Turn the engine until No. 1 piston is almost at TDC on the compression stroke (both valves closed) and the timing pointer on the timing case at the 10 deg. BTDC graduation on the flywheel damper (see **FIG 3:6**).

Lift off the distributor cap and see that the rotor arm is pointing towards that segment in the cap servicing No. 1 cylinder. Slacken the clamp bolt and rotate the distributor body slightly anticlockwise to ensure that the points are closed and then very slowly in a clockwise direction until the points just start to open. At this point tighten the clamp bolt.

A more accurate way to determine the exact moment when the points break is to connect a 12-volt bulb between the primary terminal and earth then, with the ignition switched on, the bulb will light up at the moment of breaking.

Stroboscopic timing:

Clean the flywheel damper so that the graduation marks are clearly visible. It may be of assistance if the 10 deg. BTDC mark is given a spot of white paint.

Remove the hoses from the vacuum regulator and plug the ends to prevent an air leak into the induction passages.

Connect the stroboscopic lamp to No. 1 sparking plug in accordance with the makers instructions.

Start the engine and run it at 600 to 800 rev/min, then aim the lamp at the graduation marks and rotate the distributor body until the specified mark appears stationary against the crankcase pointer. Tighten the distributor clamp bolt and recheck.

Remove the lamp and replace the vacuum hoses.

3:4 Sparking plugs

The plugs recommended for use in these cars are Bosch W.200.T.35 or the equivalent from other makers, and the correct gap is .028 to .032 inch (.7 to .8 mm). They should be removed for cleaning and inspection at regular intervals and the gap adjusted if necessary by bending the earth electrode only.

Plugs are best cleaned on a sand blasting machine which will usually have facilities for testing the plug under pressure. The threaded portion of the plug should be cleaned up with a wire brush before refitting. The original gasket should only be washed again if it has not been compressed into a thin washer.

The condition of the sparking plugs can be useful in providing information about the internal condition of the engine and also its state of tune, mixture strength etc.

Examine the firing end of the plugs and observe the type of deposit. Normally it will be a thin powdery coating of a light brown or greyish tan colour. This is the effect of mixed high-speed and low-speed driving with an engine in good tune.

If the deposits are white or slightly yellow, they indicate long periods of constant-speed driving or much low-speed city driving.

Wet black deposits are due to oil entering the combustion chamber past worn pistons and bores, past broken piston rings or down valve stems. Do not confuse this oily deposit with the wetness on plugs due to excessive fuel being introduced into the combustion chamber through over-choking. The cure for oil contamination is an engine overhaul.

Dry, black, fluffy deposits are the result of running with a rich mixture, or incomplete fuel combustion due to defective ignition. Excessive idling may also be a cause.

Overheated sparking plugs will have a white, blistered look about the electrodes, and these may be heavily eroded. The cause may be weak mixture, poor cooling, defective ignition or sustained high speeds with heavy loads.

It is false economy to run an engine with old sparking plugs and a new set should be fitted every 10,000 miles.

3:5 HT leads

Renew high-tension cables if they are defective in any way. Inspect them regularly for broken or deteriorated insulation which could be a cause of misfiring particularly in wet weather.

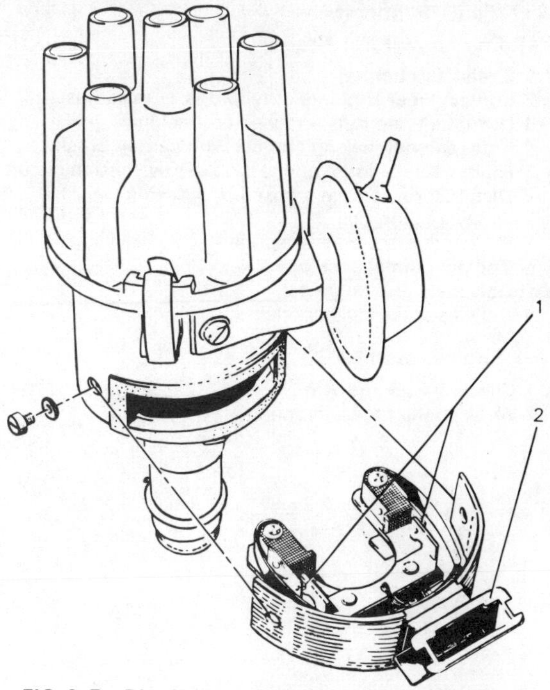

FIG 3:7 Distributor with electronic control device

Key to Fig 3:7 1 Triggering contacts 2 Electrical connection

When renewing an HT cable push it through the knurled terminal nut then bare about $\frac{1}{4}$ inch of the wire, fit the split brass washer and fan out the wire strands over the face of the washer. Screwing the nut into its socket will secure the cable.

3:6 Fuel injection

On engines fitted with electronic fuel injection a modified distributor is used having a contact device with two triggering contacts as shown in **FIG 3:7**.

These are mounted below the centrifugal governor and are actuated by a cam on the distributor shaft. Their purpose is to supply information to the control unit about engine speed for the determination of time and duration of injection with the additional data supplied by the pressure sensor.

Timing the ignition:

Instructions given in **Section 3:3** should be amended by the following:

Remove the hose for the air cleaner at the inlet duct and disconnect the hose to the distributor vacuum governor from the inlet duct.

Adjust the engine speed to between 700 and 800 rev/min.

Turn the distributor to give a firing point of 10 deg. BTDC.

3:7 Fault diagnosis

(a) Engine will not fire

1 Battery discharged
2 Contact breaker points dirty, pitted or maladjusted
3 Distributor cap dirty, cracked or 'tracking'
4 Rotor arm not making contact with carbon brush
5 Faulty cable or loose connection in low-tension circuit
6 Distributor rotor arm cracked or 'tracking'
7 Faulty ignition coil
8 Broken contact breaker spring
9 Contact points stuck open
10 Defective ignition switch
11 Plug leads wrongly connected

(b) Engine misfires

1 Check 2, 3, 5 and 7 in (a)
2 Weak contact breaker spring
3 High-tension plug or coil leads wet, cracked or perished
4 Sparking plug(s) loose
5 Sparking plug insulation cracked
6 Sparking plug gap incorrectly set
7 Ignition timing too far advanced
8 Excessive wear of distributor spindles and bushes

(c) Engine lacks power

1 Check 2 and 3 in (a) and check (b)
2 Ignition timing retarded
3 Defective centrifugal or vacuum units in distributor
4 Vacuum unit suction pipe disconnected or leaking
5 Sparking plugs worn out
6 One plug lead detached

CHAPTER 4

THE COOLING SYSTEM

4:1 Description

The engine is cooled by a conventional sealed water cooling system assisted by a ducted speed-regulated fan. An overflow or expansion tank is included to allow for operation under all climatic conditions without losing coolant, which should only require changing every two years.

The general layout of the system is shown in **FIG 4:1** which shows how the water is circulated through the system by a pump driven by a belt from a pulley on the forward end of the crankshaft. The water flows along a duct through the upper part of the engine then downwards around the cylinder walls and through the cylinder head emerging at the front end of the engine again into a space immediately below the thermostat, from which it passes either directly back to the pump or is diverted through the radiator according to the position of the thermostat valve which is responsive to the temperature of the coolant.

The action of the thermostat is clearly illustrated in **FIGS 4:2** and **4:3**. In the first diagram, with the thermostat in the cold position, the passage to the radiator is closed by the upper valve in the thermostat housing and all coolant flow is downwards through the bypass pipe and back to the pump inlet.

As the temperature rises the upper valve commences to open and the lower valve flap starts to cover up the bypass pipe until at a predetermined temperature the bypass is completely closed and all coolant circulation is through the radiator. It should be mentioned here that the water for the cars heater system is taken from the inner bypass circuit and so is brought quickly up to working temperature.

A space is left in the top of the expansion tank to act as an air cushion and permits the coolant to expand without any loss and ensures that as the temperature decreases the coolant is sucked back into the main system and keeps it filled and so helps to reduce corrosion.

The valve in the expansion tank filler cap is designed to open at a pressure of 10 lb/sq inch (.7 kg/sq cm). There is also a valve which opens when there is a partial vacuum in the system and admits air into the expansion tank.

4:2 Draining and filling the system

To drain the system it is necessary to open the drain cock on the engine and also disconnect the lower radiator hose. The expansion tank is emptied by unbolting it from its mounting and then raising it in the air so that the water

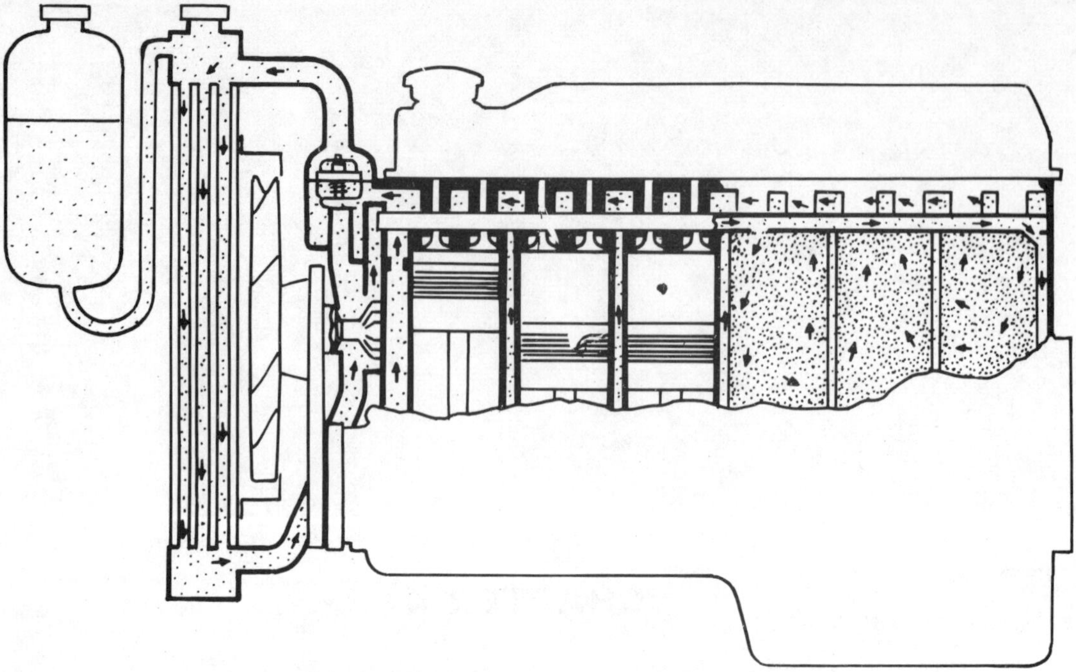

FIG 4:1 Layout of cooling system

runs into the radiator, or of course it can be turned upside down and the water poured into a suitable container.

Before refilling the cooling system it should be thoroughly flushed out with clean water preferably through a hosepipe inserted in the filler cap and allowed to flow throughout the system until it comes out without any further signs of sediment or discolouration.

The mixture recommended as a coolant in these engines is a mixture of 50 per cent ethylene glycol and 50 percent water. This mixture is used all the year round and provides protection against frost down to —35°C (—32°F) and should be changed every other year. If Volvo antifreeze, which is red in colour, is already in the engine, it should not be mixed with other brands of antifreeze.

When filling with coolant through the aperture on top of the radiator, the heater control should be set to maximum heat and the radiator filled to the top and the cap replaced. Fill also the expansion bottle to the MAX mark.

Run the engine for a few minutes at various speeds, top up if necessary and fit the cap on the expansion bottle. After a short drive check the level again.

4:3 The radiator

Removal of the radiator is as follows:

Take off the filler cap and drain the system by disconnecting the lower radiator hose.

Remove the expansion tank and hose and empty it. Remove the upper radiator hose.

Unscrew the bolts securing the radiator and the fan cowling. Lift off the radiator.

Refitting is a reversal of the removal procedure, after which the system must be refilled as described in **Section 4:2**.

4:4 The water pump

To remove the pump it is first necessary to take off the radiator as previously described in **Section 4:3**. Slacken the alternator mounting bolts to free the belt, then remove the bolts securing the pump to the engine and pull it away.

Thoroughly clean the pump and check the parts (see **FIG 4:4**) for excessive wear or corrosion and renew if necessary.

Use a new joint gasket when refitting and make sure that the sealing rings on the upper side of the pump locate correctly. Press the pump upwards against the cylinder head extension so as to ensure a satisfactory joint there, and see that the sealing rings at the water pipes are not damaged and make a sound joint when the pipes are fully pressed home.

Insert the securing bolts and tighten them up evenly. Refit the belt and tighten as follows:

4:5 The fan belt

This takes the drive from the pulley on the forward end of the crankshaft to the water pump and fan pulley and also to the alternator, and it is by adjusting the position of this latter component that the correct tension on the belt is obtained.

The belt should be tensioned so that it can be deflected by $\frac{3}{8}$ inch when a load of 15 to 20 lb is applied to the belt between the water pump pulley and the alternator pulley as shown in **FIG 4:5**.

The amount of force applied will depend on the location of the alternator tensioning bolt in its elongated slot between the long and short belt positions. With the bolt in the long belt position the load applied should be 15 lb

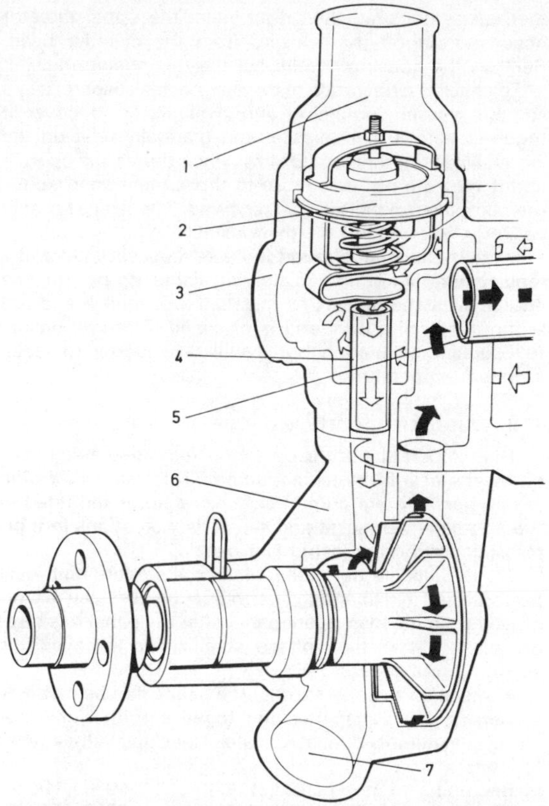

FIG 4:2 Coolant flow with thermostat closed

Key to Fig 4:2 1 To radiator 2 Thermostat 3 Cylinder head 4 Bypass pipe 5 Distributing pipe 6 Water pump 7 From radiator

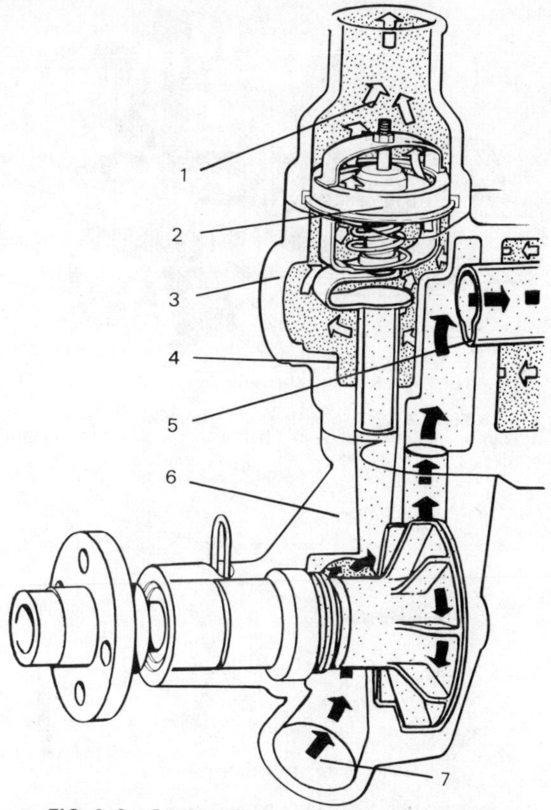

FIG 4:3 Coolant flow with thermostat open

Key to Fig 4:3 1 To radiator 2 Thermostat 3 Cylinder head 4 Bypass pipe 5 Distributing pipe 6 Water pump 7 From radiator

and at the short end of the slot it should be 20 lb. Between these two extremes the force applied should be in proportion.

If a new belt is being fitted, the tension should be checked and if necessary readjusted to take up the initial stretching.

Make sure that all the alternator securing bolts are loosened when adjusting otherwise excessive loads may easily be applied. Note also that oblique loading of the alternator is to be avoided. If a lever is to be used for moving the alternator into position it should be placed between the engine and the drive end bracket.

4:6 The fan

The type of cooling fan which is fitted as standard to these cars is speed regulated with a so-called slip-coupling the function of which is to ensure that the fan blades do not exceed a certain speed irrespective of the engine speed. The fan has five blades which are mounted asymmetrically in order to keep down the noise level.

Refer to **FIG 4:6**. The fan coupling consists of the casing 11 to which the plastic blade assembly is secured by the bolts 2. The casing is in two halves, but they cannot be separated for repairs and in the event of a failure the fan coupling must be replaced complete.

The hub 8 is a light fit on the flange of the water pump 6 to which it is locked by the centre bolt 7. This hub is provided with a disc of friction material 9 surrounded by oil. At low engine speed the degree of slip is minimal and good cooling is obtained at these times.

As the engine speed increases, the speed of the water pump increases accordingly and at about 2600 rev/min the degree of slip begins to be seen and increases rapidly with the result that at full engine speed the fan should not be doing more than 3000 to 3500 rev/min. In this way the noise output is reduced when compared with a conventionally driven fan at the same engine speeds. It is also claimed that the power loss is reduced.

On cars exported to the USA a fixed fan is used fitted with blades which straighten out at higher speeds. It is designed to give a particularly good cooling effect at low speeds.

4:7 The thermostat

This is of the wax type and is identified by the marking 82° this being the temperature C at which the valve begins to open (177 to 182°F). It should be fully open at 90°C (194°F).

To remove the thermostat, drain sufficient water out of the system to bring the coolant level below the

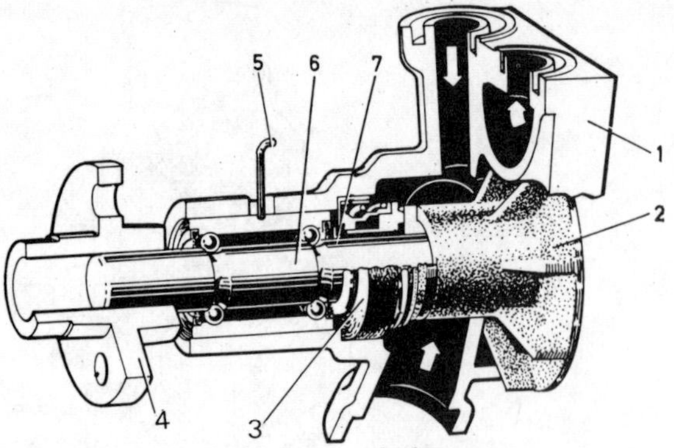

FIG 4:4 Section through the water pump

Key to Fig 4:4 1 Housing 2 Impeller 3 Seal ring 4 Flange 5 Lock spring 6 Shaft with ball bearings (integral unit) 7 Wear ring

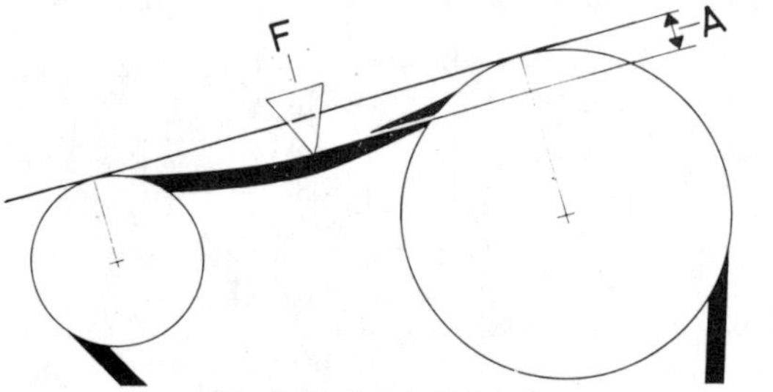

FIG 4:5 Fan belt tension

Key to Fig 4:5 F=15 to 20 lb (7 to 9 kg) A=⅜ inch (10 mm)

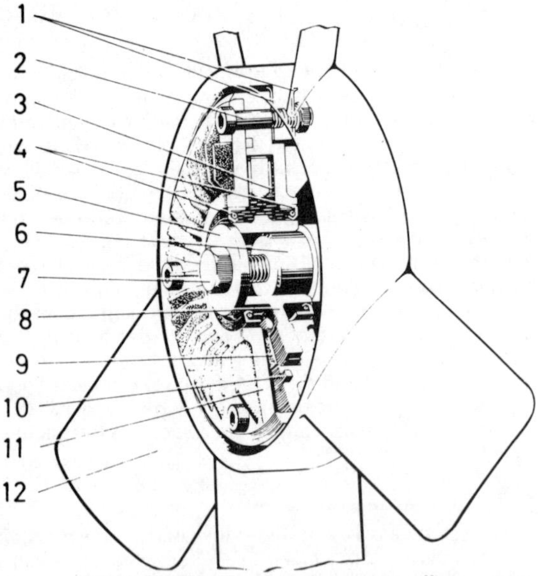

FIG 4:6 The fan and viscous coupling

Key to Fig 4:6 1 Washers 2 Bolt 3 Oil 4 Seals 5 Washer 6 Flange, water pump 7 Centre bolt 8 Hub 9 Friction material 10 Rubber ring 11 Casing 12 Fan blade

thermostat housing, then disconnect the upper radiator hose and unbolt the housing from the cylinder head. Removė the housing and lift out the thermostat unit.

To check the operation of the thermostat, suspend it in a suitable vessel containing sufficient water to cover it together with a thermometer and gradually heat up the water. Note the temperatures at which the valves operate and if they are not very close to those mentioned above the complete unit should be renewed. Always use a new gasket when refitting the thermostat.

If the thermostat is found to be seriously at fault and a replacement is not immediately available, do not run the engine with the faulty unit installed, but omit it and run without it until a new unit is obtained. This will ensure full coolant circulation but it will take longer to reach working temperature.

4:8 Water temperature gauge

The temperature of the coolant is measured electrically be means of a bi-metal instrument. The transmitter unit, which passes more current as it heats up, is mounted in the engine water jacket and sends its indications to a bi-metal gauge on the instrument panel.

These units are not repairable and the entire unit must be replaced if damaged. The indicating dial can be removed from the instrument panel after the panel has been detached. When the voltage stabilizer is removed the securing nuts are accessible.

A check on the operation of the gauge can be made by immersing the transmitter unit together with a thermometer in a quantity of heated water. Checking values are as follows:

Beginning of green area (at 'C')	40°C (105°F)
Dividing line between green areas	70°C (150°F)
Dividing line between green and red areas	100°C (212°F)

If an ohmmeter is available the resistance of the two units can be checked. The indicating head should have a resistance of about 12.5 ohms and the transmitter unit approximately 200 ohms.

4:9 Fault diagnosis

(a) Overheating

1 Broken or loose fan belt
2 Low coolant level
3 Ignition retarded
4 Weak fuel mixture
5 Choked exhaust system
6 Faulty thermostat
7 Faulty temperature gauge or sender

(b) Loss of coolant

1 Leaking hoses or joints
2 Faulty head gasket
3 Cylinder head cracked
4 Cylinder head bolts loose

(c) Poor circulation

1 Radiator blocked
2 Engine water passages obstructed
3 Fan belt loose
4 Thermostat defective
5 Perished or collapsed hoses

CHAPTER 5

THE CLUTCH

5:1 Description

The clutch fitted to these cars is a conventional diaphragm spring type consisting of a pressure plate and the diaphragm spring in a sheet metal casing. The complete assembly is riveted together and cannot be dismantled and a failure must be rectified by renewal.

The clutch is operated, in the case of lefthand drive cars, by means of a cable system between the clutch pedal and the release lever, but on righthand drive cars a hydraulic system is used.

5:2 Clutch pedal adjustment

Hydraulic operation

The correct amount of free play with this type of operation is obtained by adjusting the thrust rod on the clutch slave cylinder as shown in **FIG 5:1**.

The correct clearance is when there is between .08 inch and .12 inch (2 to 3 mm) play at the end of the release lever and this is obtained by slackening off the locknut 10 and rotating the screwed thrust rod 11 in the thrust sleeve 6 as required to give the necessary free movement.

Cable operation:

The correct adjustment is when there is between .16 and .20 inch (4 to 5 mm) free play at the end of the clutch release lever. This adjustment will normally be made by screwing the fork (3 in **FIG 5:2**), on the end of the clutch cable as necessary to obtain the specified dimension after loosening the locknut 2.

If this adjustment is not sufficient for any reason, such as the renewal of the clutch cable, the attachment for the cable outer casing can be moved by means of the nuts 1.

Renewing a clutch cable:

First unhook the return spring for the release lever then disconnect the cable.

Unscrew the rear nut and remove the outer casing from the clutch housing.

Disconnect the cable from the clutch pedal, then unscrew the nut for the cable casing and remove the cable.

The new cable is fitted in the reverse order to removal after which the pedal play must be adjusted.

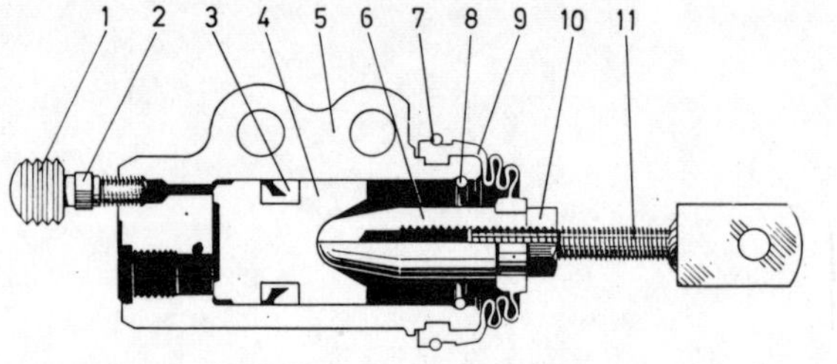

FIG 5:1 Hydraulic slave cylinder showing clutch adjustment

Key to Fig 5:1 1 Rubber cover 2 Venting nipple 3 Piston seal 4 Piston 5 Cylinder 6 Thrust sleeve 7 Circlip 8 Stop ring 9 Rubber cover 10 Locknut 11 Thrust rod

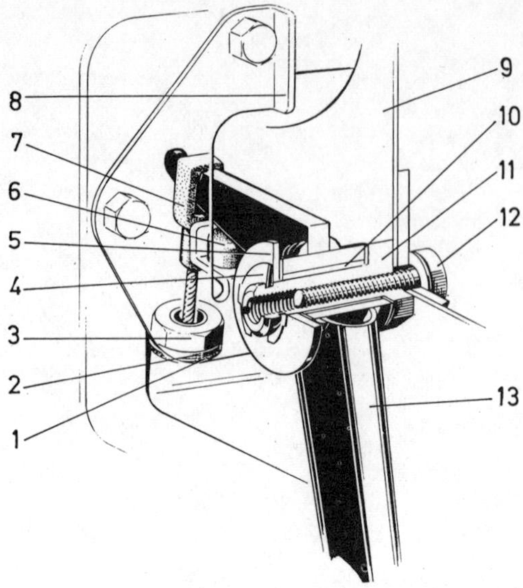

FIG 5:3 The pedal carrier

Fig 5:3 1 Rubber bushing 2 Washer 3 Nut 4 Lockwasher 5 Washer 6 Rubber stop 7 Clutch wire 8 Stop bracket 9 Bracket 10 Bush 11 Pedal shaft 12 Bolt 13 Clutch pedal

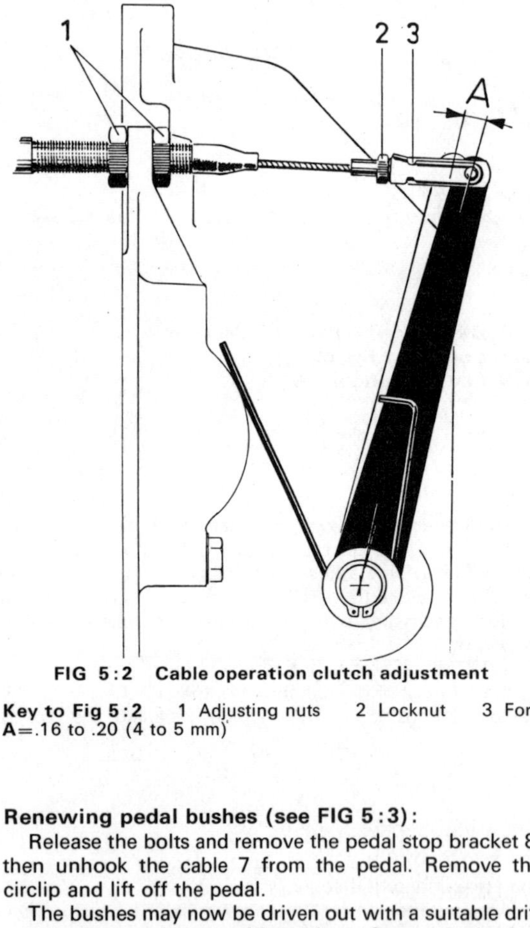

FIG 5:2 Cable operation clutch adjustment

Key to Fig 5:2 1 Adjusting nuts 2 Locknut 3 Fork **A**=.16 to .20 (4 to 5 mm)

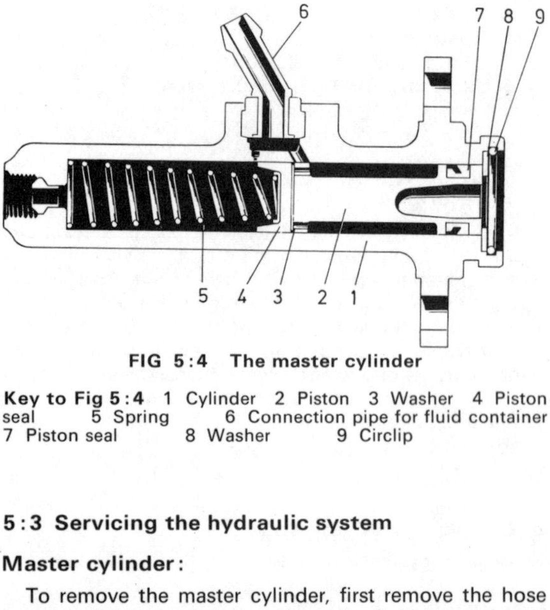

FIG 5:4 The master cylinder

Key to Fig 5:4 1 Cylinder 2 Piston 3 Washer 4 Piston seal 5 Spring 6 Connection pipe for fluid container 7 Piston seal 8 Washer 9 Circlip

Renewing pedal bushes (see FIG 5:3):

Release the bolts and remove the pedal stop bracket 8, then unhook the cable 7 from the pedal. Remove the circlip and lift off the pedal.

The bushes may now be driven out with a suitable drift and the new ones pressed into place. Grease the bushes well before fitting the pedal shaft which also should be renewed if it is worn. This is held in place by the bolt 12.

Replace the pedal on its shaft and secure with the circlip. Hook on the wire to the pedal, fit the stop bracket and adjust the free movement as described earlier.

5:3 Servicing the hydraulic system

Master cylinder:

To remove the master cylinder, first remove the hose from the fluid reservoir and allow the fluid to run into a clean container, then disconnect the pressure pipe from the master cylinder.

Remove the bolt in the clutch pedal then release the two securing bolts and lift off the master cylinder (see **FIG 5:4**).

Take off the rubber cover and extract the thrust rod.

Remove the circlip 9 and take out the washer 8, piston 2 together with the piston seal 4 and the return spring 5.

Remove the outer piston seal 7. Wash all parts in white spirit and inspect for wear or damage. New seals should always be used when reassembling. Other parts should be renewed according to their condition.

Dip all parts in clean brake fluid before assembly and then fit them together in the reverse order to dismantling. Make sure that the venting hole in the rubber cover is at the bottom.

Refit the pipes, top up with fluid and bleed the system.

Slave cylinder:

Disconnect the pipe and unhook the return spring. Disconnect the fork from the clutch release lever, remove the securing bolts and lift off.

Remove the rubber cover 9 and the thrust rod and sleeve assembly. Take off the circlip 8 and extract the piston.

Clean and inspect all the parts, renewing as necessary and reassemble in the reverse order. Bleed the system and adjust the free travel of the clutch release lever.

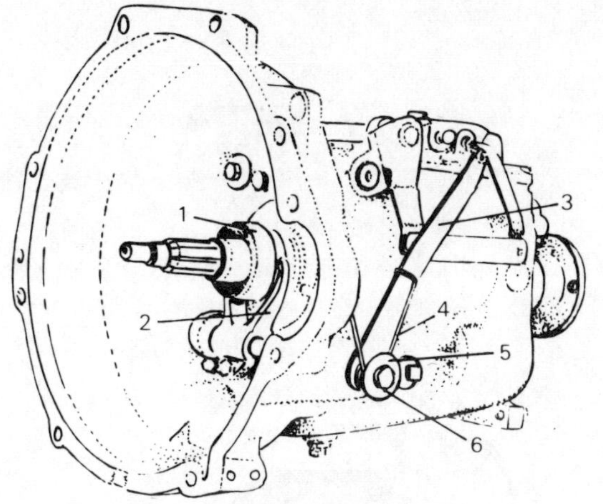

FIG 5:5 Clutch release mechanism

Key to Fig 5:5 1 Release bearing 2 Release fork 3 Release shaft and lever 4 Return spring 5 Washer 6 Circlip

5:4 Bleeding the hydraulic system

Make sure that the fluid reservoir is full, then remove the rubber cap on the bleeding nipple on the slave cylinder and fit a length of rubber or plastic hose to it, allowing the free end to be immersed in a quantity of brake fluid in a clean glass jar.

Enlist the services of an assistant and open the bleed valve while the pedal is being fully depressed. Hold it down and close the bleed valve. Release the pedal, open the bleed valve and repeat the procedure until the fluid expelled into the jar is completely free from air bubbles. Close the bleed valve, refit the rubber cap on the nipple and top up the reservoir.

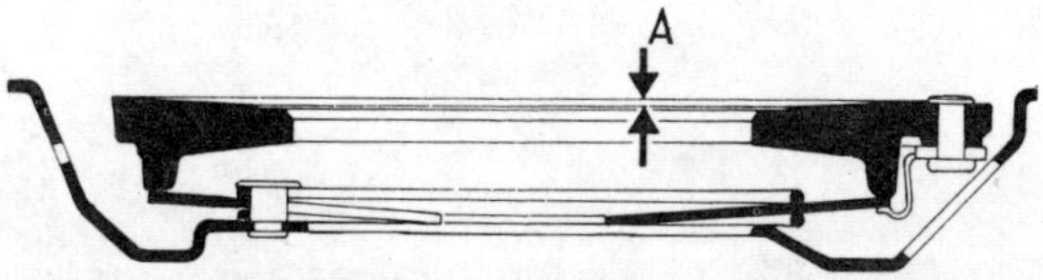

FIG 5:6 Checking the curvation of pressure plate. A= distance between straight edge and inner diameter of pressure plate, must be less than .0012 inch (.03 mm)

5:5 Servicing the clutch

Remove the gearbox as described in **Chapter 6**.

Slacken the bolts holding the clutch to the flywheel by loosening them diametrically two turns at a time to prevent possible distortion.

Remove the clutch and clutch plate.

Release mechanism (see FIG 5:5):

Remove the bolt in the release fork 2, take out the release bearing 1 and pull out the release shaft.

Old worn bushes should be knocked out using a suitable drift and new bushes pressed in.

Apply a layer of grease to the sleeve of the release bearing before fitting in position. Hold the release fork in place and insert the release shaft and secure.

Inspection:

Examine the pressure plate for scoring or heat damage on the friction surface and check its curvature with a steel rule or straightedge laid diagonally over the friction surface. Measure the distance between the straightedge and the inner diameter of the pressure plate (see **FIG 5:6**). This must not exceed .0012 inch (.03 mm).

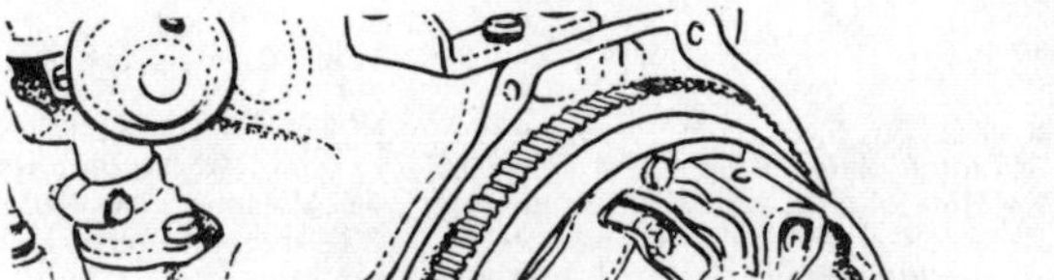

FIG 5:7 Fitting the clutch with mandrel SVO 2824

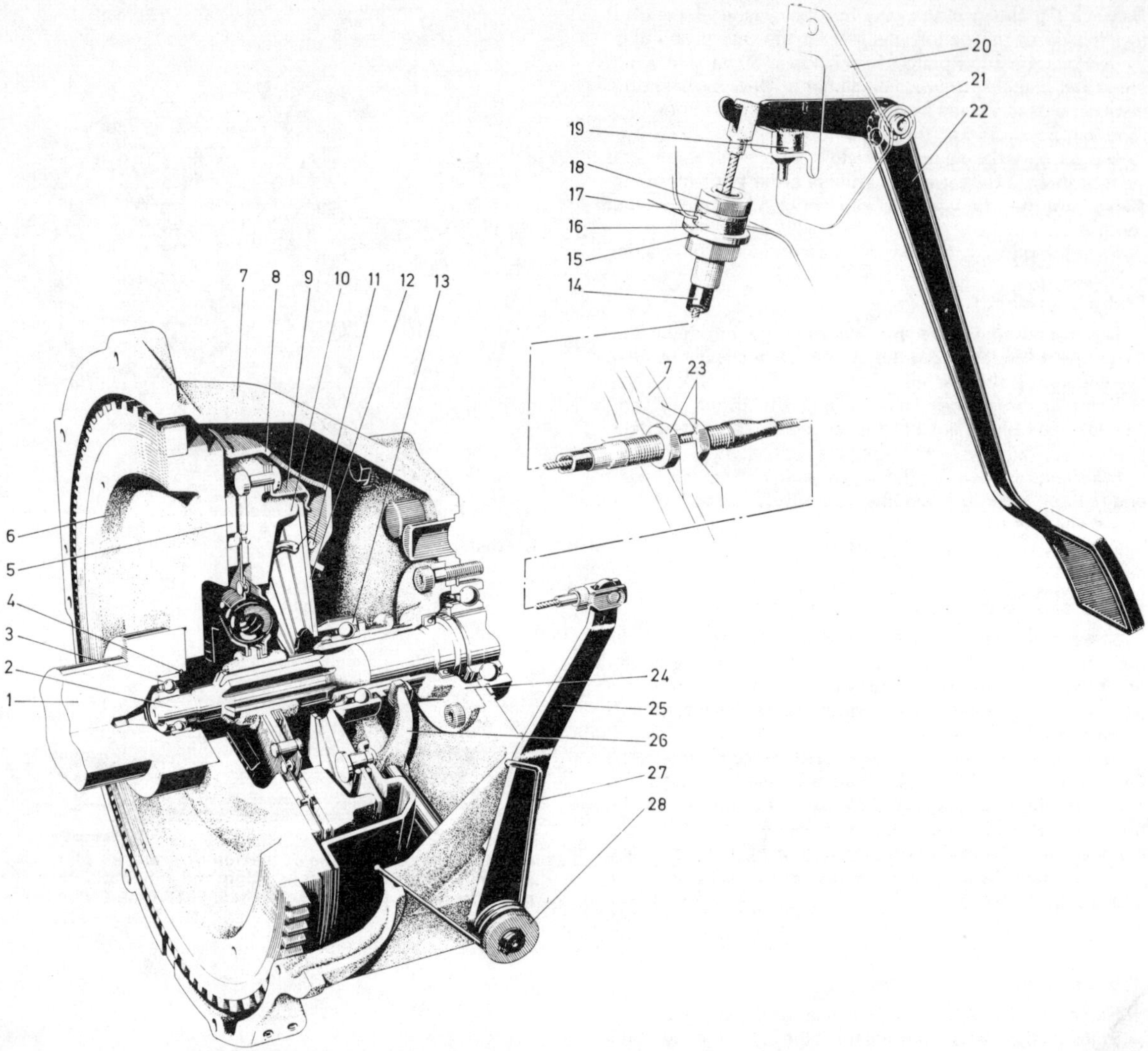

FIG 5:8 Components of clutch assembly: cable release

Key to Fig 5:8 1 Crankshaft 2 Clutch plate shaft (input shaft, gearbox) 3 Support bearing in crankshaft 4 Circlip 5 Clutch plate 6 Flywheel 7 Flywheel casing 8 Clutch cover 9 Retainer 10 Thrust plate 11 Support rings 12 Pressure spring 13 Release bearing 14 Clutch wire 15 Washer 16 Rubber bush 17 Washer 18 Nut 19 Rubber stop 20 Stop bracket 21 Pedal shaft 22 Clutch pedal 23 Adjusting nuts 24 Cover, gearbox 25 Lever and release shaft 26 Release fork 27 Return spring 28 Washer

There must also be no crowning or clearance between the straightedge and the outer diameter of the pressure plate. Carry out these checks at several different points.

Check that the clutch facings, flywheel and pressure plate are not damaged and free from oil. Wash in clean petrol and dry with a clean cloth.

Fitting:

Set up the clutch plate with the longest side of the hub towards the rear, together with the clutch against the flywheel and insert tool SVO.2824 or other suitable mandrel into the pilot bearing in the flywheel as shown in **FIG 5:7** so that the guide journal on this centres the pilot bearing in the flywheel.

Refit the six securing bolts and tighten them diagonally two turns at a time to a torque of 15 lb ft then remove the mandrel.

Refit the gearbox according to the procedure given in **Chapter 6**, and adjust the clutch pedal play as described in **Section 5:2**. A sectional view of the complete clutch installation with cable operation is given in **FIG 5:8**.

5:6 Fault diagnosis

(a) Drag or spin

1 Oil or grease on linings
2 Misalignment between engine and clutch shaft
3 Leaking master cylinder or pipeline
4 Binding driven plate
5 Driven plate distorted
6 Dirt of foreign matter in clutch
7 Air in hydraulic system
8 Incorrect adjustment
9 Cable binding
10 Diaphragm faulty

(b) Fierceness or snatch

1 Check 1, 2 and 3 in (a)
2 Worn friction linings

(c) Slip

1 Check 1, 3, 8 and 9 in (a), check 2 in (b)
2 Weak diaphragm spring
3 Piston seized in master cylinder
4 Dirt in hydraulic system

(d) Judder

1 Check 1 and 2 in (a)
2 Pressure plate not parallel to flywheel
3 Splined shaft bent
4 Buckled plate
5 Worn release mechanism

CHAPTER 6

GEARBOX AND OVERDRIVE

6 : 1 Description

The gearbox type M400, or M410 when coupled to an overdrive, is a conventional fourspeed and reverse type having synchromesh engagement on all four forward speeds. Helical cut gears are used and all except reverse are in constant mesh with one another, and for this reason the mainshaft gear is journalled with needle bearings. The internal arrangement of the gearbox and changing mechanism can be seen in the cut-away view of **FIG 6 : 1**.

6 : 2 Maintenance

This is confined to a periodical check on the oil level and topping up as required with the recommended grade of oil. For the type M400 gearbox a gear oil of specification SAE.90 is advised although an engine oil of SAE.30 is permissible as an alternative. The capacity is approximately 1.1 pints (.6 litre). When overdrive is fitted, an engine oil of the same viscosity is recommended and the capacity for the combined units is $2\frac{1}{2}$ pints (1.4 litres).

After the first oil change at 3000 miles, the oil should be drained out and renewed at intervals of 25,000 miles by removing the drain plug underneath the gearbox. This is best done after a run when the oil will be warm and will run out more easily.

6 : 3 Removing the gearbox

Take the weight of the engine on a suitable rig such as SVO.2727 as shown in **FIG 6 : 2**, noting that the lifting hook is secured round the exhaust manifold. Securely jack up the car and drain the oil from the gearbox.

Remove the gearlever and disconnect the upper mounting bolts from the radiator, the exhaust manifold flange nuts, the battery, the throttle shaft and clutch wire from the flywheel housing.

Remove the supporting member under the gearbox then disconnect the bracket for the exhaust pipe, the propeller shaft and the speedometer cable.

Lower the rear end of the engine about two inches and and release the leads for the reversing lights and overdrive when fitted.

Support the gearbox on a suitable jack, remove the bolts in the clutch casing and pull the gearbox to the rear and downwards.

Refitting the gearbox is a reversal of the above procedure.

6 : 4 Dismantling the gearbox

These instructions also apply to the type M410 after the overdrive has been removed, and will be facilitated if the box can be supported in a fixture which will permit swivelling and inverting.

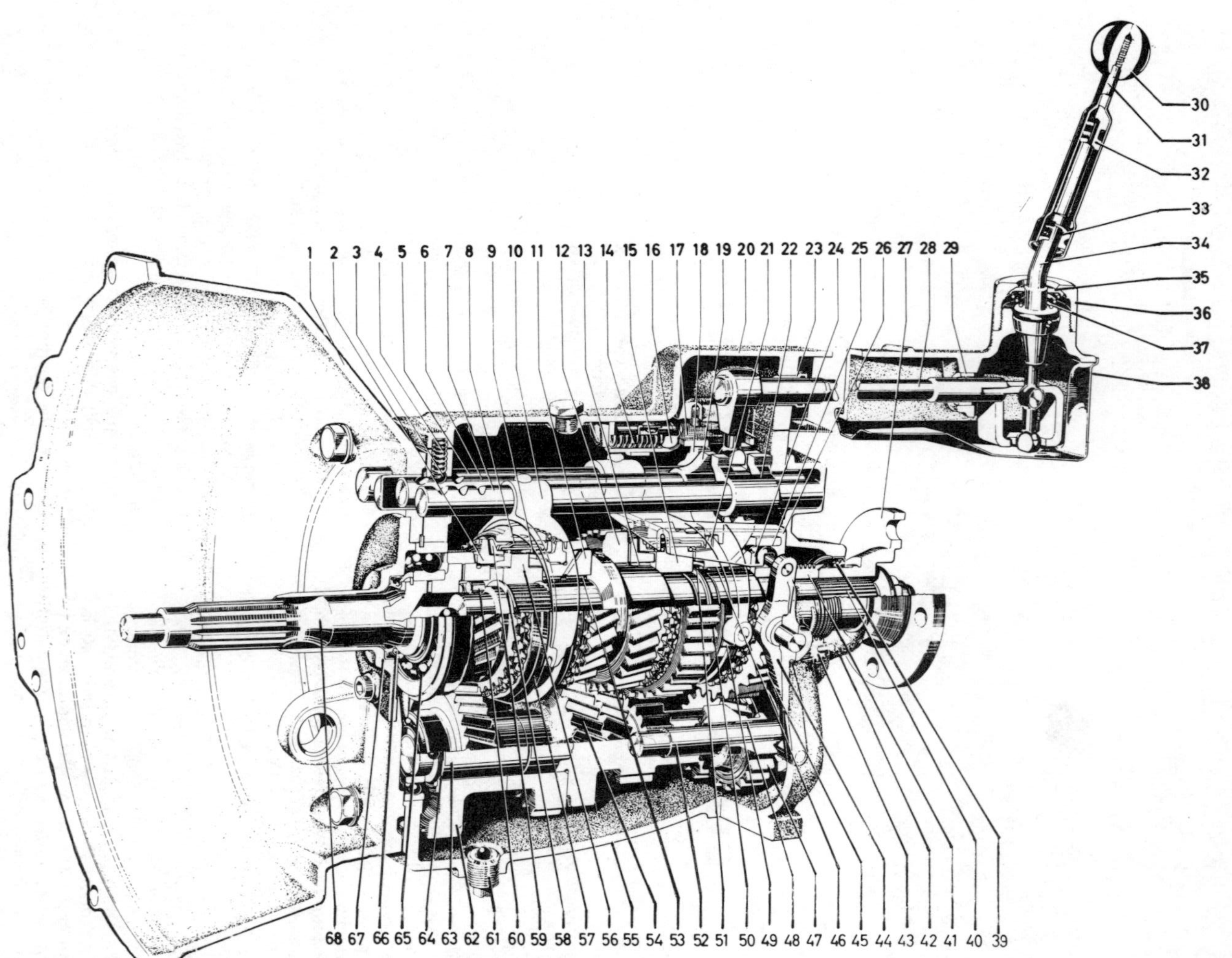

FIG 6:1 Cut-away view of gearbox

Key to Fig 6:1 1 Clutch casing 2 Engaging ring 3 Interlock ball 4 Spring 5 Selector rail, reverse gear 6 Selector rail for 1st and 2nd gears 7 Selector rail for 3rd and 4th gears 8 Flange 9 Spring 10 Selector fork 11 Gearwheel, 3rd speed 12 Gearwheel, 2nd speed 13 Needle bearing 14 Spring 15 Synchronizing hub, 1st to 2nd gears 16 Interlock ball 17 Sliding plate 18 Flange 19 Selector fork, 1st and 2nd gears 20 Gearbox cover 21 Synchronizing cone 22 Flange 23 Bush 24 Thrust washer 25 Ballbearing 26 Selector fork, reverse gear 27 Flange 28 Shaft 29 Bush 30 Gearlever knob 31 Gearlever, upper section 32 Rubber bush 33 Rubber bush 34 Gearlever, lower section 35 Washer 36 Cover 37 Spring 38 Protective casing 39 Oil seal 40 Mainshaft 41 Speedometer drive 42 Rear cover 43 Speedometer pinion 44 Shift lever 45 Gearwheel, 1st gear 46 Needle bearing 47 Reverse gear 48 Bush 49 Slide register 50 Engaging sleeve and gearwheel for reverse gear 51 Circlip 52 Reverse gearshaft 53 Needle bearing 54 Gearwheel 55 Gearbox housing 56 Synchronizing hub 57 Engaging sleeve 58 Circlip 59 Synchronizing cone 60 Needle bearing 61 Drain plug 62 Gearwheel 63 Countershaft 64 Ballbearing 65 Ballbearing 66 Oil seal 67 Cover 68 Input shaft

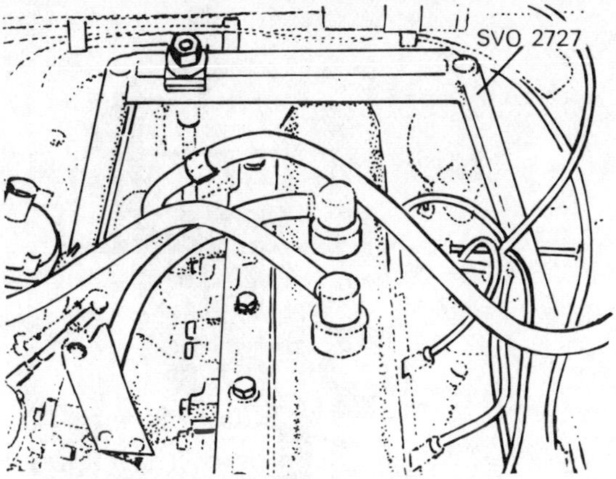

FIG 6:2 Supporting the engine

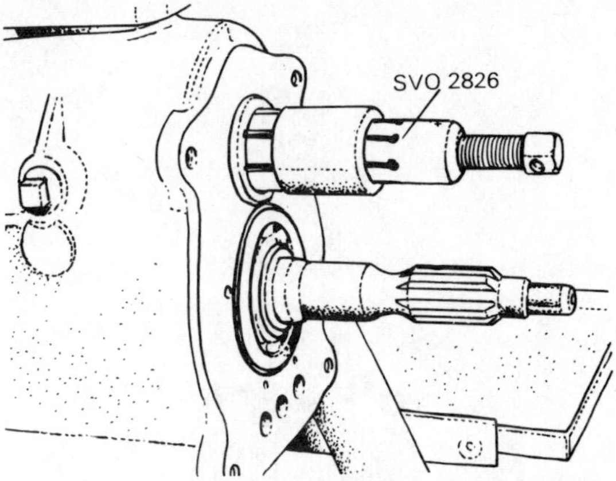

FIG 6:3 Removing intermediate shaft front bearing

Unbolt and lift off the top cover, remove the springs and the interlock balls for the selector rails.

Slacken the nut for the flange using SVO.2837 and then pull off the flange with a puller such as SVO.2261. Remove the release bearing. Release the bolts and remove the cover for the input shaft. The bolts for the clutch casing can now be released and the casing removed.

Turn the gearbox upside down and pull out the front bearing of the intermediate shaft with tool SVO.2826 as shown in **FIG 6:3**, then remove the rear cover and pull off the rear bearing of the intermediate shaft using SVO.2827 if available.

Turn the gearbox to its normal position, taking care that the shaft is not allowed to drop heavily on to the bottom of the casing. Unscrew the bolts for the selector forks, push the selector rails backwards and drive out the tensioning pin in the flange of the rails. Push out the selector rails, noting that the forks must be held so that they do not jam on the rails. Remove the selector forks.

Remove the speedometer gear. Pullout the rear bearing of the mainshaft (SVO.2828). If the bearing sticks in the casing, push the mainshaft forwards so that its drive and synchronizers go against the intermediate shaft drive. To prevent this, place a flat piece of iron between the front end of the mainshaft and the gearbox housing.

On M410 models the bolt in tool SVO.2828 should be removed and replaced with SVO.2832, as shown in **FIG 6:4** to remove the rear bearing.

Extract the input shaft and remove the synchronizing ring, also the thrust washer from the rear end of the mainshaft.

Using tool SVO.2829 if available, lift up the mainshaft as shown in **FIG 6:5**, after pushing the engaging sleeve for 1st and 2nd gear to the rear.

Pull out the reverse shaft and remove the gear. Pull out the oil seals from the front and rear covers.

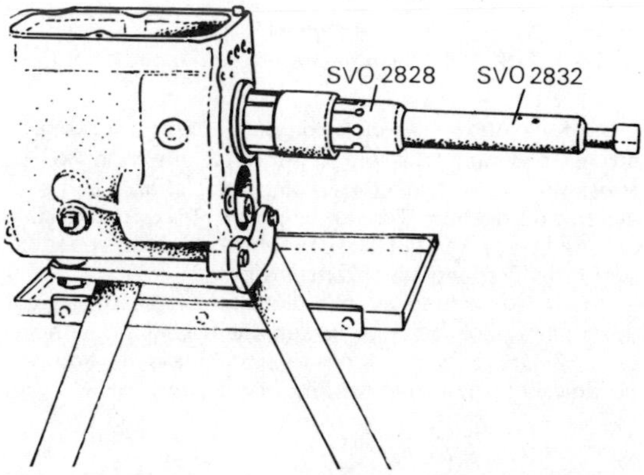

FIG 6:4 Removing mainshaft rear bearing (M410)

The mainshaft:

Remove the lifting tool SVO.2829, if it was used, and then take off the first-speed gear, the needle bearing and the synchronizing cone.

Remove the engaging sleeves and synchronizer flanges. Remove the circlips for the synchronizer hub.

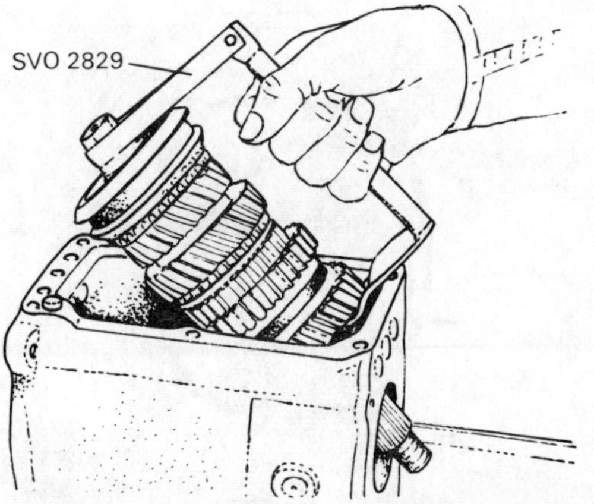

FIG 6:5 Lifting out the mainshaft assembly

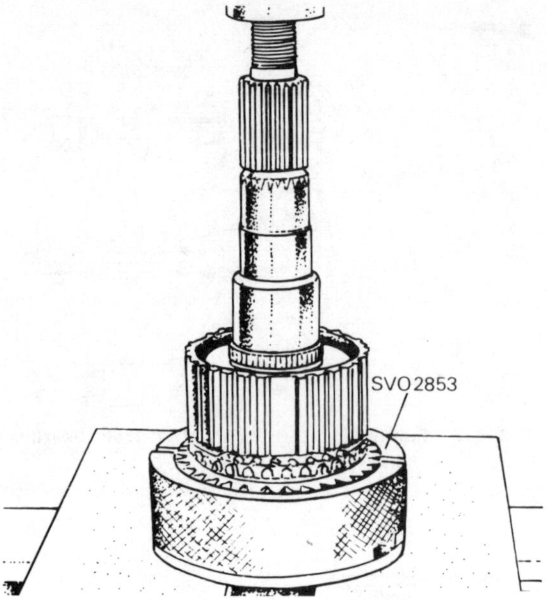

FIG 6:6 Dismantling the mainshaft

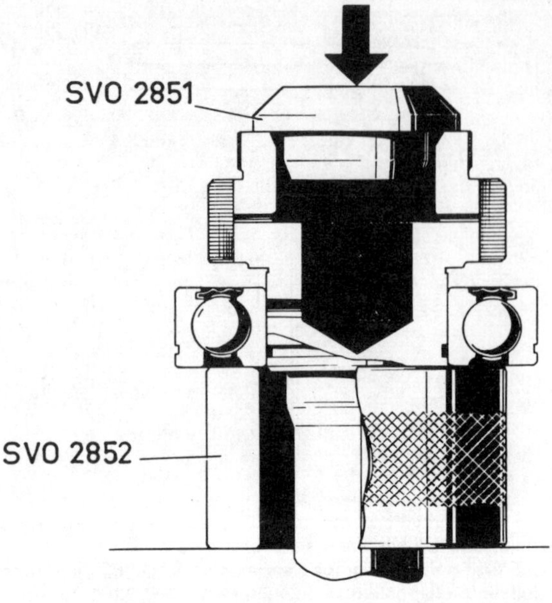

FIG 6:8 Fitting the ballbearing on the input shaft

Fit tool SVO.2853 on to the mainshaft then place it in a press and support it with the tool as shown in **FIG 6:6** Press off the 2nd speed gear and the 1st and 2nd speed synchronizing hub. Turn the shaft in the opposite direction and place it in the press to remove the 3rd speed gear and the 4th speed synchronizing hub.

After dismantling all the parts, clean them in white spirit and check for wear or damage, replacing as necessary. Examine particularly the ballbearings and synchronizers for possible scoring or cracking.

6:5 Assembling the gearbox

First assemble the two synchronizers, making sure that the snap rings are correctly fitted. Reference to **FIG 6:7** will make this clear, then place tool ring SVO.2852 in a press and position the 3rd/4th speed synchronizer, cone, 3rd speed gear and needle bearing, making sure that the synchronizing flange locates correctly in the grooves in the synchronizing cone. Press in the mainshaft, at the same time turning the 3rd speed gear in order to check that the gearwheel and the needle bearing fit correctly. Using a new circlip of the correct size fit it in its groove.

Position the 1st/2nd speed synchronizer, cone, 2nd speed gear and needle bearing on the ring tool SVO.2852. Ensure that the gear ring on the engaging sleeve comes forwards and that the flanges fit correctly in the grooves in the cone. Press the mainshaft into place and at the same time turn the 2nd speed gear to see that it does not get locked. Secure with a new circlip.

Fit the 1st speed gearwheel with its needle bearing and synchronizing cone on to the mainshaft, then fit the lifting tool SVO.2829 if available (see **FIG 6:5**).

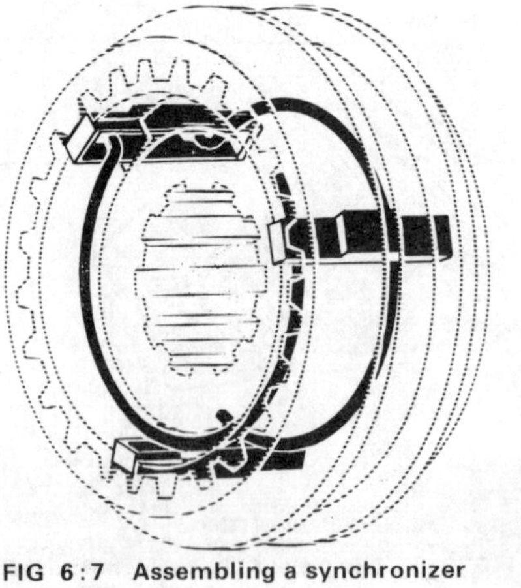

FIG 6:7 Assembling a synchronizer

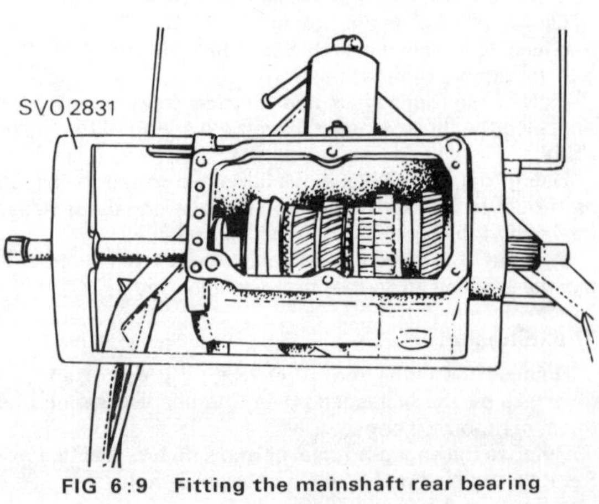

FIG 6:9 Fitting the mainshaft rear bearing

Press new oil seals on to the front and rear covers and then press the ballbearing on to the input shaft using the tools shown in **FIG 6:8** and secure with a well fitting circlip.

Place the reverse shaft gearlever on to the bearing pin in the gearbox casing, then fit the reverse gear and the reverse gearshaft. This shaft must be level with the rear end of the casing or a maximum of .08 inch (.2 mm) below.

Place the intermediate shaft in the bottom of the gearbox casing, then fit in the mainshaft. Remove the lifting tool and fit the thrust washer on the mainshaft.

Fit the rear ballbearing on to the mainshaft and fit the press tool SVO.2831 over the bearing and mainshaft as in **FIG 6:9**. Press the bearing on to the shaft, noting that if the bearing does not locate in the housing the spindle on the tool can be unscrewed and a flat piece of iron placed between it and the front end of the gearbox casing. The bearing should then be satisfactorily pressed into position.

Fit the needle bearing in the input shaft. Fit the loose synchronizing cone in the 3rd/4th speed synchronizer, placing it correctly with the flanges in the grooves. Insert the input shaft into the housing and on the pin of the mainshaft.

Turn the gearbox upside down and press the insert drift into the press tool SVO.2831 as shown in **FIG 6:10** and press on the intermediate shaft bearings. Fit the clutch housing using a new gasket.

Fit the selector forks, flanges and selector rails, making sure that the flange for the reverse gear fits correctly in the gearlever. Fit the bolts and new tensioning pins.

Rotate the gearbox so that the rear end is uppermost and drive the intermediate shaft forwards so that its front bearing lies against the clutch casing. Fit in shims for the intermediate shaft rear bearing so that they lie level with or not more than .002 inch (.05 mm) below the rear end. This dimension may be seen in **FIG 6:11**.

Fit the large speedometer gear. Fit a new gasket with the rear cover, noting that the gasket must be compressed to ensure that the intermediate shaft has a clearance of between .008 and .010 inch (.2 and .25 mm).

Press on the flange and fit the washer and nut, which is tightened to 80 to 110 lb lt (11 to 14 kg m).

Place the interlocking balls and springs in position, then fit the gearbox cover and gasket. Fit the cover over the input shaft. Fit the release bearing.

6:6 The overdrive

The overdrive unit is of the epicyclic type and is mounted on the rear end of the gearbox. The system is engaged by electro-hydraulic means and gives a step-up ratio of .797:1, which is available only when top gear is engaged. It is switched on by means of a switch placed underneath the steering wheel, which closes the circuit via a switch on the gearbox to a solenoid mounted on the overdrive unit which in turn operates the control valve bringing the overdrive into operation.

A cut-away view of the unit is given in **FIG 6:12**, but it must be stressed that servicing this component is a job for a qualified service station with the requisite specialist equipment. The owner driver is advised to limit his operations to a few simple maintenance details.

The electrical circuit is shown in **FIG 6:13** and is self-explanatory. The switch 4 on the gearbox is shown closed, a position obtained only when top gear is engaged.

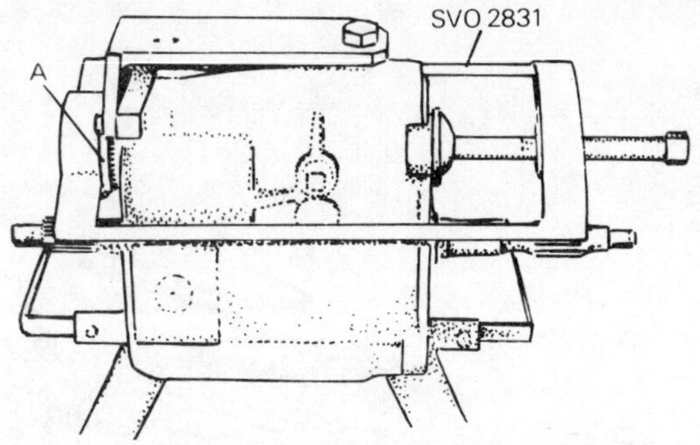

FIG 6:10 Fitting the intermediate shaft bearing. A shows insert drift

Checking the oil pressure:

This is best done on the road, but can be carried out with the car jacked up, provided suitable precautions are taken.

Remove the plug under the operating valve and connect a suitable pressure gauge (SVO.2834).

Drive the car in direct drive at about 25 mile/hr (40 km/hr), when the pressure indicated should be about 21 lb/sq inch (1.5 kg/sq cm). Then engage the overdrive and check that the pressure rises to 510 to 550 lb/sq inch (36 to 39 kg/sq cm).

Disengage the overdrive and check the time taken for the pressure to drop back to the first reading. This time must not exceed three seconds.

The relief valve (see FIG 6:14):

Remove the baseplate and the prefilter, taking care to catch the oil which will be released and noting that if the vehicle has just come in from a run this may be VERY HOT.

Remove the plug under the relief valve (SVO.2836). This allows the extraction of the large piston of the relief valve, the spring and the spring retainer and also the low-pressure spring. Then pull out the small piston unit with spring and retainer, also the cylinder and end washer.

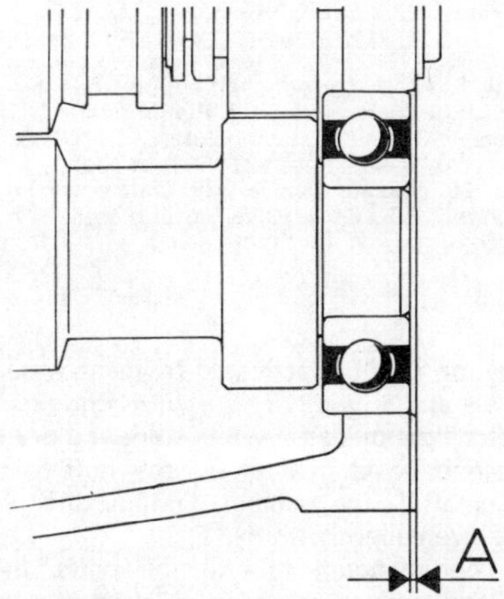

FIG 6:11 Clearance for intermediate shaft. A=.002 inch (0 to .05 mm) maximum

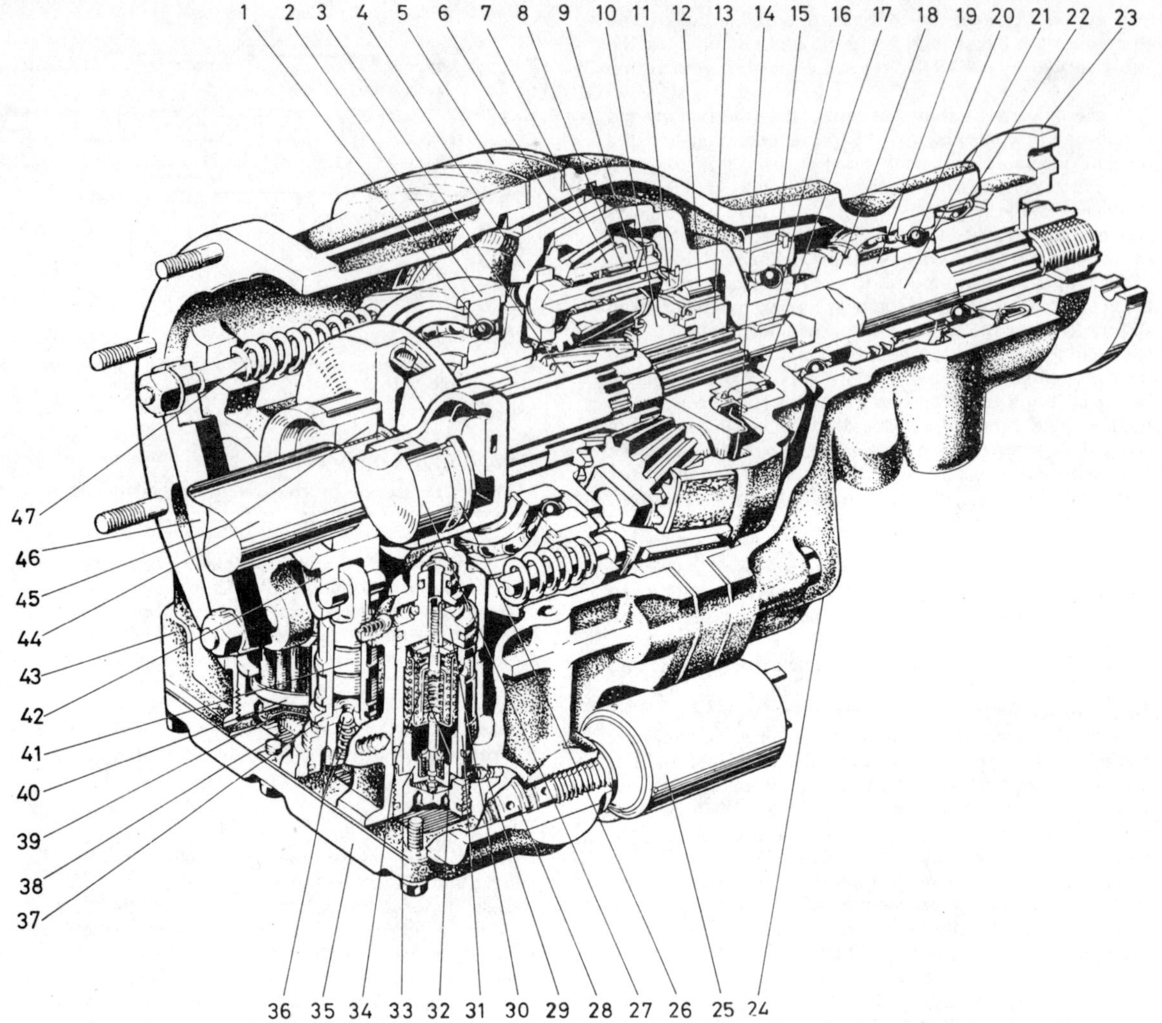

FIG 6:12 Cut-away view of overdrive unit

Key to Fig 6:12 1 Output shaft support bearing 2 Thrust bearing retainer 3 Sunwheel 4 Clutch sliding member 5 Brake ring 6 Clutch member outer lining 7 Planet gear 8 Needle bearing 9 Shaft 10 Planet carrier 11 Oil thrower 12 Unidirectional clutch rollers 13 Unidirectional clutch 14 Oil trap 15 Ballbearing 16 Bush 17 Thrust washer 18 Speedometer driving gear 19 Spacer 20 Ballbearing 21 Output shaft 22 Oil seal 23 Coupling flange 24 Rear casing 25 Solenoid 26 Piston seal 27 Piston 28 Operating valve 29 Orifice nozzle 30 Cylinder top 31 Cylinder 32 Spring 33 Large piston 34 Small piston 35 Base plate 36 Check valve for oil pump 37 Pump cylinder 38 Magnet 39 Prefilter 40 Fine filter 41 Pump plunger 42 Connecting rod 43 Front casing 44 Input shaft (gearbox mainshaft) 45 Eccentric 46 Bridge piece 47 Spring

This operation may be facilitated by using a pair of long-nosed pliers and a piece of wire with a hooked end.

Wash all the pieces in white spirit and dry with compressed air to avoid picking up any fluff from a cloth. Examine carefully for wear or damage and replace any which are even slightly faulty.

Before commencing to refit the parts, the internal channels and orifices should be blown clear with compressed air.

Fit new O-rings on the end washers, cylinder and plug, and dip the parts in clean engine oil. Installation is made in the following order: End washer, cylinder, small piston, low-pressure spring, large piston and finally the plug which should be tightened to a torque of 16 lb ft (2.2 kg m).

See that the magnet is in position on the baseplate, then fit it together with the prefilter using a new joint gasket.

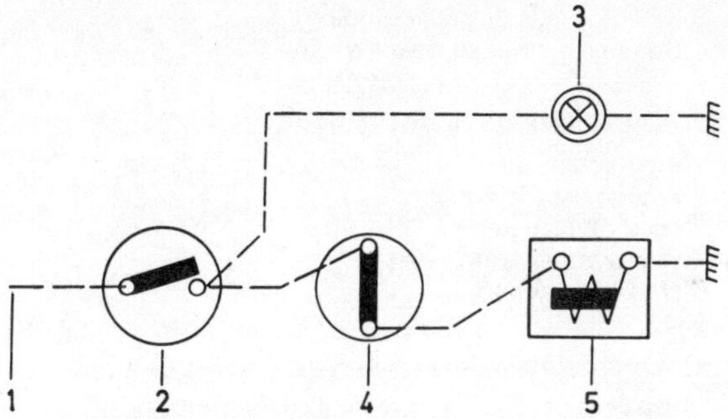

FIG 6:13 Overdrive electrical circuit diagram

Key to Fig 6:13 1 Lead from fusebox 2 Swith for overdrive 3 Indicator lamp for overdrive 4 Switch on gearbox 5 Solenoid on overdrive

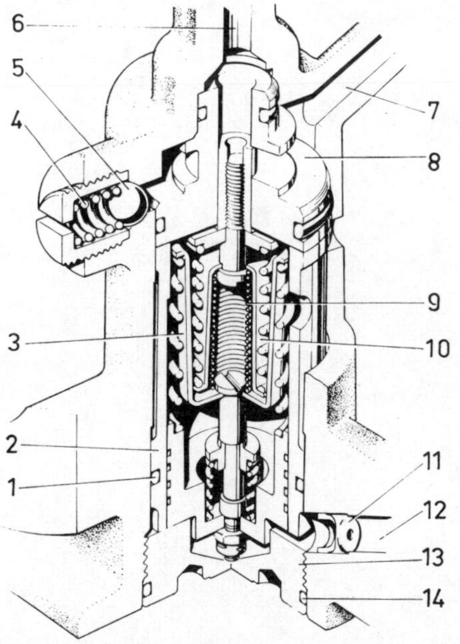

FIG 6:14 Sectional view of the relief valve

Key to Fig 6:14 1 O-ring 2 Cylinder 3 Large piston unit 4 Spring 5 Valve ball 6 Channel for oil pump 7 Channel to mainshaft 8 End piece 9 Spring 10 Small piston unit 11 Nozzle 12 Channel from control valve 13 Plug 14 O-ring

The check valve:

This also is accessible after the removal of the baseplate and prefilter. Remove the plug (SVO.2836) and take out the non-return valve spring, ball and body. Wash in clean white spirit and dry carefully.

A new O-ring should be obtained and also any other parts where wear or damage is found.

The parts are reassembled in the reverse order, the plug being tightened to a torque of 16 lb ft (2.2 kg m).

The filter:

This should be cleared while the baseplate is detached and is just a matter of unscrewing the plug and taking out the seal ring and the fine mesh filter.

Clean the filter in white spirit and blow dry, then refit it together with a new seal and tighten the plug.

Reference to **FIG 6:15** will assist in these operations.

6:7 Removing the overdrive

Removal of the unit will be facilitated if the car is first driven with the overdrive engaged and then with it disengaged **with the clutch pedal depressed.** The latter is important in order to avoid torsional stresses in the shaft between the planet carrier and the unidirectional clutch.

Carry out the operations detailed in the first four paragraphs of **Section 6:3, Removing the gearbox,** then:

Disconnect the cables to the solenoid and unscrew the bolts securing the overdrive unit to the intermediate flange. The overdrive can now be pulled straight back until it is free from the mainshaft in the gearbox and lowered away.

Reinstallation is of the reverse of the above. Fill with the recommended grade of oil and check the level again after driving for a few miles.

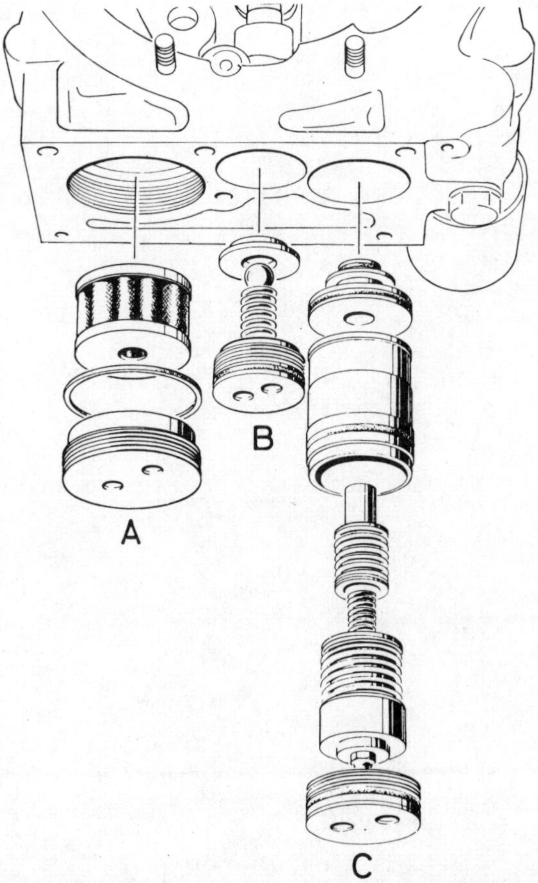

FIG 6:15 Showing location of A Fine filter, B Check valve, C Relief valve

6:8 Fault diagnosis

(a) Jumping out of gear

1 Worn bearings on shafts or gear
2 Worn grooves in selector rails
3 Weak springs
4 Worn gearwheels
5 Gearbox out of alignment

(b) Noisy gearbox

1 Insufficient oil
2 Worn or damaged bearings
3 Worn gears

(c) Difficulty in engaging gears

1 Clutch not releasing
2 Worn synchronizers
3 Selector rails or gears binding
4 Bearing bushes or gears worn

(d) Overdrive does not engage

1 Insufficient oil
2 Faulty electrical circuit
3 Low oil pressure
4 Faulty non-return valve
5 Oil filter choked

(e) Overdrive will not release

Important. Do not reverse in overdrive.

1 Solenoid valve sticking
2 Faulty electrical circuit
3 Mechanical damage in unit
4 Sticking unidirectional clutch

CHAPTER 7

AUTOMATIC TRANSMISSION

7:1 Description of automatic transmission

The Borg Warner Model 35 automatic transmission comprises two main components, a fluid flywheel and a hydraulically operated gearbox embodying a set of epicyclic gears with controls providing three forward speeds and a reverse.

Both the fluid flywheel, or hydrokinetic converter, and the gearchange mechanism share a common oil supply and pump. The gearchanges are effected by the application of internal clutches and external brake bands to elements of the planetary gears in ordered sequence. This is set by the selection of gear from a lever by the driver, engine speed as regulated by the throttle control and torque as determined by a governor.

Dealing first with the hydrokinetic converter, this comprises an impeller, bolted to the engine crankshaft through a special adaptor plate, the outer blades of which circulate the fluid through the peripheral vanes of a turbine rotor coupled to the gearshaft, the fluid returning through inner vanes of the rotor and a stationary set of vanes back to the impeller (see **FIG 7:1**).

The shape of the vanes is such that, when the impeller is turning at a rate faster than that of the turbine rotor, the drive is combined with a degree of torque multiplication. This ranges from 2:1 at full throttle with the car stationary in gear, decreasing to 1:1 when impeller is running at about ten per cent above rotor speed. From this point the device acts as a simple fluid coupling, without torque multiplication. It is this feature that enables a threespeed gear train to be used to give better than the normal performance possible with a fourspeed manual gearbox.

The transmission can be considered as two distinct mechanisms, a mechanical group, comprising planetary gears, clutches and band brakes, and a hydraulic group of pumps, valves, regulators and a governor.

The physical arrangement can be seen from the sectional view in **FIG 7:2**, the torque converter being on the left, the gear trains on the right and the hydraulic channels and valves in the section beneath. The hydraulic governor is in the extension housing with the speedometer drive beyond.

A schematic view of the transmission is given in **FIG 7:3**, with a more detailed cutaway view of the clutch and gear trains in **FIG 7:4**. The front clutch 6, links the input shaft 5, with the forward sun gear 13. The rear clutch 7 links the input shaft 5 with the reverse sun gear 17, the latter being locked by the external brake band 8, in certain gear configurations. A unidirectional clutch 9, prevents

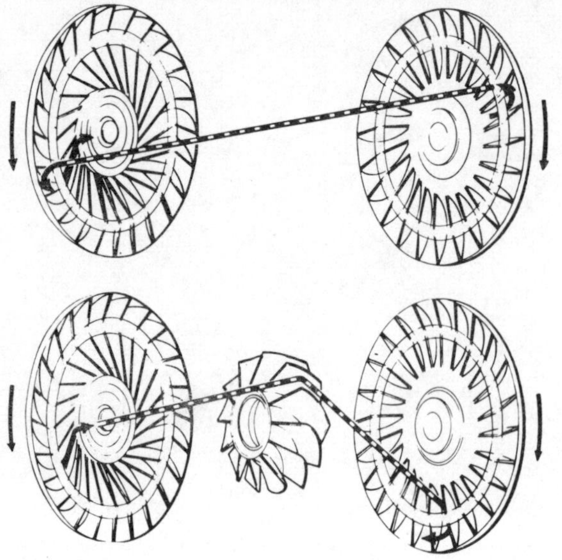

FIG 7:1 Diagram showing function of torque converter

the pinion carrier 11, from rotating in a direction opposite to that of the engine and permits the gearbox to freewheel in first gear. The rear brake band 10, when applied, locks the pinion carrier against rotation in either direction while the annulus 12 transmits the drive from the planetary pinions 15 and 16.

The planetary gear set comprises two sun gears, two sets of pinions, a pinion carrier and a ring gear or annulus. The teeth are helical involute throughout for quietness and efficient torque transmission. In all forward gears, the drive is through the forward sun gear 13 (see **FIG 7:5**), leaving by the ring gear 12. In reverse, the drive is through the reverse sun gear 17. Six pinions in all are mounted on the planet carrier. Three are long pinions meshing between the reverse sun gear 17, and the internal teeth of the annulus at one end and between the forward sun gear 13, via the second set of three pinions 15, and the annulus teeth at the other.

Selection of gear is primarily, by the gear selection lever on the steering column or console. This provides 5 positions, **Neutral, Drive, Reverse, Lock-up** and **Park,** indicated by the initial letters on a scale adjacent to the lever.

In the two drive positions, D and L, the bottom gear is mechanically selected on depression of the lever, changing

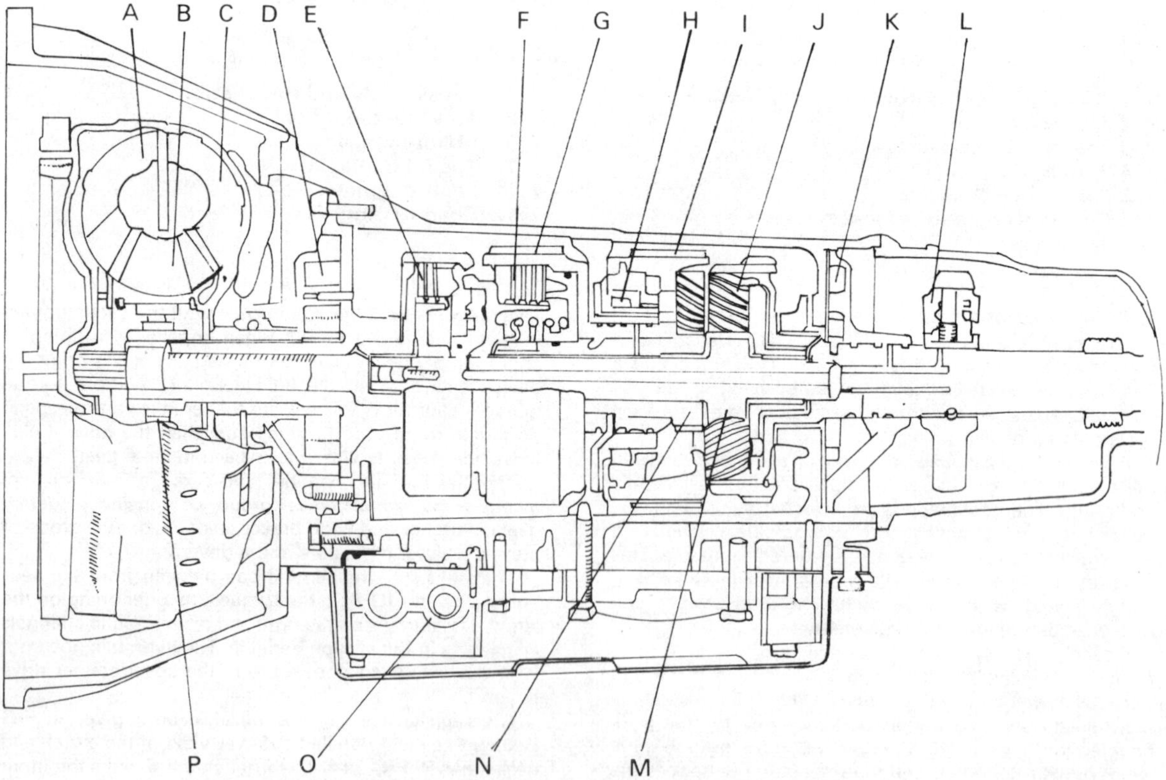

FIG 7:2 Section view of transmission unit

Key to Fig 7:2 **A** Turbine **B** Stator **C** Impeller and cover **D** Front pump **E** Front clutch **F** Rear clutch **G** Front brake band **H** One-way clutch in gearbox **I** Rear brake band **J** Planetary gear set **K** Rear pump **L** Governor **M** Reverse sun gear **N** Forward sun gear **O** Control system **P** One-way clutch in converter

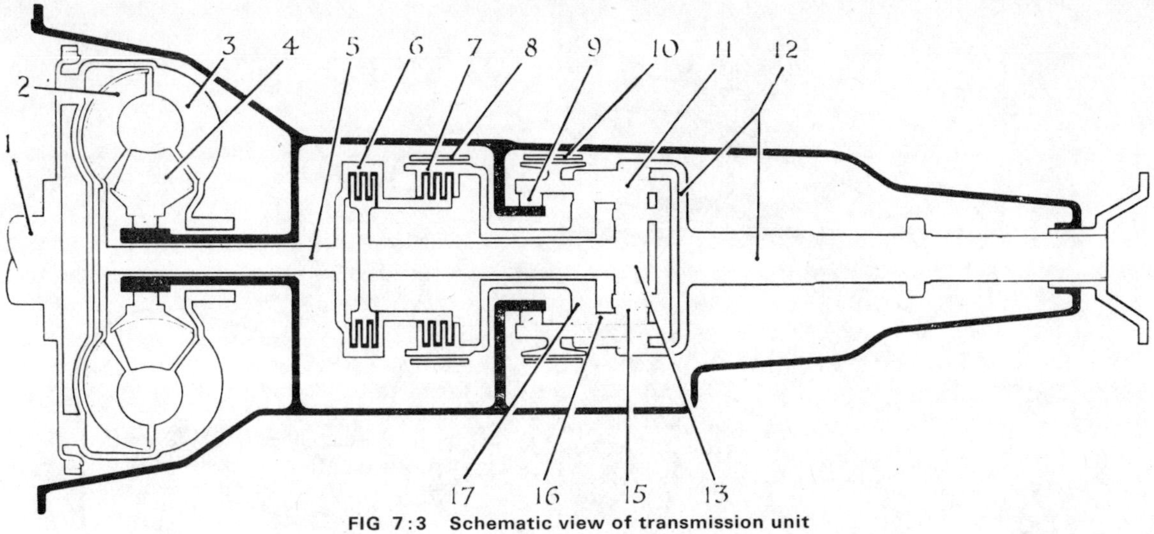

FIG 7:3 Schematic view of transmission unit

Key to Fig 7:3 1 Crankshaft 2 Turbine 3 Impeller 4 Stator 5 Input shaft 6 Front clutch 7 Rear clutch 8 Front brake band 9 Unidirectional clutch 10 Rear brake band 11 Pinion carrier 12 Annulus and drive shaft 13 Forward sun gear 14 Parking pawl teeth 15 Short planetary pinion 16 Long planetary pinion 17 Reverse sun gear

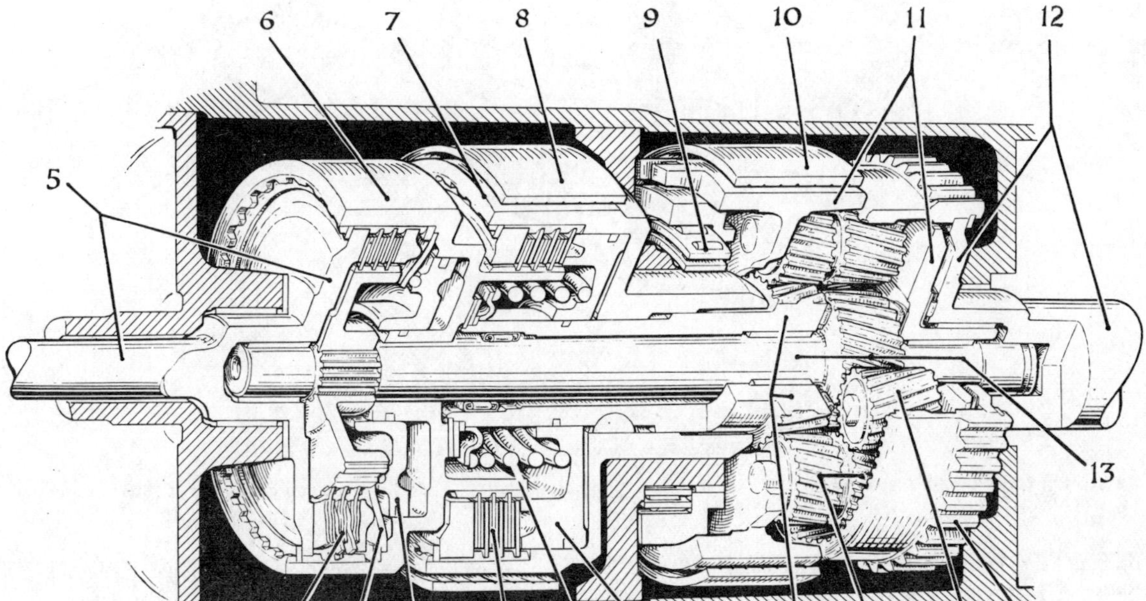

FIG 7:4 Cut-away section of clutches and planetary gears

Key to Fig 7:4 1 Crankshaft 2 Turbine 3 Impeller 4 Stator 5 Input shaft 6 Front clutch 7 Rear clutch 8 Front brake band 9 Unidirectional clutch 10 Rear brake band 11 Pinion carrier 12 Annulus and drive shaft 13 Forward sun gear 14 Parking pawl teeth 15 Short planetary pinion 16 Long planetary pinion 17 Reverse sun gear 18 Rear clutch piston 19 Rear clutch return spring 20 Rear clutch plates 21 Front clutch piston 22 Front clutch diaphragm spring

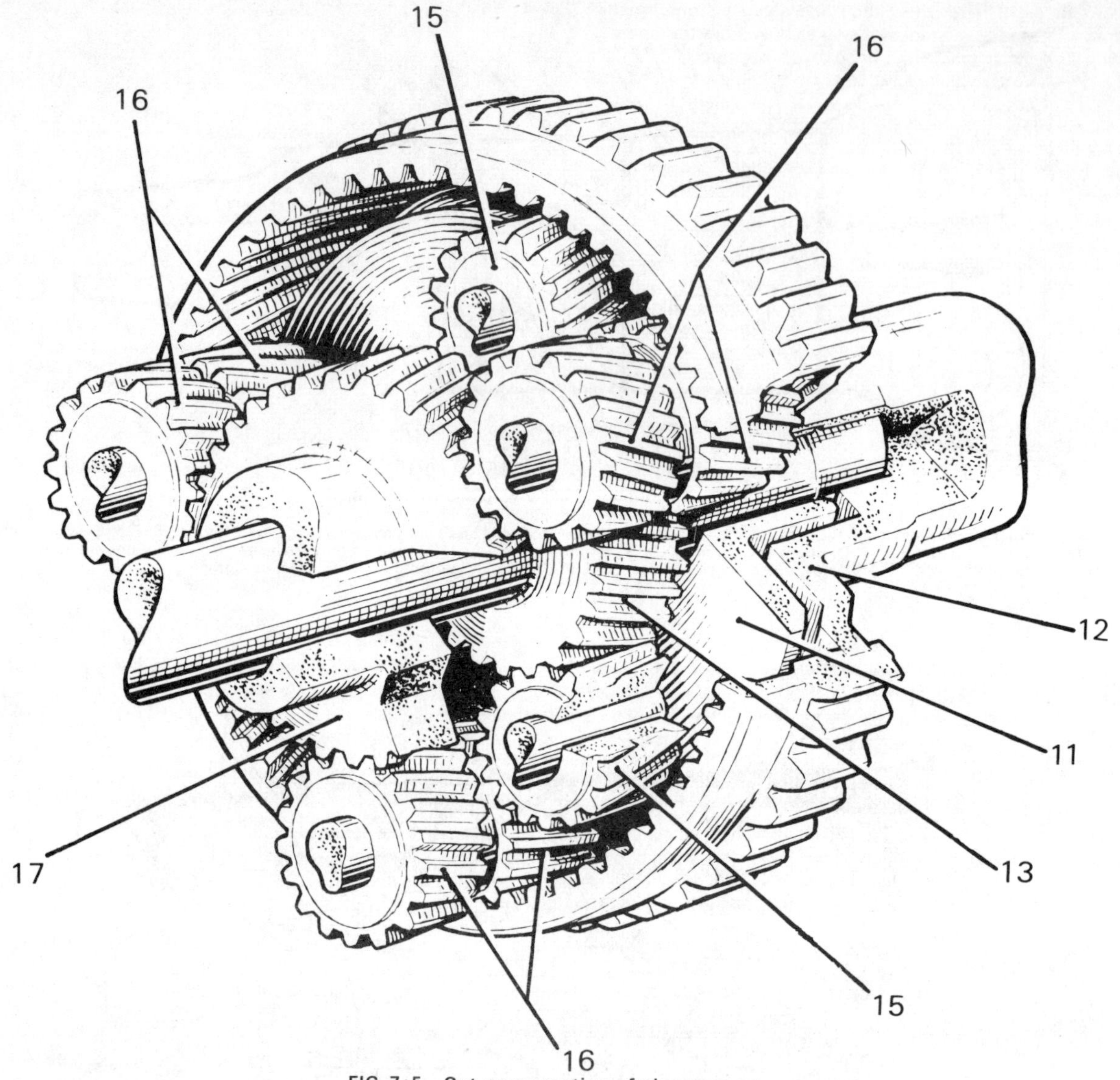

FIG 7:5 Cut-away section of planetary set

Key to Fig 7:5 11 Planet carrier 12 Ring gear and output shaft 13 Forward sun gear 15 Short planet pinion 16 Long planet pinion 17 Reverse sun gear

up then being automatic according to throttle setting and torque. This is done by the hydraulic control mechanism. In P, the car is braked positively by a pawl mechanism providing a third brake apart from the hand and footbrake. **It must never be engaged while the car is in motion or serious damage to the transmission will result.**

The hydraulic control derives its supply of oil from two pumps, one driven from the input shaft and the other from the output shaft, to give pressures ranging from 57 lb/sq inch to 160 lb/sq inch according to speed. The dual pump arrangement ensures a maintenance of supply in the event of an engine failure while the car is still moving. Part of the output is routed to the hydraulic converter and part is converted to lower pressures in regulator valves for other purposes within the transmission.

Apart from non-return valves, there are eight valves (two regulator, two shift, one manual, one throttle, one servo orifice and one modulator) a governor, two brake servos and two clutch servos interconnected by a complex network of channels. The manual valve is operated mechanically by the gear selector lever and the throttle valve by a cam linked with the throttle by a cable. All others are hydraulically operated and provide the automatic feature of the transmission.

The function of the manual valve, mechanically linked to the gear selector lever, is to direct the hydraulic fluid to, or exhaust it from, the clutch and servo pistons. In this manner the initial stages of power flow from the engine, through the gears, to the drive shaft is set up.

The throttle valve is set by a cam, cable-linked to the throttle control. Depression of the accelerator pedal, therefore, acts on both the carburetter butterfly valve and the throttle valve in a proportion set by the shape or contour of the cam. Actually, this is two valves in a common body each having a separate function and interlinked by a spring. The first is the downshift valve the function of which, at full accelerator depression, is to delay upshifts or effect downshifts at maximum engine speeds. This is the 'kick-down' feature which enables the driver to achieve the effect of a changedown with a manual gearbox to get increased acceleration if needed.

The second is the throttle valve proper which floats between the downshift valve spring and its own return spring, the return force being amplified by governor controlled throttle pressure. It transmits hydraulic pressure, via the primary regulator valve, to control the clutch and servo units operating on the brake bands of the sun wheel and annulus. This regulates the clutch and brake band capacities to suit current operating conditions.

The governor valve is centrifugally operated and regulates the pressure to the modulator, shift and servo orifice valves according to output shaft speed. The regulator valves are, in effect, pressure reducing valves modifying the pump pressures to suit the requirements of the hydrokinetic converter, overall lubrication and the exhaust to the pump inlets. The modulator valve acts as a hydraulic relay applying the differing pressures required by the throttle valve according to the condition of the governor.

Though the underlying principles of the transmission are relatively simple, their translation into an effective and smooth running, reliable mechanism is the result of much development and experiment with valve dimensions, spring pressures and channel proportions all of which are permanently set in the dimensions of the component parts. The only adjustments are the purely mechanical ones of taking up wear in the planetary brake bands, the linkage between the carburetter and the downshift cam and the link between the gear selector lever and the manual valve. The sole faults that are likely to occur in the valve and hydraulic system are those due either to the use of wrong hydraulic fluid, to allowing the fluid level to fall too low or to the admission of dirt or grit into the hydraulic system.

The adjustments to the linkages are made while the transmission is in the car. Adjustments to the planetary brake bands necessitate removal of the unit to a bench.

7:2 Gear selection

The gear selector lever is mounted below the steering wheel on the right or left, according to whether the car is right or lefthand drive (see **FIG 7:6**).

Movement of the gearlever between Drive (D) and Neutral (N) is normal but the lever must be depressed for engagement of the three other positions. Return from the Lock-up (L) or Reverse (R) positions is effected without further depression of the lever but once the Park (P) position has been selected, the lever must again be depressed to release.

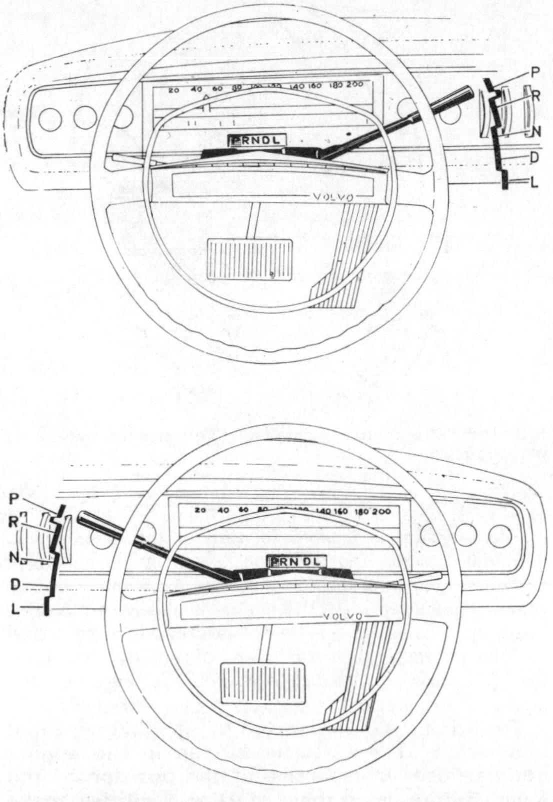

FIG 7:6 Gear selector lever. Top, lefthand drive. Bottom, righthand drive

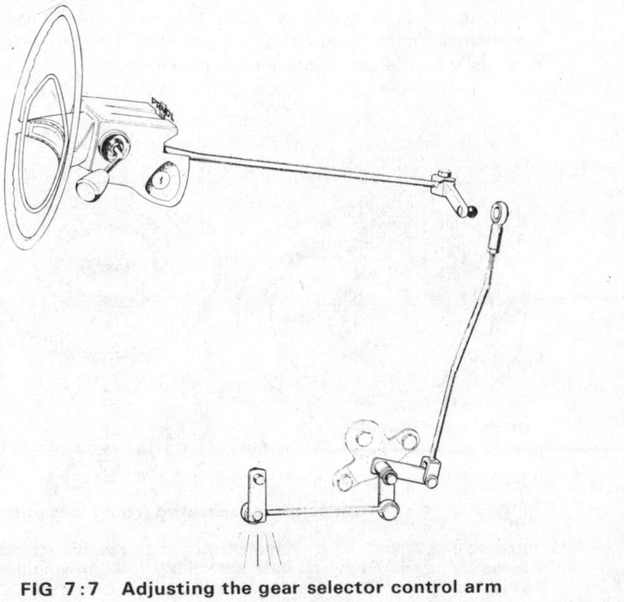

FIG 7:7 Adjusting the gear selector control arm

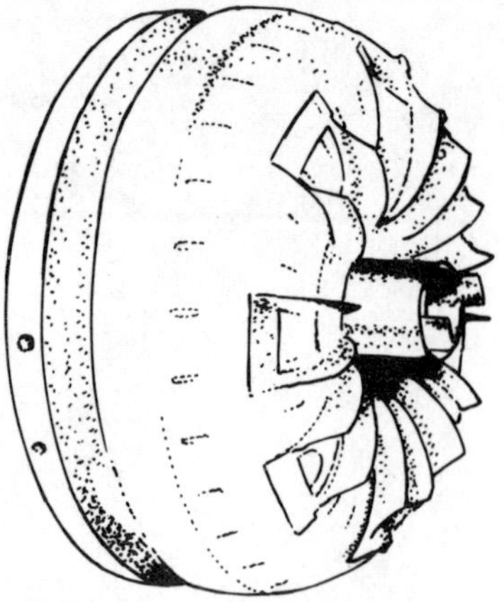

FIG 7:8 The torque converter. The starter gear ring is not shown

The indicator is located forward of the lever and is illuminated when the panel lights are switched on. A switch mounted on the transmission unit inhibits operation of the starter when the engine is in any of the drive positions. This switch is in the solenoid circuit of the starter and, should the engine stall in any of the drive positions, the lever must be returned to N before it can be started again.

The engine can be started by handle or manual depression of the starter button in the engine compartment irrespective of the position of the lever. Before using these starting facilities, make sure that the gear selector is set in P.

Should the linkage come out of adjustment, resetting is simple. All that is necessary is to disconnect the ball joint (see **FIG 7:7**) at the lower end of the lever arm, move the lever into position D, then, at the gearbox end, first move the selector arm to the rear as far as it will go. This is the Parking (P) position. Then move it forward three 'clicks' of the gear detent, and adjust the ball socket on the rod to fit easily on the ball head. Finally check each position by

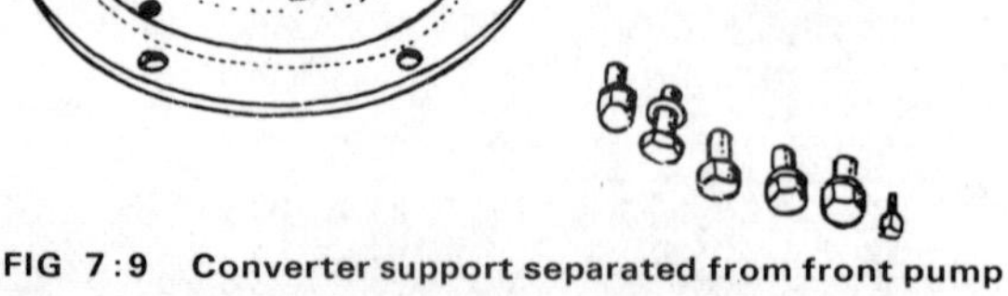

FIG 7:9 Converter support separated from front pump

Key to Fig 7:9 **A** Pump adaptor and converter support assembly **B** Body and bush assembly **C** Driving gear **D** Driven gear

the feel or sound of the detent engagement and lock the socket on the rod.

The selector indicator is a separate unit the pointer of which is linked with the lever by a Bowden cable.

The use of the L position is to keep the car running in the second gear, either as a means of controlling a coast downhill, or as an alternative to using the 'kick-down' to give increased acceleration while in top gear. At speeds below 5 mile/hr, the use of the L position automatically keeps the engine in first gear. **L should not be selected at speeds above 50 mile/hr, except in an emergency.**

The parking position P, is particularly useful for holding the car on steep gradients but it should always be applied in addition to, and not as a substitute for, the handbrake. If it is released without the hand or footbrake being applied, the car will immediately commence to roll and attempts to re-engage it can only result in damage.

When stopping on slight upward gradients, if the engine tick-over has been properly set, the car will remain stationary in Drive and not roll back. If the gradient is a little steeper, roll-back can be stopped by a small application of the accelerator ready for a quick move off. On level ground, the engine should be set to give a very slow crawl forward. The footbrake should always be applied before selecting gear and the foot transferred to the accelerator after the gear has been engaged. A very slight kick can be felt as the servo clutches operate.

7:3 The torque converter

The torque converter is a sealed unit with the impeller as an integral part of the housing, a stator mounted on a unidirectional clutch supported on the tube projecting from the gearbox and the turbine rotor splined to the gearshaft housed within the tube. Cooling blades and a drive ring are welded to the outer casing of the converter and the general view when extracted from the gearbox is shown in **FIG 7:8**. The sleeve seen projecting from the converter provides the drive to the front pump rotor, the projections fitting into the slots visible in **FIG 7:9**. Within this sleeve is the converter support tube, the splined end carrying the unidirectional clutch and stator. The gearshaft passes through the support tube to enter the splined boss of the turbine rotor.

The three units, impeller, stator and rotor, are self-supporting within the converter and the withdrawl of support tube or shaft does not affect their mechanical relationship. The hydraulic fluid from the pump enters the converter via an annular clearance between the sleeve and support tube, returning via a similar clearance between support tube and gearshaft.

The starter ring gear is shrunk on to the drive ring and the whole is mounted on an adaptor plate secured to the flywheel flange on the engine crankshaft by four special bolts with hardened steel washers, similar bolts and washers being used to secure the drive ring to the adaptor plate (see **FIG 7:10**).

Two types of starter ring are fitted. The first, with double-chamfered teeth can be used either with inertia type of pre-engaged starters. Rings with single-chamfered teeth can be used only if the intertia type of starters is fitted. The same procedure and comments apply to renewal of the ring gear as already outlined for a manual gearbox in **Chapter 1, Section 1:10.**

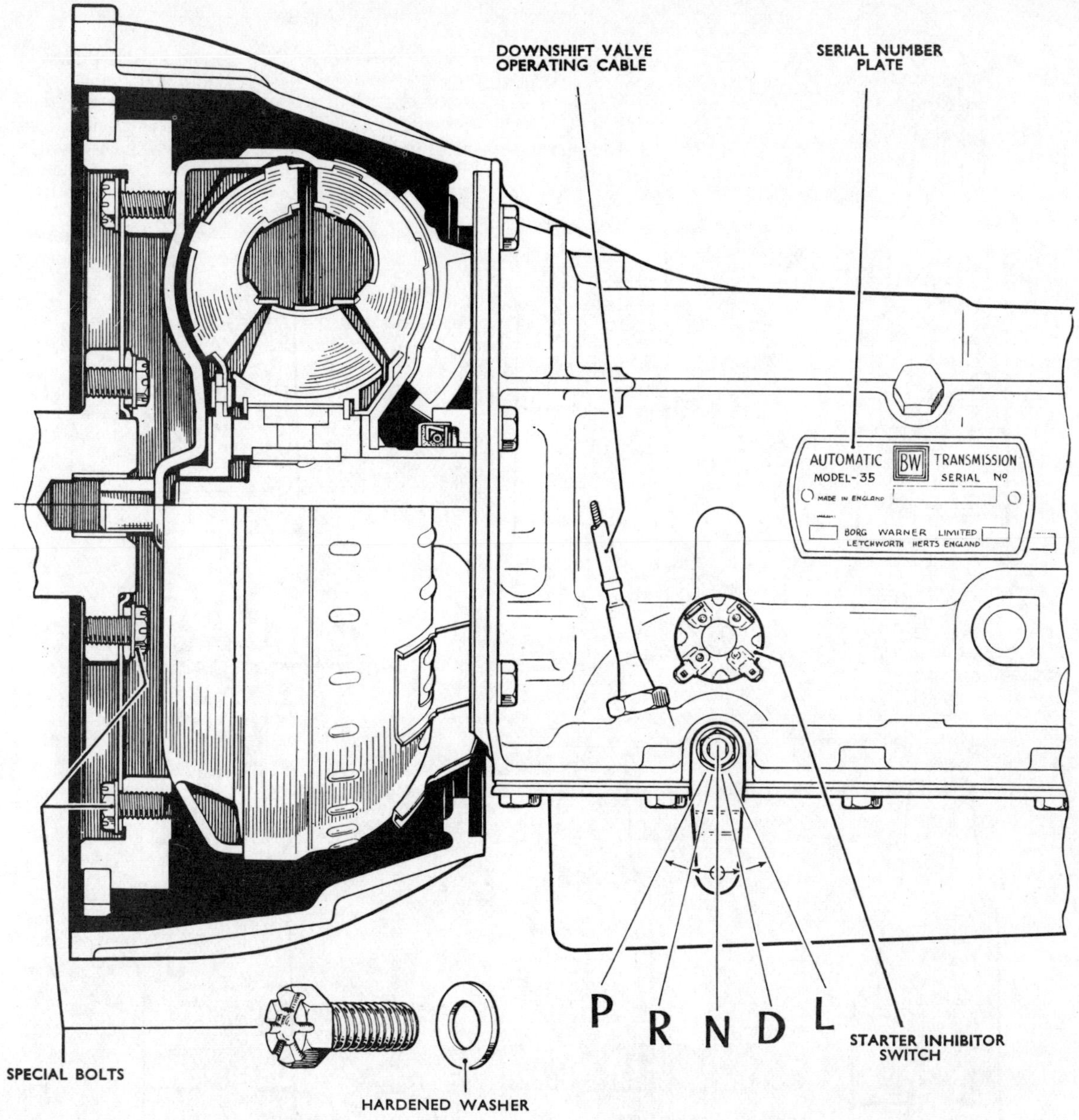

FIG 7:10 Part section through converter and housing showing the bolts securing the adaptor plate to the crankshaft flange and the location of the selector lever inhibitor switch, downshift cable and serial number plate

7:4 Power flow in gears

Torque transmission, or power flow, in the various gears is shown diagrammatically in **FIG 7:11**.

In the first of these, the gear selector is set in either N or P. The front and rear clutches are released and the rotor shaft turns without transmitting torque to either of the sun wheels. The only difference between the two positions is that, in P, the pawl brake is applied mechanically through linkage with the selector shaft and, purely for constructional reasons, the rear brake band is applied if the engine is running.

When the Drive position is selected, the front clutch is applied connecting the converter to the forward sun gear. The unidirectional clutch prevents the pinion carrier from turning and the torque is transmitted through the pinions to the annulus providing a gear reduction of 2.39:1. On

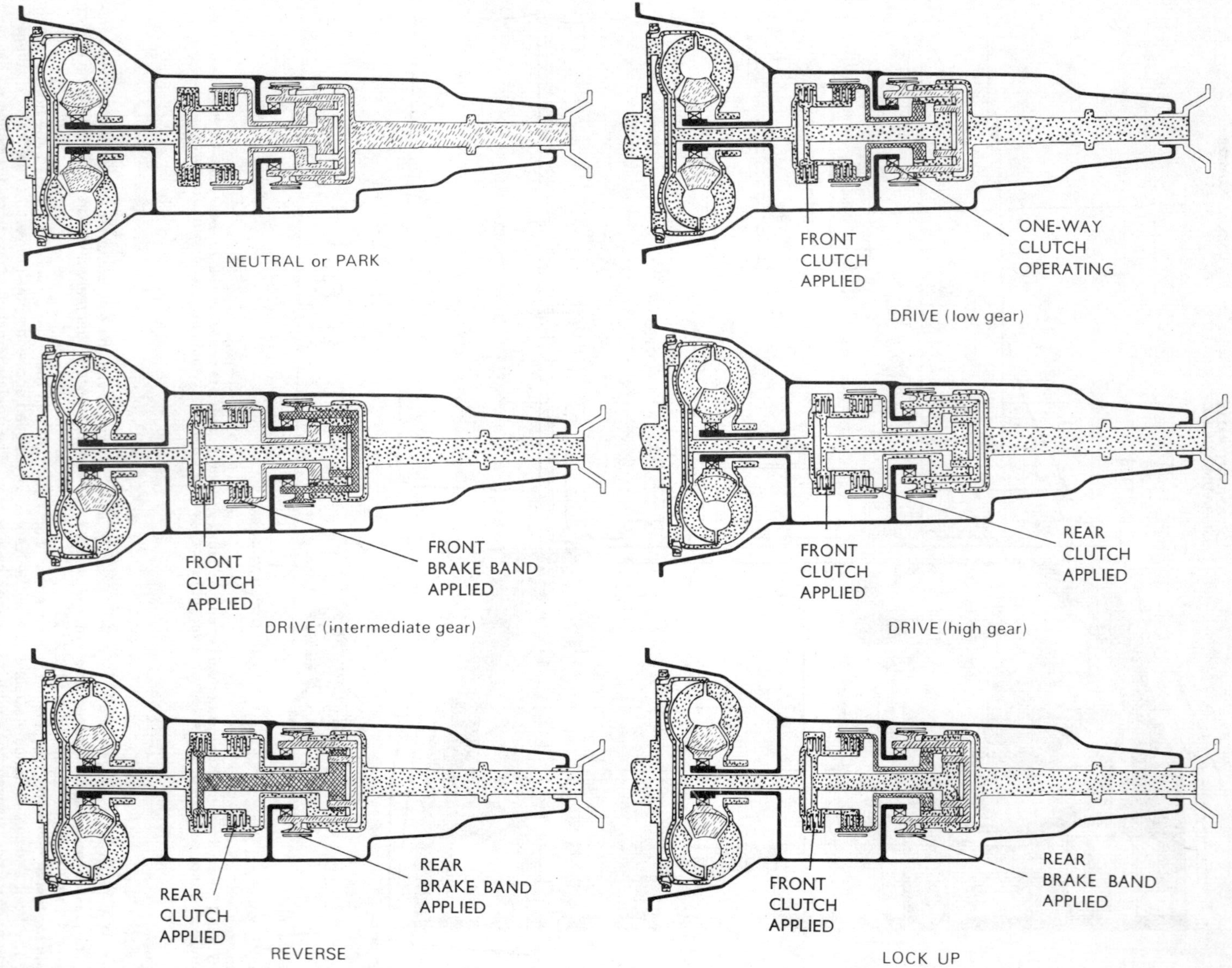

FIG 7:11 Power flow diagrams for main selector positions

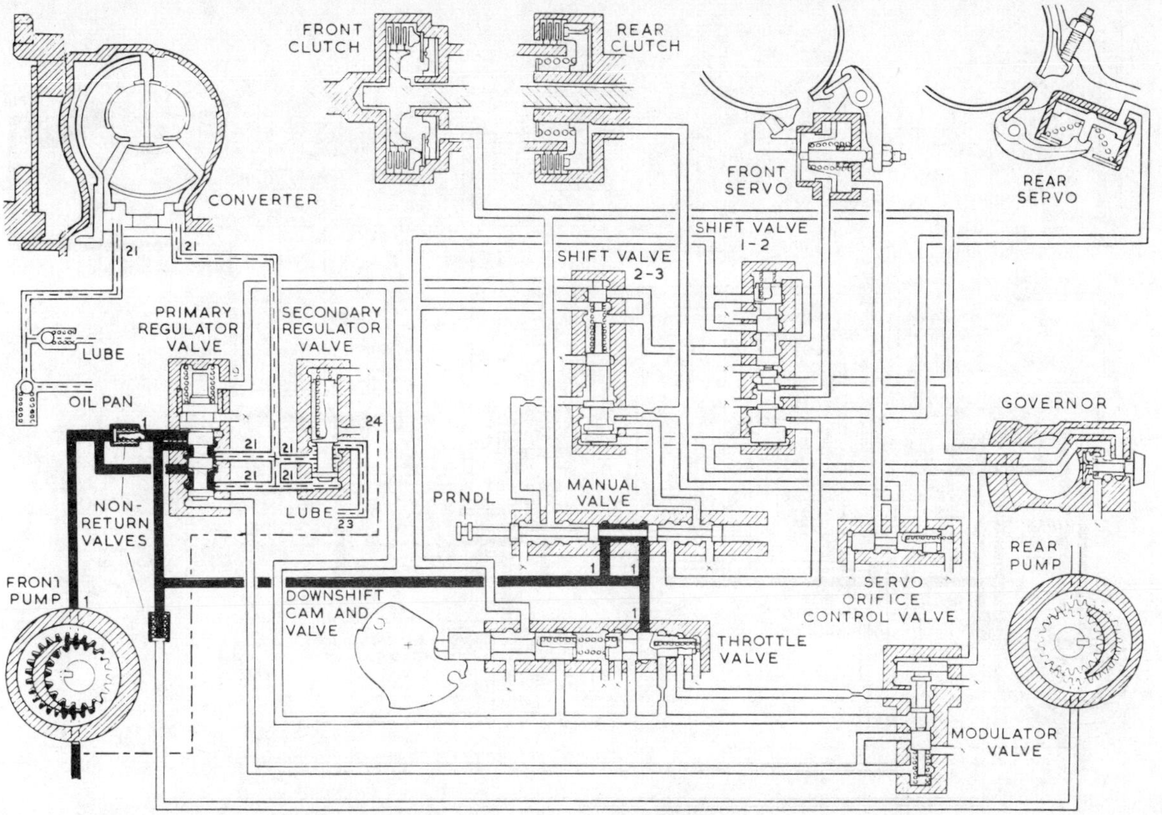

FIG 7:12 Operation of hydraulic circuit in N

the overrun, the unidirectional clutch releases the forward drive and the car freewheels.

At a suitable point, set by the combination of governor pressure and throttle setting, the front brake band is applied holding the reverse sun gear, which has been freewheeling, stationary. This has the effect of reducing the gear ratio to 1.45:1.

With a further increase in engine speed for a given throttle setting, the front clutch is applied, connecting the converter to the forward sun gear. At the same time, the front brake band is released. With both sun gears now locked together, the gearing rotates as a whole to give a direct drive from converter to drive shaft.

Changing up and down from second to top gear is, therefore, effected by switching the locking between front band and rear clutch, while changes between bottom and second are effected by applying or releasing the front brake band.

When Reverse is selected, the front clutch is released and both the rear clutch and rear brake band are applied. The latter holds the pinion carrier stationary and the drive is now through the rear sun wheel, via the gears on the carrier to the annulus and drive shaft, the intermediate gear in the pinion carrier reversing the direction of rotation of the annulus to that of the converter. The reduction ratio is now 2.09:1.

If Lock-up (L) is selected instead of D, the rear brake band is applied instead of using the unidirectional feature of the built-in clutch. The gear ratio is the same as for Drive, namely 2.39:1, but the car can no longer freewheel and the engine can therefore be used for braking when descending hills. The other features of the L drive are inherent in the hydraulic system, but, in effect, the application of L when the car is stationary inhibits a change-up into second gear while a shift from Drive to L in second or top gear produces an immediate changedown into the gear below. Only one change is possible without further movement of the lever unless the speed of the car is reduced by braking to below 5 mile/hr. The same effect can be achieved between 5 and 20 mile/hr by use of the accelerator kick-down with the selector lever in L.

7:5 The hydraulic system

The hydraulic system is complex and not easy to understand or dismantle. Even garage mechanics of long experience and skill have to undergo a course at the makers before they are able to dismantle, repair and readjust the hydraulics satisfactorily, so it is not advisable for the owner/mechanic to attempt to dismantle the assembly even under the most favourable home garage conditions. Fortunately, the makers supply a valve and body assembly

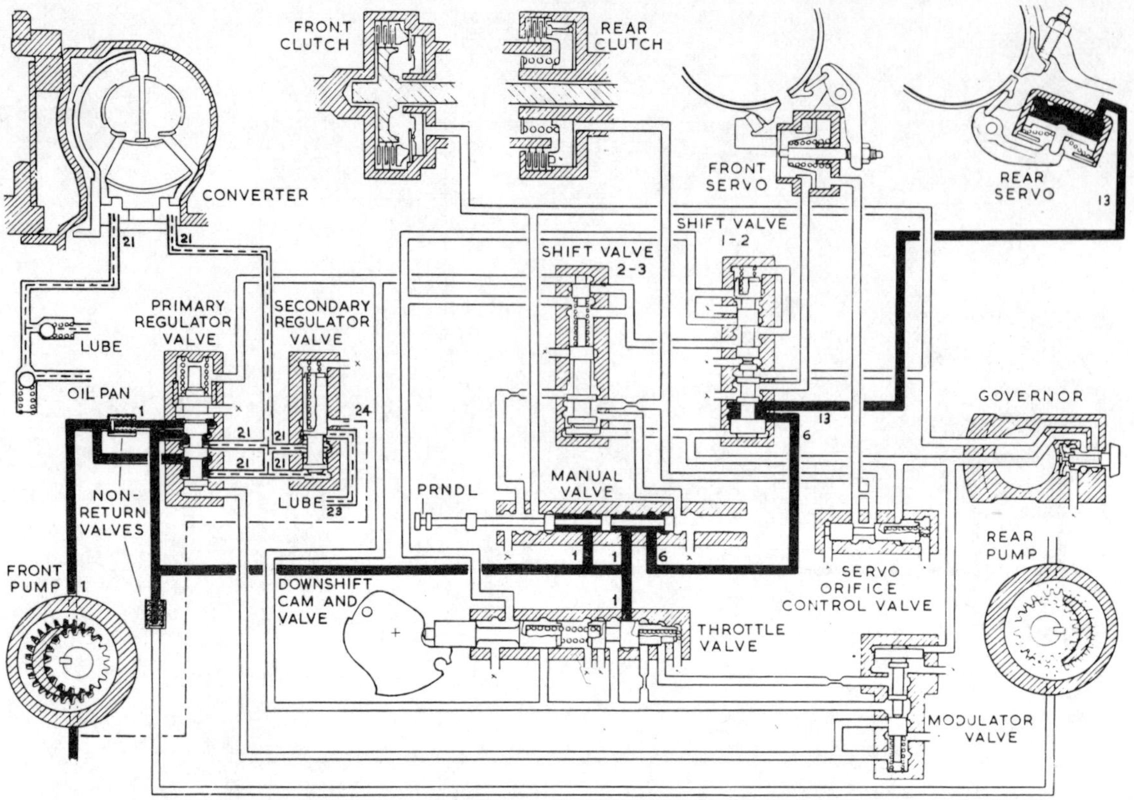

FIG 7:13 Operation of hydraulic circuit in P

as a complete unit and, should trouble be traced to this area of the transmission, replacement of the unit is the recommended remedy. The procedure is dealt with in **Section 7:6**.

Operation of the system in the various settings of selector lever and throttle are outlined below with schematic diagrams to enable the owner/mechanic to appreciate something of what is going on during a journey.

Lever in Neutral (N) (see FIG 7:12):

With the engine running, the front pump circulates the fluid to the primary regulator valve, manual valve and throttle valve, the former adjusting pressure to the hydrokinetic converter and, via the secondary regulator valve, lubrication for the gear trains. A non-return valve blocks the line from the rear pump which, at this stage, is not pumping unless the car is coasting or being towed. Both clutches are free and neither of the servo brake bands are applied.

Lever in Park (P) (see FIG 7:13):

With the engine running, the hydraulic system is the same as for Neutral with the addition of a feed to the rear servo brake band. An extension to the selector rod lever setting the manual valve operates a toggle mechanism inserting a robust pawl into dog-teeth integral with the driven shaft annulus or ring gear.

Strictly speaking, the application of the rear servo brake band has no useful purpose but the arrangement is the result of an extremely simple design of manual control valve.

Lever in Reverse (R) (see FIG 7:14):

With the engine running and the front pump circulating the hydraulic fluid, the manual valve opens the line to shift valves 1/2 and 2/3. The former redirects the pressure to apply the rear servo while the latter applies the rear clutch and via the servo orific valve (which serves no purpose at this stage) the front servo. The function of the throttle pressure line is to regulate the degree of pressure applied to the clutches and servos to suit the torque as a function of engine speed and throttle setting.

The application of the clutches and brakes is then as described in **Section 7:4** for Reverse.

Lever in Drive (D) (see FIGS 7:15, 7:16 and 7:17):

The manual valve applies pressure to the front clutch at the same time opening the hydraulic lines to the shift valve 2/3, 1/2 and to the governor valve. As the car moves

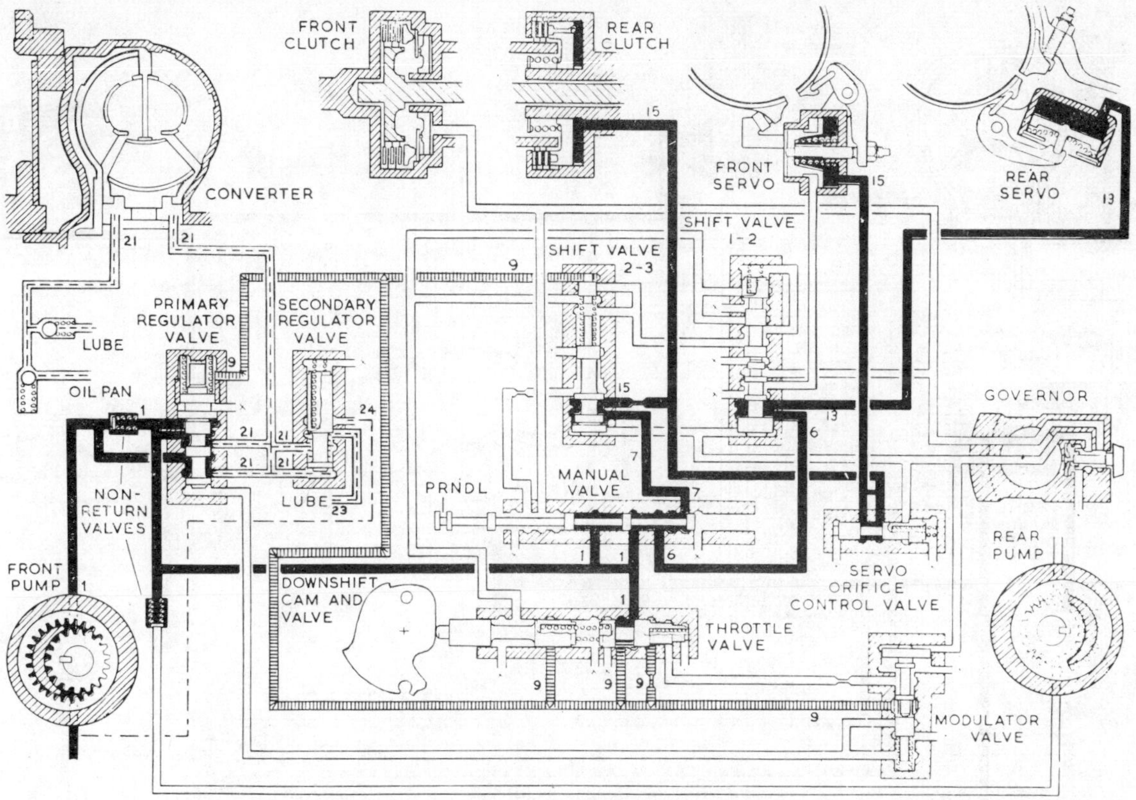

FIG 7:14 Operation of hydraulic circuit in R

forward, the rear pump commences to operate and, as soon as the pressure is sufficient to overcome the non-return valve spring, adds its flow to that of the front pump.

With the throttle in full open position as illustrated, the pressure 9, regulated by the modulator valve balancing governor pressure against feedback throttle pressure, opposes the throttle pressure in the primary regulator valve to adjust line pressure in the interests of smooth gear-shifts. As the engine speed increases with fall-off in torque for a given throttle setting, the governor commences to regulate the flow and pressure of fluid to the shift valves, servo orifice valve and modulator valve 2, balancing the throttle pressure 9, so adjusting the degree of application of the front clutch.

The rear pump now takes over, the control of flow through the primary regulator valve, supplying the converter and lubrication, being set by the opposing forced and modulated throttle pressures 9 and 8. The former is controlled by the setting of the throttle valve and the latter by the modulator valve which, in turn, is regulated by governor pressure 2 (see **FIG 7:16**).

The shift takes place when the governor pressure 2 at one side of the 1/2 shift valve opposes the internal spring pressure and shift valve plunger pressure 10, to a point at which line pressure 5 is admitted to the front servo line 19, applying the front brake band. In the kick-down position as shown, the downshift cam has opened the throttle pressure line 9, to the modulated throttle pressure line 11, opposing the governor pressure in the two shift valves. The action of these is then inhibited and the changedown takes place or change-up is prevented, at least until the kick-down has been stopped or excessively high engine speed has caused the governor to resume control.

As the engine speed increases with reduced torque in intermediate gear, the governor pressure 2 also increases until a point is reached at which shift valve 2/3 also moves up to open the line 15, to both the rear clutch, applying it, and to the servo orifice control valve which regulated by governor pressure 2. When this is sufficient to move the piston, fluid is admitted to the opposite side of the front servo and the brake band is released. With the two clutches engaged, the through drive is effected.

Any further retardation merely serves to reduce the throttle pressure and the transmission remains in top. Even when the car is coasting with the throttle closed, as in **FIG 7:17**, the existence of governor pressure is sufficient to prevent changedown. The only conditions which will induce a changedown is a serious fall in speed with load, resulting in a fall in governor pressure, or a sudden rise in throttle pressure as would result from a heavy depression of the accelerator either of which, or a combination of both, will result in shift valve 2/3 closing to release the rear clutch and permit the 1/2 valve side of the front servo

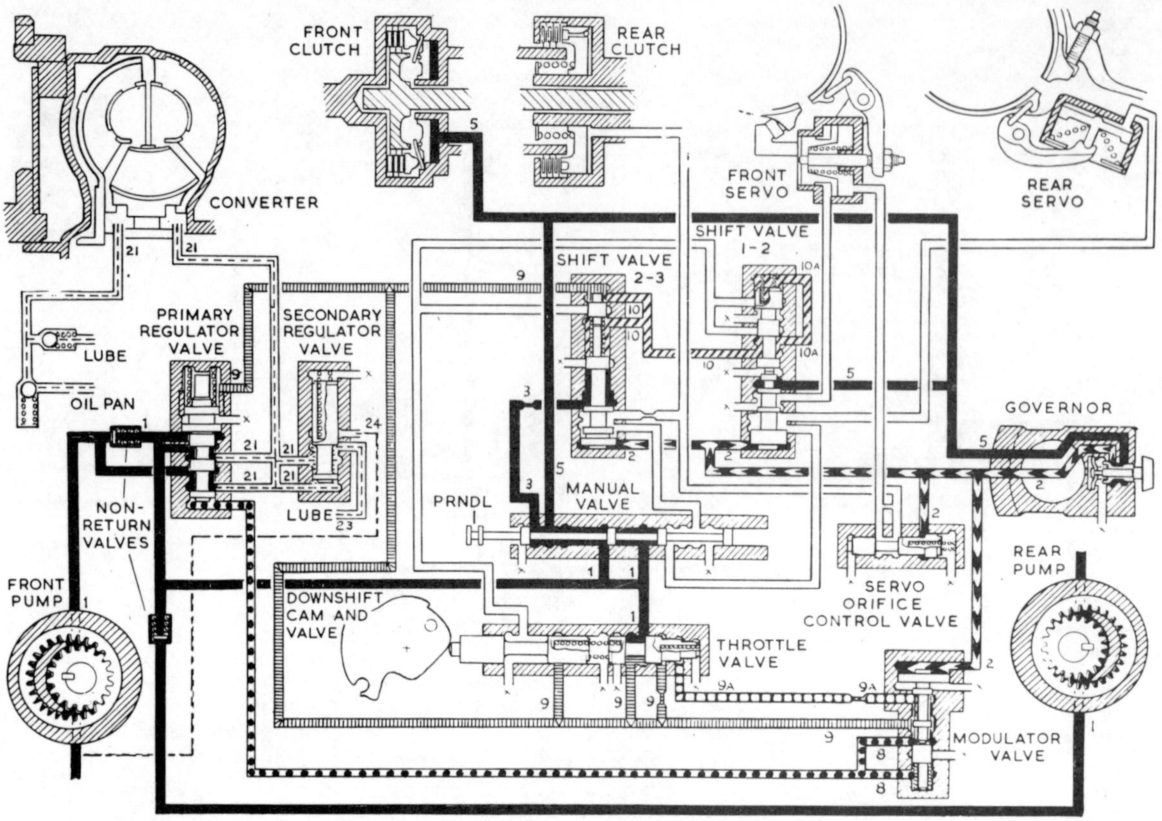

FIG 7:15 Operation of hydraulic circuit in D (Low)

to overcome the rapidly falling counter pressure from the servo orifice control valve.

It must be appreciated that the operation of the valves and hydraulic pressures is not a step-by-step process but a constantly varying and inter-related condition which is functioning entirely in accordance with road and engine speed conditions, related to throttle opening, on a pre-arranged performance graph. The examples shown are merely typical conditions existing at selected points on this performance graph. Even the application of the clutches and servos is a graduated process giving smooth transitions from gear-to-gear, not just an on-off step. The exception to this is the front clutch which is directly applied by selection of any of the forward gears, the feed coming from the manual valve alone. The other three controls are dependent upon the position of the shift valves.

Lock-up:

The one position that has not been considered is the Lock-up (L) state (see **FIG 7:18**). Here the manual valve has sealed off the pressure to the shift valve 2/3 and provided a direct feed via 6 and 13 to the rear servo. Governor pressure acting on the two shift valves is unable to effect any changes and the bottom gear remains selected from a standing start.

If the transmission is already in D and running in top gear (see **FIG 7:17**), the effect of moving the manual valve to L is to open the line 3, from shift valve 2/3 to exhaust and the line 15 pressure drops releasing the rear clutch. A downshift to second gear results, governor pressure moving shift valve 1/2 up to seal off 6 and couple 13 to exhaust while opening 5 to 19 the front servo release. This is then the condition in **FIG 7:16**.

7:6 Dismantling and inspection

The transmission and converter are best removed from the car as separate units. The gearbox is first removed, unbolting it from the torque converter housing, leaving both housing and converter in place on the engine crankshaft casing. The converter and housing can then be removed as a second operation.

Dealing first, with the transmission, from underneath the car, drain the fluid from the gearbox. **If the engine has been running recently before dismantling is commenced, take care when doing this as the temperature of the fluid rises to scalding point.**

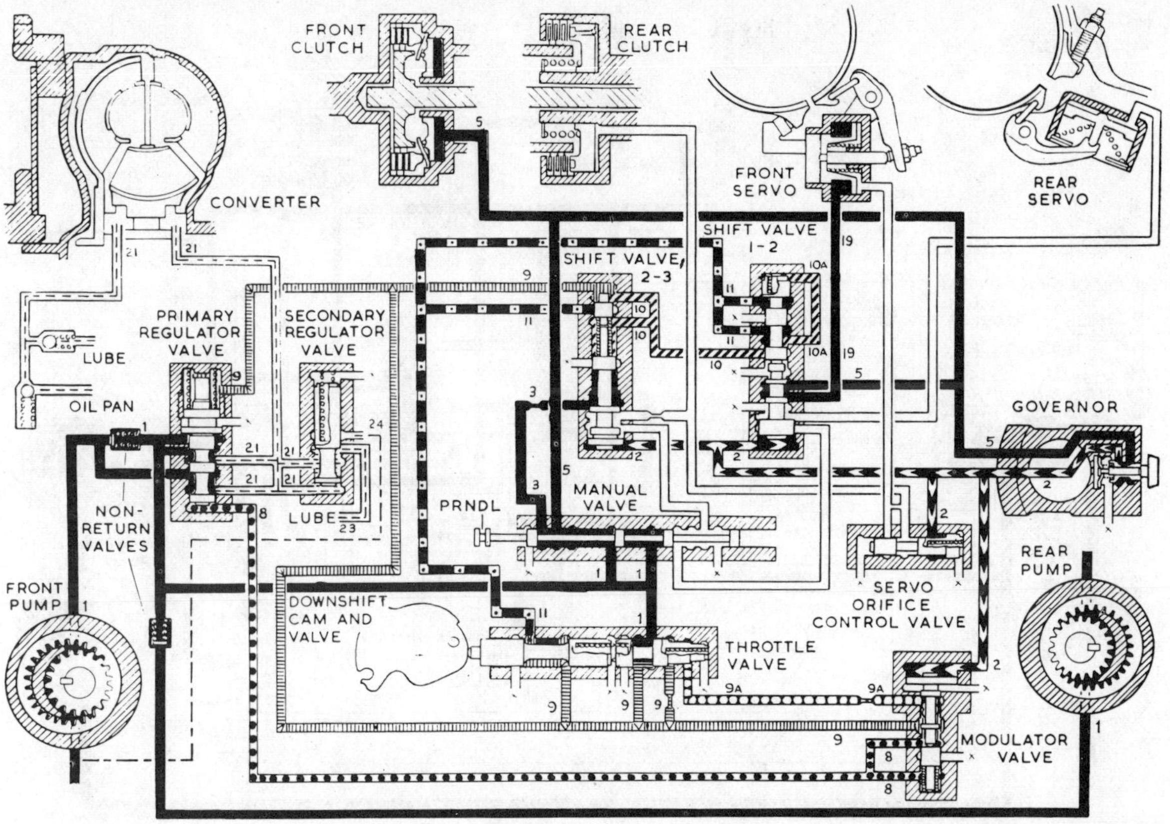

FIG 7:16 Operation of hydraulic circuit in D (Intermediate)

The drain plug has a hollow hexagon (Allen) head and requires an Allen key $\frac{1}{4}$ inch A/F to remove it (see **FIG 7:19**).

Disconnect the battery, drain the radiator and remove water hose, air cleaner and, possibly, rocker cover and distributor cap. Disconnect the throttle operating shaft and vacuum brake cylinder hose from the inlet manifold. On the transmission, disconnect the downshift cable and sleeve at the carburetter end, the fuel feed pipe to the fuel pump and the transmission filler tube at the cylinder head end. Undo the filler tube clamp and remove the filler tube. Disconnect the leads to the starter motor and the oil gauge feed pipe together with any other feature likely to be strained or broken on lowering the rear end of the engine.

Under the car, disconnect and remove the exhaust pipe and silencers as far back as necessary. Loosen and remove the speedometer cable and disconnect the leads to the starter inhibitor switch on the transmission. Remove the propeller shaft, identifying the ends for reinstatement later, and then disconnect the operating shaft from the gear selector lever at the side of the transmission and the reinforcing bracket under the oil panel.

Support the engine on a sling as described in **Chapter 1**. Unbolt and remove engine crossmember and the rear engine mounting brackets. Lower the engine sufficiently to be able to reach the gearbox to converter housing nuts, and undo the bolts, commencing with the lower ones. Place a container under the converter to catch any fluid draining from it when the transmission is removed, then withdraw the unit from the converter and lower it on to a trolley for conveyance to the bench (see **FIG 7:20**).

Next, unbolt and remove the converter housing and unbolt and remove the starter motor. Through the aperture vacated by removal of the air grilles, and using the special cranked spanner designed for the purpose, loosen and remove the four bolts attaching the converter to the adaptor plate, ease the converter clear and lower on to the trolley.

There may be some variations in the above procedure made necessary by difference in the location of controls and mountings on left and right-hand drive models but these should become evident as dismantling proceeds.

Clean the exterior of the transmission and converter housings and drain the hydraulic fluid from the transmission through the drain hole in the pan if this has not already been done.

Examine the converter body for signs of damage and check that the sleeve with the turbine rotor within rotates in the bearing without roughness or excessive friction. If any trouble has been experienced or there is any suspicion as to its efficient operation, fit a new converter returning

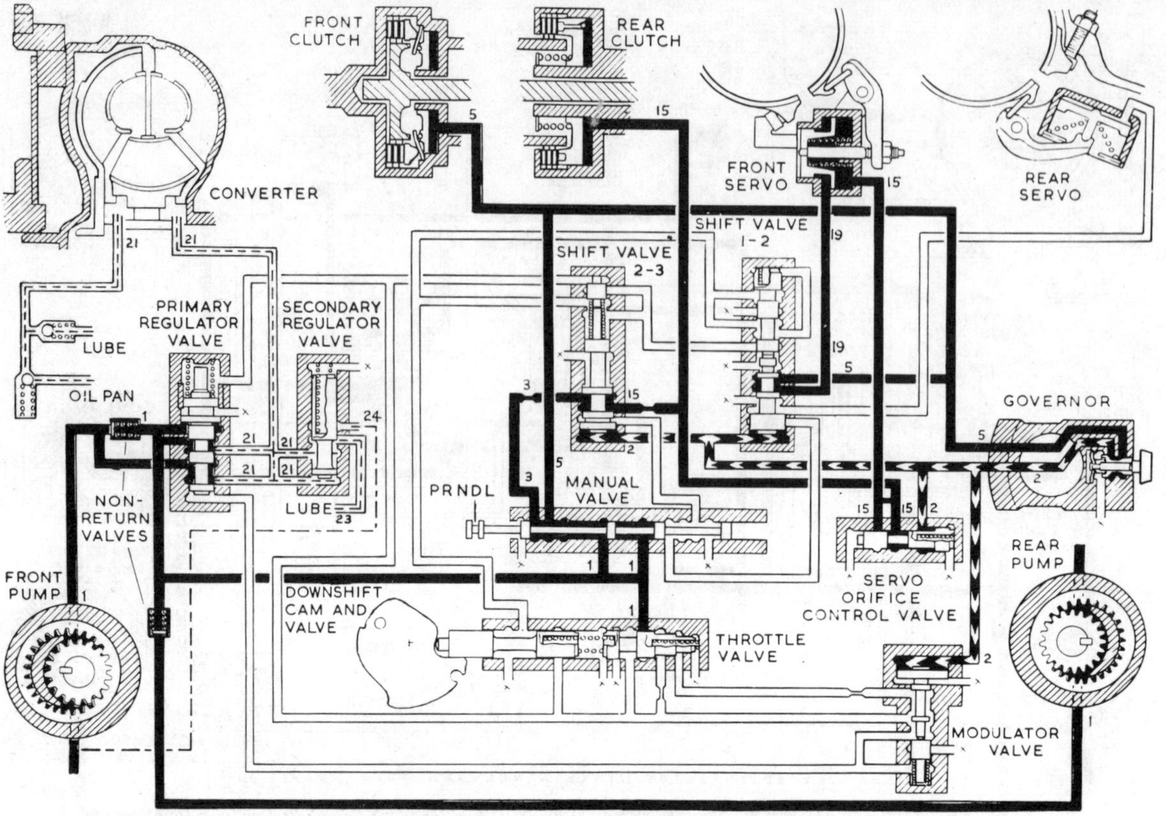

FIG 7:17 Operation of hydraulic circuit in D (High)

the other to the makers for reconstruction. **The units, being welded together, are not suitable for local repair.**

Turn the transmission over and mount on a suitable cradle with the hydraulics section uppermost (see **FIG 7:21**). Unbolt and remove the oil pan. The pan supports four oil tubes each of which is a push fit into its socket. These can easily be damaged if the gearbox is allowed to rest its weight on the oil pan, so be careful. With the pan removed, carefully lever out the tubes, noting their positions for reinstatement. Unscrew the four studs securing the two filters in place, clean the filters in petrol or carbon tetrachloride and allow to dry. **Do not use any fluffy material to wash or wipe down.**

Now remove the valve body assembly by extracting the three $\frac{7}{16}$ inch bolts indicated in **FIG 7:22**. (Two of these may have already been extracted when removing the filters.) Detach the cable from the downshift cam and carefully lift clear of the four oil tubes in the front of the gearbox. The two larger diameter tubes are the front pump inlet and outlet and the smaller are the feed and return for fluid to the converter. **Do not attempt to dismantle the valve body assembly.** The front pump may now be removed giving access to the gear train from the front clutch end.

The two clutch assemblies may now be extracted, the front clutch by just pulling clear and the rear assembly, complete with forward sun gear, by easing through the open front clutch band. Separation is a second procedure. The clutch band can then be squeezed together to free it from the servo and withdrawn through the front opening. The servo unit is secured by two $\frac{5}{16}$ inch bolts.

To remove the planet gears, the centre support must first be extracted. This is secured by two centre screws and the forward screw of the pair retaining the rear servo unit. Separation of the support and gears assembly is external to the casing after extraction. The rear brake band can now be extracted through the front end, tilting it slightly on withdrawal.

To reach the governor and rear pump, the rear housing must first be removed. The governor can be serviced on the drive shaft. To remove the pump, unscrew the five bolts and spring washers and withdraw the pump together with the drive shaft and ring gear as a unit and dismantle on the bench.

Examine all bushes, thrust washers, friction surfaces of clutch plates and drums for signs of scoring and the brake bands for signs of burning. Replace all oil seals and any parts obviously damaged or worn.

The foregoing brief summary of dismantling assumes that minimum work is needed and, in the majority of cases, it is only to service one part which is suspect. For a fuller instruction, secure from the agent a workshop manual on the Borg-Warner gearbox.

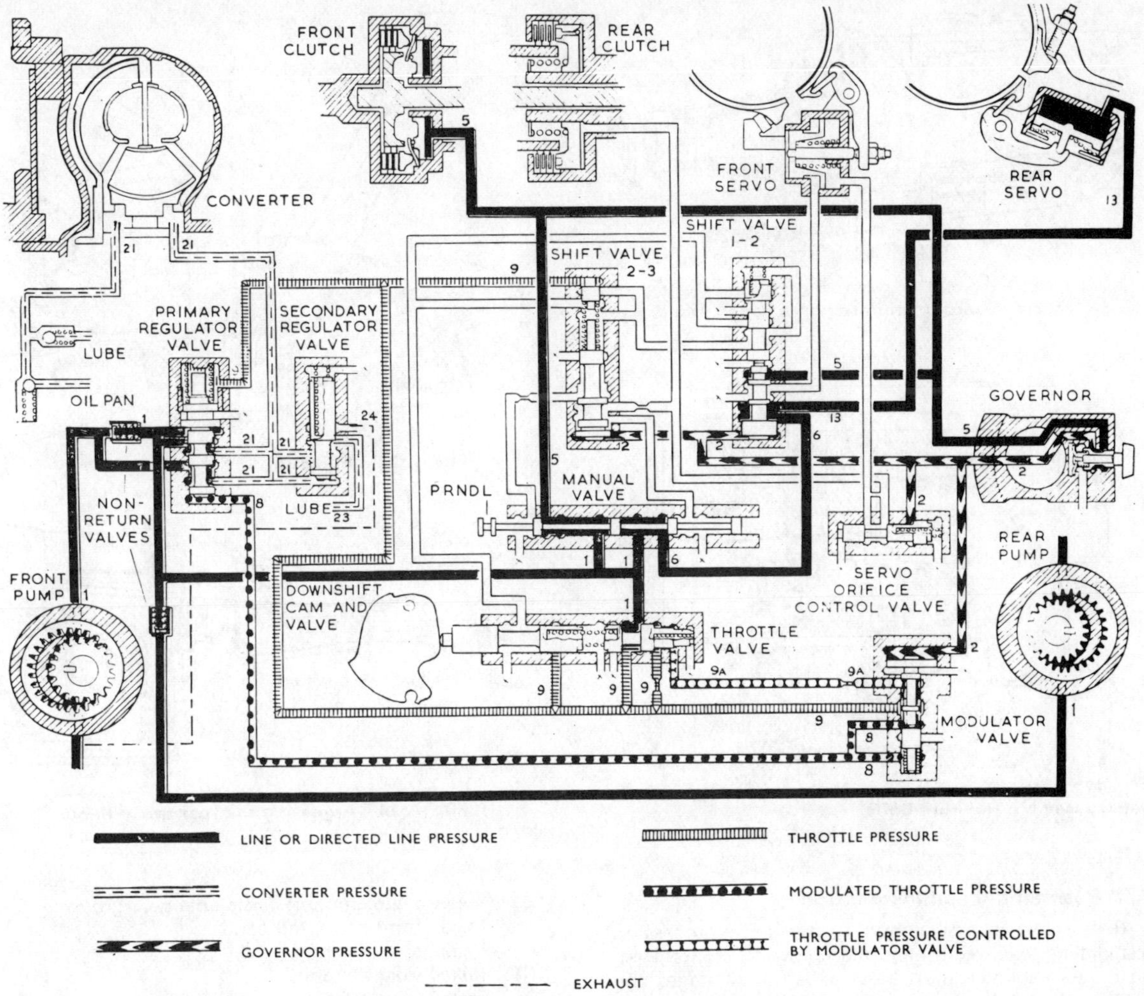

FIG 7:18 Operation of hydraulic circuit in L

FIG 7:19 Showing position of transmission drain plug

FIG 7:20 Transmission unit in jacking fixture

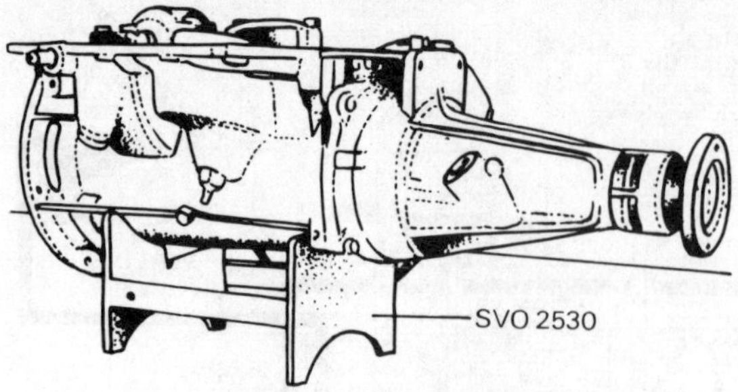

FIG 7:21 **Gearbox mounted on a bench stand**

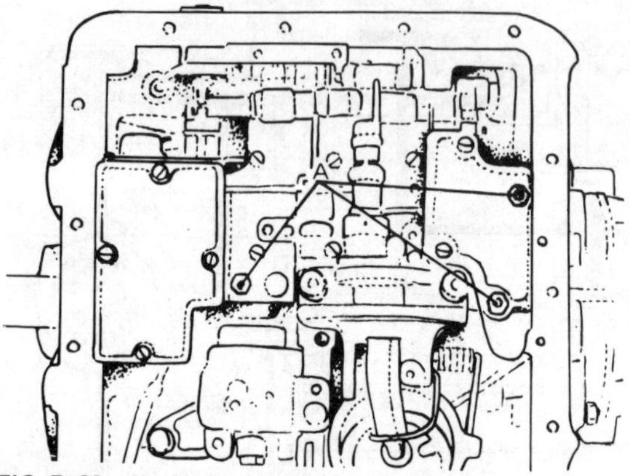

FIG 7:22 **Underside of transmission showing at A the valve assembly securing bolts**

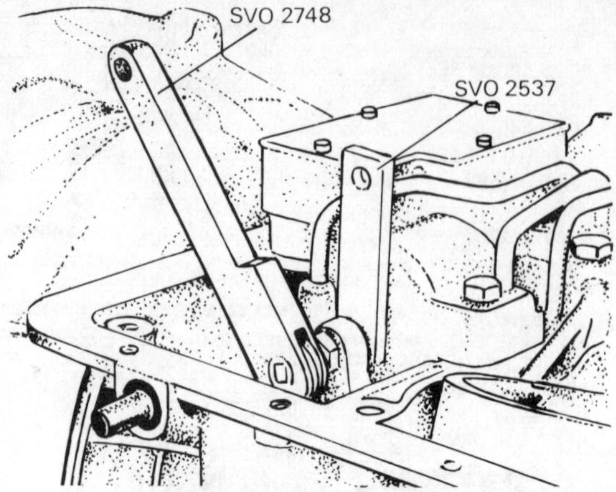

FIG 7:23 **Adjusting the front brake band**

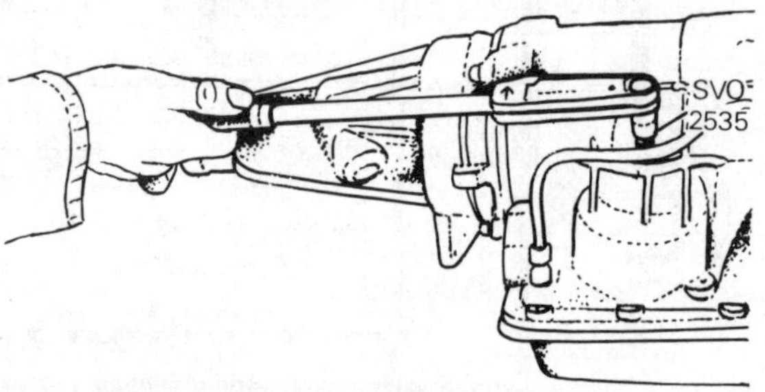

FIG 7:24 **Adjusting the rear brake band**

7:7 Reassembly and installation

Reassembly is a straightforward reverse process to dismantling, bearing in mind the following points. First, absolute cleanliness must be observed at all stages and the use of rags should be dispensed with or, at the minimum, only lint-free materials. Freshly washed nylon rag is quite suitable.

Always renew all gaskets and oil seals. Immediately before reassembly, clean all parts in petrol or carbon tetrachloride and dip in clean transmission fluid to facilitate installation.

All nuts and screws must be tightened to the appropriate torque as detailed in the Appendix as many of the threads are of light-alloy and over-tightening may damage them and render the fixing insecure. Be particularly careful not to cross threads when inserting. If possible, start the thread with the fingers and take up slack with a tubular socket spanner without the use of a tommy bar or other lever device, using the torque wrench as the final stage.

From full dismantling, the assembly sequence is:

(a) Insert shift rod, lever and parking pawls
(b) Insert drive (output) shaft and annulus
(c) Install rear pump
(d) Fit governor and speedometer drive pinion
(e) Install rear band and servo
(f) Insert centre support and planet gear group
(g) Install front servo and band
(h) Install rear clutch
(i) Install front clutch
(j) Install front pump
(k) Fit extension housing
(l) Fit pump and converter oil tubes and install valve assembly
(m) Fit four supply tubes and install oil pan.
(n) Install converter and housing in car
(o) Reinstall transmission on housing in car
(p) Reconnect propeller shaft and resupport gearbox on mounting
(q) Remake all connections, electrical and mechanical, dissembled during the preparatory phase of dismantling.

Adjustments:

During the reassembly certain adjustments have to be made. The first of these is for the front brake band (see **FIG 7:23**) and procedure is as follows. Slacken the adjustment locknut. With a torque screwdriver tighten the adjusting screw to a torque of 10 lb ft, then slacken off exactly four turns and secure with the locknut. **This is done with the oil pan removed.**

The rear brake band adjustment is external on the right-hand wall of the case (see **FIG 7:24**). Again, slacken the locknut, tighten the adjusting screw to a torque of 10 lb ft and slacken off one complete turn. Tighten the locknut.

To adjust the starter inhibitor switch, mounted above the gearshift lever on the transmission, place the selector lever in the D or L position. Couple the reverse connections (see **FIG 7:25**) (these tabs are set over at 45 deg.) to a battery and lamp and screw in the switch body to the unit until the lamp is extinguished. Make a mark on the body against a mark on the transmission casing and transfer the connections to the other two tags. Screw in further, counting the number of turns and parts of a turn, until the lamp is again extinguished. Turn back half this number to achieve a mid-point setting and secure with the locknut. Remake the proper connections.

To set the throttle downshift valve cable, warm up the engine and set the idle speed to 700 rev/min. Check that the inner and outer cables are correctly attached.

Screw up the threaded sleeve until it is $\frac{1}{32}$ inch (1 mm) from the stop which is crimped on to the cable and then fully press down the accelerator pedal and check that (a) the throttle is fully open and (b) the line pressure at converter stall speed is at least 160 lb/sq inch (11 kg/sq cm).

Stall speed check:

For this test it is necessary to connect an accurate tachometer to record the engine speed. It will also be necessary to have the road wheels firmly braked and chocked.

Having warmed up the engine and checked the oil level, select and apply full throttle for not more than ten seconds or overheating will occur. Compare the tachometer reading with the following table.

Rev/min	*Condition*	*Rectification*
2100 approx.	Satisfactory	—
over 2200	Transmission slip	Check transmission unit
below 1500	One-way clutch slip	New converter
1500 to 1800	Engine down on power	Check engine

7:8 Tow start and tow

Emergency starts, such as may be necessitated by a low charged battery, may be made by tow or push starting. Although the term 'tow start' is used, it includes starting by pushing the car from behind and this is preferable as, once the engine starts, the tendency is for the car to run away from the pushing vehicle instead of running into it from behind. Procedure is as follows:

Set the selector switch in **N** and, with the ignition switched off, push the car from behind (or tow) until a speed of about 25 mile/hr is reached. Set the choke, switch on the ignition and move the gear selector to the **L** position. When the engine starts, move the selector lever to **N** and apply the brakes. Alternatively, move the selector lever to **D** and drive away.

In the event of total engine failure and providing that the transmission is in order, the car may be towed with the selector lever in **N**. The only precuation necessary is to check that the oil level is up to the high mark. If, however, the transmission is out of order and the case of the car not being operational, the propeller shaft must be disconnected at the differential end and supported underneath the car before towing commences. **Towing with the shaft connected and a faulty transmission may cause serious internal damage to the Borg-Warner gears and/or converter.**

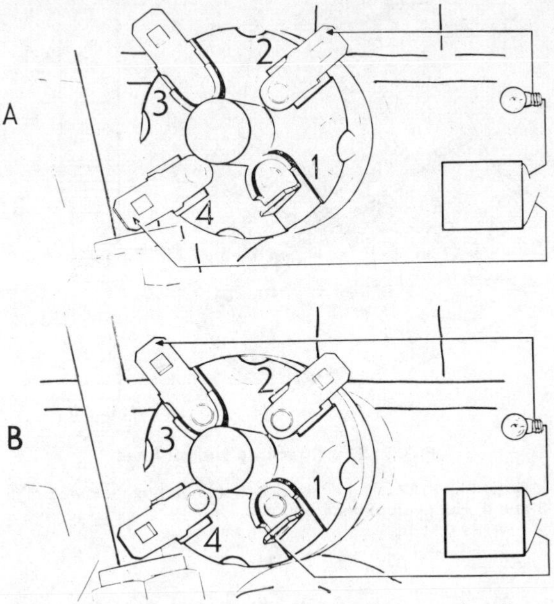

FIG 7:25 Inhibitor switch connections and adjustment

Key to Fig 7:25 **A** Reversing light contacts **B** Starter inhibitor contacts

7:9 Maintenance

Maintenance is restricted to periodic checks of the hydraulic fluid using the dipstick in the breather tube to the rear of the engine. This should be done every 3000 miles and the check must be carried out on a level surface after the fluid has attained normal running temperature and while the engine is running. Bring the level up to the 'high' mark **but do not overfill** (see **FIG 7:27**).

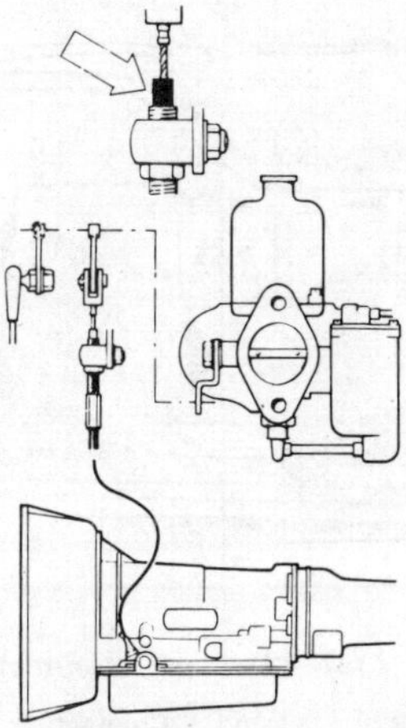

FIG 7:26 Adjusting the downshift cable

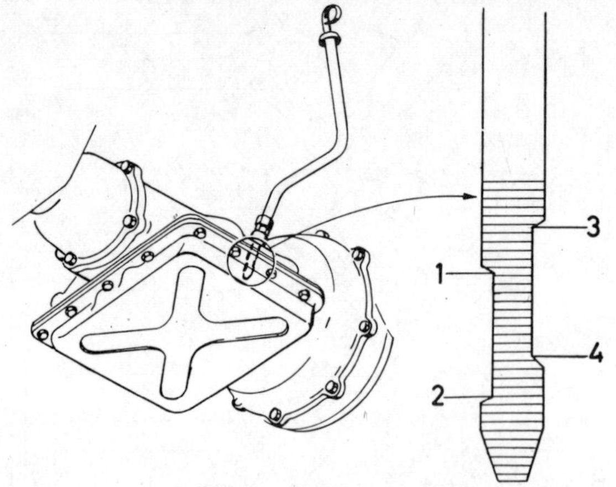

FIG 7:27 Checking the oil level

Key to Fig 7:27 1 and 2 Cold gearbox max. and min. 3 and 4 Hot gearbox max. and min.

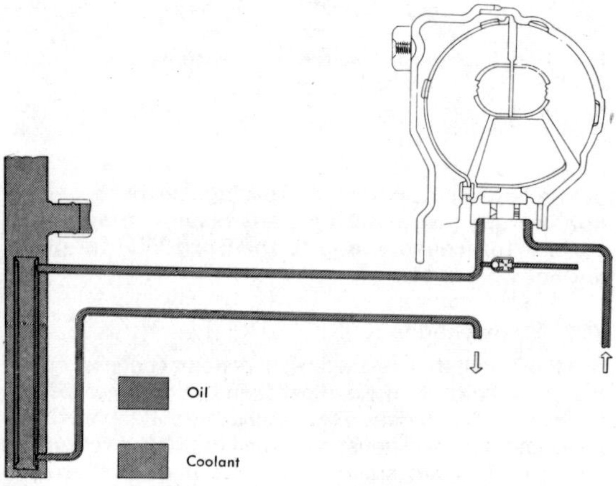

FIG 7:28 Oil cooler layout

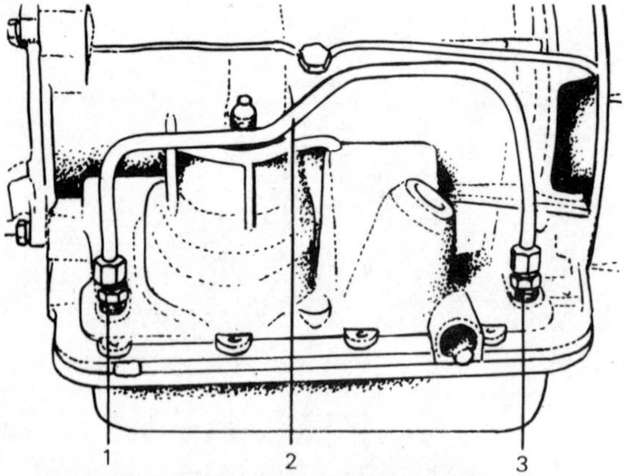

FIG 7:29 Oil cooler connections

Key to Fig 7:29 1 and 3 Connection nipples for cooler 2 Connecting pipe when cooler is not fitted

Routine fluid changes are unnecessary. At each service period, check the condition of the oil pan underside and the ventilating grilles beneath the converter housing. Clear away any caked road dirt or mud as the surfaces play an important part in cooling.

7:10 The oil cooler

On some cars, depending on the climatic conditions in which it is expected to operate, an oil cooler is fitted to prevent overheating of the transmission fluid. This forms part of the bottom tank of the engine radiator and is connected as in **FIG 7:28**.

If required, this can also be fitted to other (later) gearboxes by removing the connecting pipe (2 in **FIG 7:29**) and connecting the oil cooler between the unions 1 and 3 on the righthand side of the gearbox. It will, of course, be necessary to change the engine radiator.

7:11 Fault diagnosis

Most faults in the transmission system can be located by a sequential process since an observed irregularity can be traced to more than one cause. The adjoining table shows how the most common symptoms can be checked to identify the cause in the quickest possible time. Clearly, those causes which do not need unit removal must be checked before the longer process is embarked upon. Intelligent use of the chart avoids this. Operations G to L do not need unit removal from the car but do need draining of the hydraulic fluid and lowering of the oil pan.

Key to Fault diagnosis Chart:

A Check fluid level
B Adjust manual linkage
C Check carburetter full throttle
D Adjust engine idling speed
E Adjust downshift cable
F Adjust rear brake band
G Examine rear servo
H Adjust front brake band
J Examine front servo
K1 Check valve block screws for tightness
K2 Remove and clean valve block
L Remove and clear governor
M Readjust starter inhibitor switch
N Check pawl mechanism
O Check fit of rear clutch supply tube
* Remove transmission unit
p Examine front pump and drive
q Check front friction band
r1 Examine front clutch assembly and forward sun wheel seals
r2 Examine plug in forward end of drive shaft
s Examine rear clutch assembly and seals
t Check unidirectional clutch
u Check rear friction band
v Examine planetary gear set
w Replace torque converter

QUICK REFERENCE FAULT DIAGNOSIS CHART
NUMBERS INDICATE THE RECOMMENDED SEQUENCE OF FAULT INVESTIGATION

Fault	Operations that do not require unit removal															Operations requiring unit removal									
	A	B	C	D	E	F	G	H	J	K(1)	K(2)	L	M	N	O	*	p	q	r(1)	r(2)	s	t	u	v	w
No automatic upshifts																									
No 1-2 shift	.	1	.	.	.	.	.	3	4	.	5	2	.	.	.	6	.	7	.	.	.	.	.	.	.
No 2-3 shift	.	1	.	.	.	.	.	.	4	.	5	2	.	.	3	6	.	.	.	.	7	.	.	.	.
Incorrect shift speeds—quality of shift affected																									
Incorrect shift speeds	.	.	1	.	2	.	.	.	5	.	3	4	.	.	6	.	.	.	.	.	.	.	.	.	.
Loss of kickdown	.	.	1	.	2	.	.	.	.	.	3	.	.	.	.	.	.	.	.	.	.	.	.	.	.
Slip on 1-2 shift	1	3	.	.	2	.	.	4	5	.	6	.	.	.	.	7	.	8	9	.	.	.	.	.	.
Slip on 2-3 shift	1	2	.	.	3	.	.	.	5	.	6	.	.	.	4	7	.	8	.	.	9	.	.	.	.
Harsh 1-2 shift	.	.	.	.	1	.	.	2	.	.	3	4	.	.	.	5	.	.	7	.	.	6	.	.	.
Harsh 2-3 shift	.	.	.	.	1	.	.	2	.	.	3	.	.	.	.	4	.	.	.	.	5	.	.	.	.
Harsh 3-2 shift	.	.	.	.	.	.	.	1	3	.	2	.	.	.	.	4	.	5	.	.	6	.	.	.	.
Harsh 2-1 shift	.	.	.	1	2	.	.	.	.	.	.	.	.	.	.	3	.	.	4	.	.	5	.	.	.
Seizure 1-2	.	.	.	.	.	1	.	.	.	2	.	.	.	.	.	3	.	.	.	.	4	5	.	.	.
Seizure 2-3	.	.	.	.	.	.	.	1	2	3	.	.	.	.	.	.	.	.	.	.	.	.	.	.	.
Loss of drive—slip on take off																									
No forward drive	1	2	.	.	3	.	.	.	.	.	4	5	.	.	.	6	.	.	7	8	.	9	.	10a	10b
No drive in reverse	1	2	.	.	.	3	6	.	.	.	5	.	.	.	4	7	.	.	.	.	8	.	9	.	.
Slip or squawk in L	1	2	.	.	3	.	.	.	.	.	4	.	.	.	.	5	8	.	6	7	.	.	.	.	.
Slip or squawk in R	1	2	.	.	3	4	5	.	.	.	6	.	.	.	.	7	10	.	.	.	8	.	9	.	.
Incorrect operation in L																									
Upshifts occur with L selected	.	1	.	.	.	.	.	.	.	3	.	2	.	.	.	.	.	.	.	.	.	.	.	.	.
Excessive downshift delay—no engine braking. L selected from 30 m.p.h.	.	1	.	.	.	.	.	2	3	.	4	.	.	.	.	.	.	.	.	.	.	.	.	.	.
Miscellaneous																									
Incorrect starter or reverse lamp operation	.	1	.	.	.	.	.	.	.	.	.	.	2	.	.	.	.	.	.	.	.	.	.	.	.
P position not holding vehicle	.	1	.	.	.	.	.	.	.	.	.	.	.	2	.	.	.	.	.	.	.	.	.	.	.
Bumpy D, L, or R engagement	.	.	.	1	2	.	.	.	.	.	3	.	.	.	.	4	.	.	5	.	6	.	.	.	.
Delayed D, L, or R engagement	1	2	.	.	.	.	5	.	.	.	4	.	.	.	3	6	10	.	7	8	9	.	.	.	.
No neutral drive in neutral	.	1	.	.	.	.	.	.	.	2	.	.	.	.	.	3	.	.	4	.	.	.	.	.	.
Drag in R	.	.	.	.	.	.	.	1	.	.	.	.	.	.	.	2	.	.	3	.	.	.	.	.	.
Overheating	1	.	.	.	.	3	.	2	.	.	.	.	.	.	.	4	.	.	.	.	.	.	.	.	5

7:12 Road testing

After an overhaul and reinstallation, carry out the following road test procedure to ensure that the transmission is in correct adjustment and fully operative.

1 Check that the starter operates only with the selector in **P** and **N** and that the reversing light operates only in **R**

2 Apply the brakes and, with the engine running at normal idling speed, select **N-D, N-L** and **N-R**. Transmission engagement should be felt in each position selected.

3 Check the converter stall speed with the transmission in **L** and **R**. Check for slip or clutch squawk.

Note: Do not stall for longer than 10 seconds or the transmission will overheat.

4 With the transmission at normal running temperature, select **D**. Release the brakes and accelerate with minimum throttle opening. Check for **1-2** and **2-3** shifts. At minimum throttle openings, the shifts may be difficult to detect. Confirmation that the transmission is in third gear may be obtained by selecting **L**, when a **3-2** downshift should be felt.

5 At just over 30 mile/hr (50 kilometre/hr), select **N**, switch off the ignition and let the car coast. At 30 mile/hr (50 kilometre/hr) switch on the ignition and select **D**. The engine should then start through the rear wheels, indicating that the rear oil pump of the transmission is operating.

6a Stop and restart using full throttle acceleration. Check for **1-2** and **2-3** shifts according to the shift speed table in the attached schedule.

b At 25 mile/hr (40 kilometre/hr) in third gear, depress the accelerator to full throttle position. The car should accelerate in third gear and not downshift to second.

c At 30 mile/hr (50 kilometre/hr) in third gear, depress the accelerator to the kick-down position. The transmission should downshift to second gear.

d At 15 mile/hr (25 kilometre/hr) in third gear, depress the accelerator to the kick-down position. The transmission should downshift to first gear.

7a Stop and restart using full throttle acceleration. Check for **1-2** and **2-3** shifts according to the shift speed table in the attached schedule.

b At 40 mile/hr (65 kilometre/hr) in third gear, release the accelerator and select **L**. Check for **3-2** downshift and engine braking. Check for rollout **2-1** downshift at about 5 mile/hr (8 kilometre/hr) and engine braking.

8 Stop, and with **L** still engaged, release brakes and, using full throttle, accelerate to 20 mile/hr (30 kilometre/hr). Check for no slip or clutch squawk and no upshifts.

9 Stop and select **R**. Release brakes and reverse using full throttle if possible. Check for no slip or clutch squawk.

10 Stop on the brakes facing downhill on a gradient and select **P**. Release the brakes and check that the parking pawl will hold the car. **Re-apply the brakes before disengaging the parking pawl.** Repeat with the car facing uphill. Check that the selector is trapped by the gate in **P**.

Approximate gearshift speeds:

	1 to 2	*2 to 3*	*3 to 2*	*2 to 1*
Full throttle	30 (48)	54 (87)	41 (66)	9 (14)
Kick-down	39 (63)	70 (112)	62 (100)	32 (51)

Speeds are given in miles/hr. Speeds in kilometres/hr are in brackets.

CHAPTER 8

TRANSMISSION AND REAR SUSPENSION

8:1 Propeller shaft and bearing

The propeller shaft is of the divided tubular type terminating at both the gearbox and differential in Hardy-Spicer pattern universal joints with sealed needle bearings. The forward section is coupled to the rear section through a third universal joint and, in addition, is supported in a ballbearing bracket secured to the underbody of the car (see **FIG 8:1**). To allow for lateral extension with oscillation of the rear axle, the front fork of the centre universal joint is terminated in a splined shaft which slides in a mating splined bush in the end of the forward section of the tubular shaft, the joint being rendered grease and weatherproof by a collapsible rubber boot (see **FIG 8:2**).

The front and rear universal joints terminate at the outer ends in flanges for bolting to the gearbox drive shaft and differential couplings respectively, the inner forks of the joints being welded integral with the tubular shaft sections.

8:2 Removal and servicing

It is usual to remove the propeller shaft in two sections, the rear section first. Unbolt the flange from the differential drive flange and lower the shaft to the floor. At the support bearing, bend back the lockwasher and unscrew the nut (7 in **FIG 8:2**) from the end of the front section. Withdraw the rear section complete with nut and bolt. Loosen the cover to the support bearing and pull the complete assembly of bearing 4, rubber housing 5 and dust covers 3 and 6 from the shaft. At the gearbox, unbolt the flange coupling and lower the forward section of the propeller shaft to the floor. Transfer all three parts to the bench and clean thoroughly.

Inspect all universal joints for wear or damage and check the tubular sections for straightness and freedom from dents or cracks, particularly in the welded areas. Examine the centre bearing and replace if necessary. It is easily withdrawn from the rubber housing and a new one inserted in its place.

Damaged or bent shaft sections must be replaced. Do not attempt to straighten a bent section and the maximum out-of-straight that can be tolerated without causing unpleasant vibration is .01 inch at the centre when the section is being rotated in centres or rolled on knife edges at the closest points to the extremities.

The universal joints can be dismantled by first removing the circlips (see **FIG 8:3**) and tapping gently on one radius of the ear of the yoke. The needle bearing will then emerge and can be extracted. Repeat for the opposite bearing. Turn the joint through 90 deg. and repeat for the other two sides. Extract the journals and spider. Wash

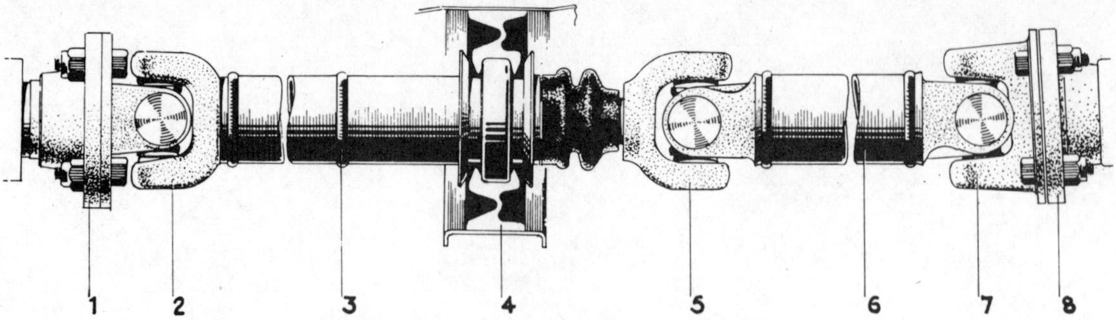

FIG 8:1 Propeller shaft and support bearing

Key to Fig 8:1 1 Flange on gearbox 2 Front universal joint 3 Front section of propeller shaft 4 Support bearing 5 Intermediate universal joint 6 Rear propeller shaft 7 Rear universal joint 8 Flange on rear axle

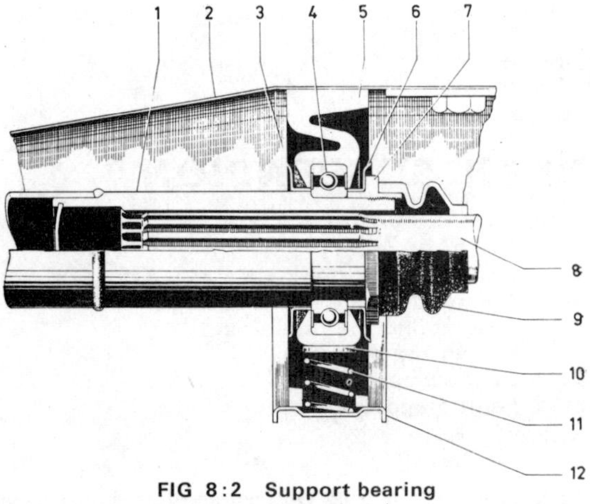

FIG 8:2 Support bearing

Key to Fig 8:2 1 Front section of propeller shaft 2 Floor tunnel 3 Dust cover 4 Ballbearing 5 Rubber housing 6 Dust cover 7 Nut 8 Rear section of propeller shaft 9 Rubber cover 10 Washer 11 Suspension spring 12 Cover

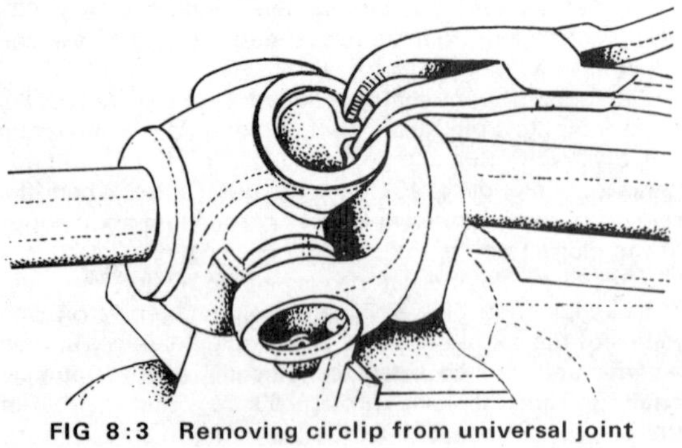

FIG 8:3 Removing circlip from universal joint

all parts in paraffin and examine for wear. Replace parts worn or marked with corrosion.

Reassemble, packing the bearings with Retinax 'A' grease filling the race about one-third full with the rollers in position. Install new gaskets and seals. **The inner yokes can be replaced only with the shaft to which they have been welded and balanced.**

Insert the journal in the flange yoke holes, gently tap the bearing assembly in position and, when all are located, fit new circlips. Tap lightly all round to relieve pressure, if any, in the assemblies.

8:3 Reassembly and installation

Refit the front section to the gearbox drive shaft flange and install the rear part in the support bearing. Secure the support bearing to the chassis. Check that the shaft runs true by rotating with the gearbox drive shaft while a dial gauge is applied to the shaft. Tighten the flange bolts down and lock.

Grease the inside splines of the forward section and the splined end of the rear section, fit a new rubber boot to the rear section and nut, then insert the rear section to the front and secure by means of the nut.

Reconnect the rear section flange to the differential flange, insert the bolts and tighten. Again check for alignment on the rear section of the shaft.

8:4 Rear axle, description

The rear axle assembly, comprising differential axle casing and halfshafts, is carried on two support arms as may be seen in **FIG 8:4**, pivoting on brackets secured to the chassis frame. The axle is attached to the support arms with levers and with two torque rods, to take up the axle torque, connecting the tubular axle casing and to the frame. There is also an anti-sway rod to prevent any relative sideways movement between the axle and the body.

The final drive unit, which is shown cut open in **FIG 8:24**, is of the hypoid type with the drive pinion below the centre of the crownwheel. A conventional differential assembly passes the drive to the two halfshafts the outer ends of which are journalled in taper roller bearings as shown in **FIG 8:5**. The bearing clearance here is not

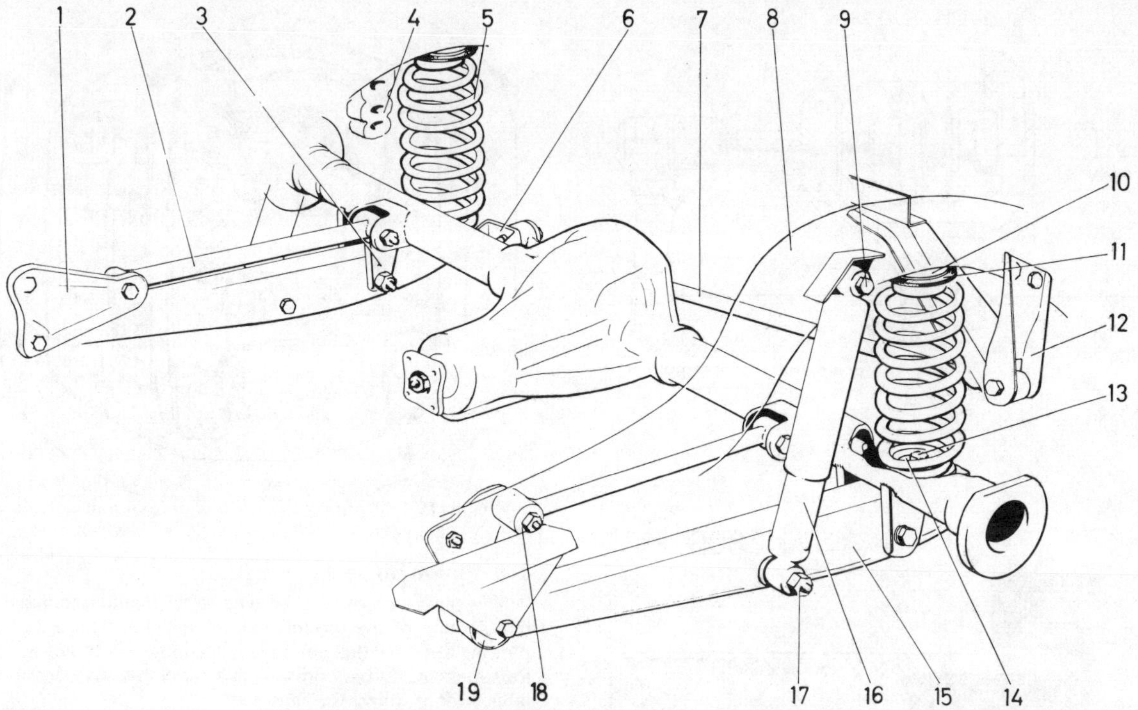

FIG 8:4 Rear axle and suspension assembly

Key to Fig 8:4 1 Bracket 2 Support stay 3 Bracket 4 Rubber buffer 5 Rear spring 6 Bracket 7 Anti-sway bar 8 Rear sidemember 9 Upper damper attachment 10 Washer 11 Rubber spacer 12 Bracket 13 Screw lower spring attachment 14 Washer 15 Support arm 16 Damper 17 Lower damper attachment 18 Front support stay attachment 19 Front bush, support arm

adjustable, being determined by the construction of the bearing clearances at other points in the rear axle are adjusted by a selection of shims.

8:5 Bearings and oil seals

Jack up the car, support it on stands and remove the wheels.

Disconnect the hydraulic supply pipes from the brake calipers then unbolt and remove the disc.

The thrust washer bolts are accessible through the holes in the drive shaft flange, unbolt these and pull out the drive shaft with a tool such as SVO.2709 (see **FIG 8:6**).

Secure press tool SVO.2838 in a vice and the drive shaft to the spindle plate. Then unscrew in the spindle so that the two arms of the tool can be placed against the bearing. Screw out the spindle and remove the bearing and lock ring. Remove the oil seal.

Before fitting the new oil seal, fill the space between the lips with grease, place it on the drive shaft together with the bearing (see **FIG 8:5** for the correct location) and a new lock ring. Using a fitting ring tool SVO.2839 as shown in **FIG 8:7**, press on the bearing and lock ring by screwing in the spindle.

Grease the bearing and fit the drive shaft, tightening the thrust washer bolts to a torque of 36 lb ft (5 kg m).

Fit the brake disc, caliper and hydraulic pipe. Bleed the brakes.

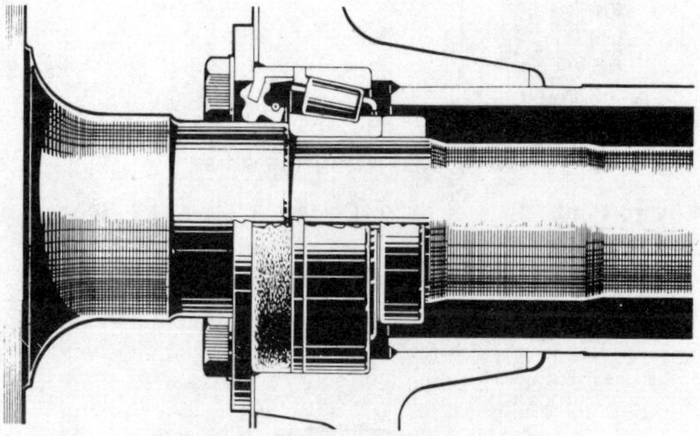

FIG 8:5 Drive shaft bearings

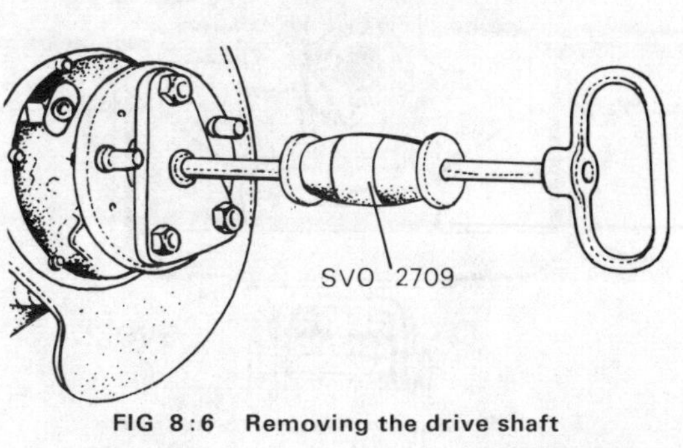

FIG 8:6 Removing the drive shaft

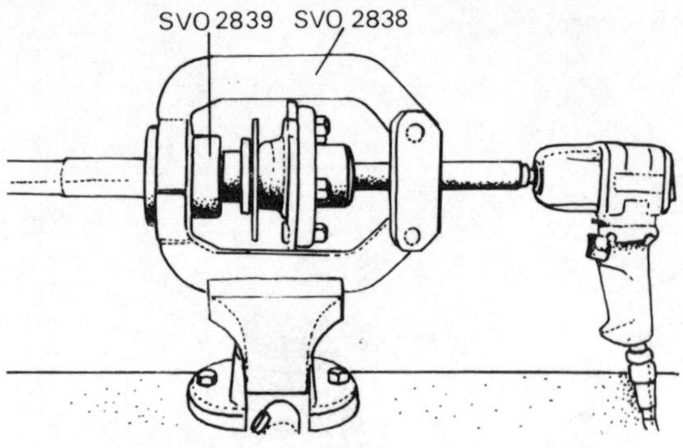

FIG 8:7 Fitting the drive shaft bearing

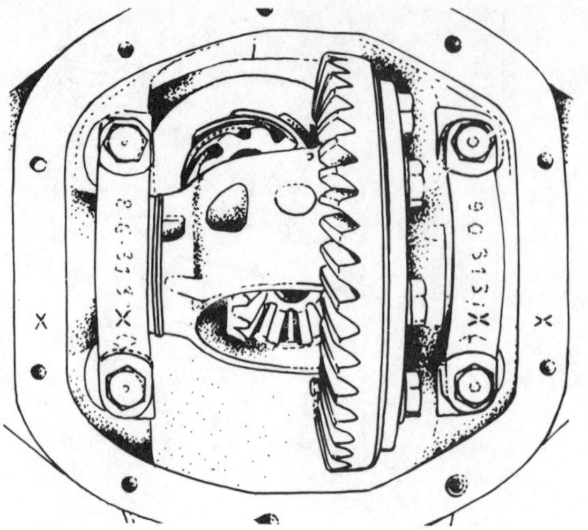

FIG 8:10 Alignment markings on cap and carrier

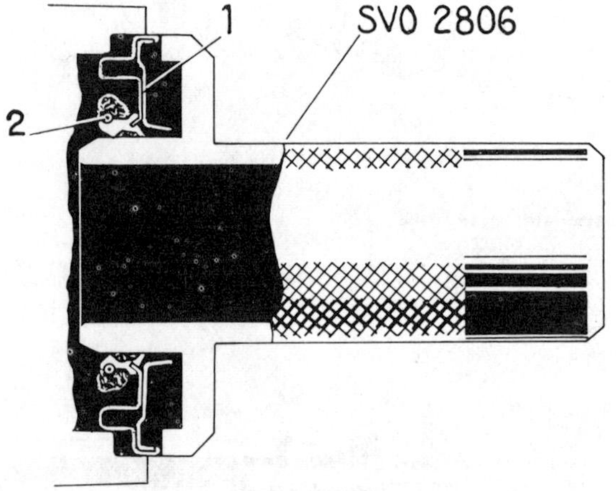

FIG 8:8 Fitting the oil seal

Key to Fig 8:8 1 Oil seal 2 Spring coil

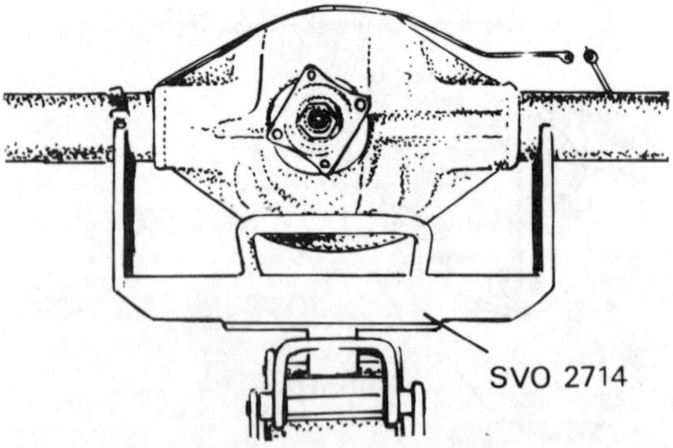

FIG 8:9 Support fixture for rear axle

8:6 Pinion oil seal

The pinion oil seal is removed after disconnecting the rear section of the propeller shaft from the flange on the pinion, but first the pinion shaft should be checked for looseness in its bearing and this remedied, as described later, before fitting the new seal.

Remove the flange nut using SVO.2837 and pull off the flange. Extract the old oil seal.

Before fitting the new seal, lubricate it well with grease and also apply a layer of grease to the coil spring, see **FIG 8:8**, in order to prevent it jumping out during the fitting operation.

Press on the flange and replace the washer and nut, tightening the nut to 200 to 220 lb ft (28 to 30 kg m). Refit the propeller shaft.

8:7 Removing the rear axle

Chock the front wheels and raise the back end of the car, supporting it on stands. Take off the two road wheels and then take the weight of the axle in the cradle fixture shown in **FIG 8:9**.

Release the upper damper attachment bolts. Disconnect the handbrake cables from the levers and brackets on the brake backplates. Disconnect the propeller shaft from the pinion flange and the brake pipe union from the rear casing.

Loosen the front attachment bolts for the support arms by about one turn then unscrew the rear bolts for the torque rods. Free the anti-sway bar from the bracket on the axle casing and remove the lower spring attachment bolts.

The jack should now be lowered to release the support arms from the springs and the bolts unscrewed which secure the axle casing to the support arms. Lower the jack and move the rear axle forwards.

8:8 Dismantling the rear axle

This is an operation which, for satisfactory completion, requires a number of special tools which may not be available to the home operator, although in most cases a suitable alternative may be found.

Place the axle in a suitable stand with the pinion pointing downwards. Remove the brake pipes and release the bolts securing the backplates and brake shoe retainers. This is done by working the holes in the drive shaft flanges. Pull out the drive shafts.

Remove the inspection cover and before proceeding any further check the alignment markings on the cap and carrier as shown in **FIG 8:10**. If these cannot be seen, mark one side with a punch before removing the caps.

Fit SVO.2394 and retainers SVO.2601 in the holes in the drive pinion carrier (see **FIG 8:11**) and tension the tool until it fits exactly into the carrier holes. Tension the bolt a further 3 to 3½ turns and lift out the differential carrier and crownwheel.

Reverse the assembly in the mounting letting the oil drain into a container and pull off the pinion flange with SVO.2261 or other suitable puller. Press out the pinion and then drive out the front pinion bearing, washer and oil seal. The standard handle SVO.1801 may be used for this with drift 2599. If necessary, drift SVO.2843 may be used for driving out the outer ring of the rear bearing on the same handle.

Clean the gasket and remove any roughness on the joint face.

The rear pinion bearing may be pulled off the pinion with puller SVO.2844 as follows: Refer to **FIG 8:12**, move the puller down over the rollers and press down the lock ring. Then pull up the puller using the bolt until the rollers lie flush with the edge of the inner race and the edge on the puller. The lock ring is tapped off with a hammer.

The differential:

First release the ring gear bolts and remove the crownwheel then drive out the locking pin and the shaft for the differential gears which are then taken out together with the thrust washers.

Pull off the differential carrier bearings with SVO.2483, taking care not to lose the shims.

After cleaning the pieces and examining for excessive wear or damage, the gears should be fitted dry into the differential carrier together with the shaft and thrust washers and the play checked by means of marking blue behind both of the side gears. If at any point the play exceeds .0024 inch (.06 mm) it should be rectified by using thicker washers of which three different sizes are available.

8:9 Assembling the final drive

Differential:

Fit the side gears and thrust washers in the carrier and 'roll' in both the side pinions simultaneously with the dished thrust washers as in **FIG 8:13**.

Drive in the shaft and check for any play which must be removed by fitting new thrust washers. Fit the locking pin.

Check that there is no damage or burring and fit the crownwheel tightening the bolts to a torque of 47 to 65 lb ft (6.5 to 9 kg m).

The pinion:

Clean thoroughly the marking surface on the pinion, if necessary using extremely fine emerycloth, then fit the adjusting ring SVO.2847 and tool SVO.2841 on the pinion as in **FIG 8:14**. Place the pinion in the carrier as in **FIG 8:15** and secure the adjusting ring by screwing in the lock screw.

The pinion should have a certain nominal measurement from the centre line of the crownwheel, but due to manufacturing tolerances there are deviations from this and this deviation is indicated on the pinion with a figure and a plus or minus sign. If a plus sign is in front of the number, the nominal measurement should be increased, and if the sign is minus the nominal measurement should be decreased. The number shows the deviation in thousandths of an inch.

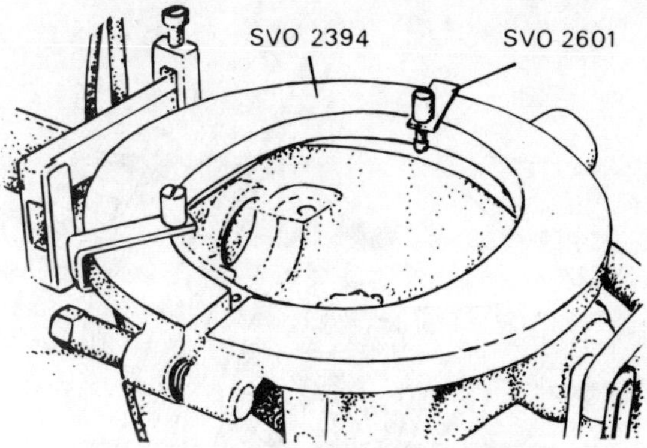

FIG 8:11 Expanding the drive pinion carrier

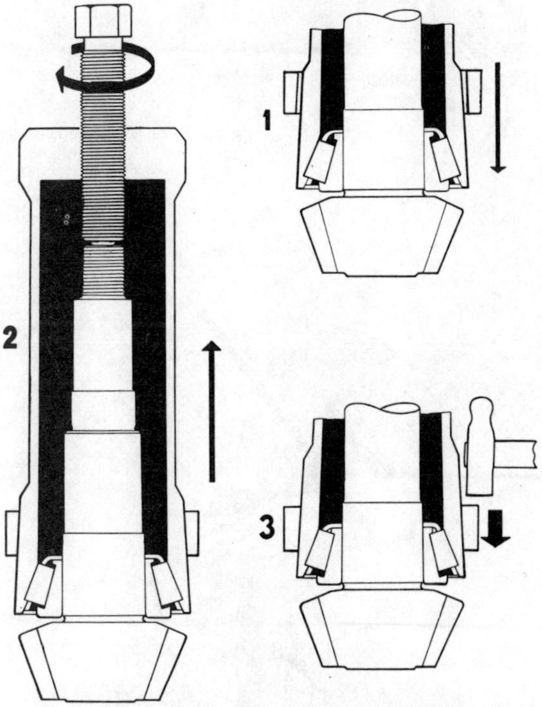

FIG 8:12 Pulling off the pinion rear bearing

Key to Fig 8:12 1 Puller is pressed down over the rollers 2 Rollers pulled up 3 Lock ring tapped into position

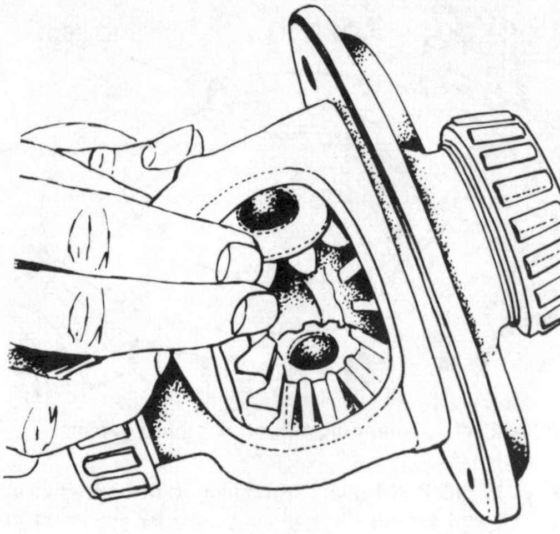

FIG 8:13 Fitting the differential gears

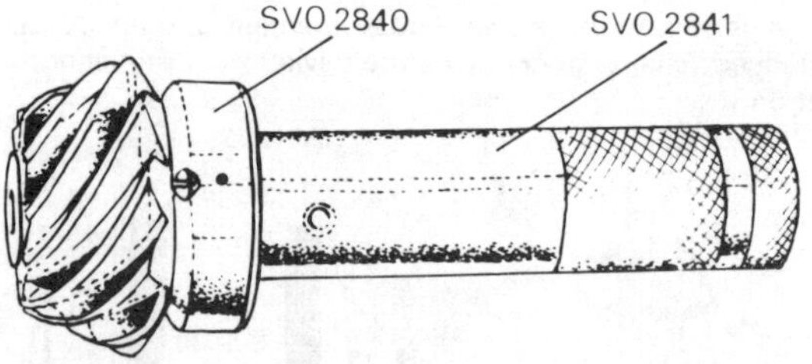

FIG 8:14 Adjusting ring and tool for pinion location

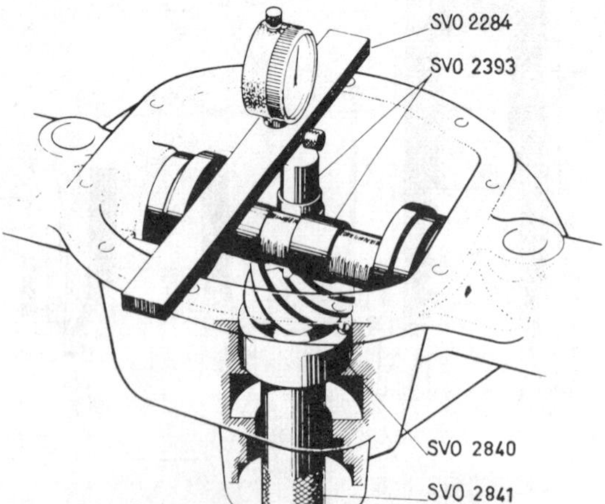

FIG 8:15 Position of the measuring tools

Refer to **FIG 8:15** and place the pinion gauge SVO.2393 on the ground surface of the pinion and the adjusting jig in the differential bearing positions. Place the indicator retainer SVO.2284 on the drive pinion carrier and zero the gauge against the adjusting jig. This may be seen in **FIG 8:16**. Move the indicator retainer so that the indicator contacts the pinion gauge (see **FIG 8:17**). If the pinion is marked — the gauge should be higher than the jig: if it is marked + the gauge should be lower than the jig with correct setting. The setting is adjusted by turning the cam on the pinion until the gauge shows the correct value. Lock the adjusting ring with the screw and remove the gauge and pinion.

Place the rear pinion bearing complete with outer ring in the measuring fixture SVO.2600. Put on the plate spring and nut, and turn the nut with the flat side upwards. The plate and the bearing are turned in each direction several times to locate the rollers correctly. Fit the adjusting ring as shown in **FIG 8:18**, position SVO.2284 and dial indicator with the measuring point of the indicator opposite the adjusting ring and set to zero. Move the pointer of the indicator to the outer ring of the bearing and the dial will show the required thickness of shims. It may not be possible to obtain the exact thickness so the following tolerances are allowed: +.0012 inch (.03 mm), —.0032 inch (.08 mm).

Press the rear bearing on to the pinion, fit the calculated shim thickness and press in both the outer rings of the bearings (see **FIG 8:19**). Insert the pinion into the casing and fit on three .03 inch (.75 mm) shims and the front pinion bearing. Fit SVO.2404 and SVO.1845 on to the front end of the pinion and pull it in (see **FIG 8:20**). Tighten the nut until the pinion is brought forward just short of the bearing positions.

Replace SVO.1845 with a washer and nut and tighten to a torque of 200 to 220 lb ft (28 to 30 kg m). Fit on the pinion gauge and the dial indicator retainer. Pull down the pinion, turning it backwards and forwards at the same time. Set the indicator to zero. Press the pinion upwards, turning it at the same time as before, and read off the clearance.

Remove the pinion. Remove shimming equal to the measured clearance +.003 inch (.07 mm) and refit the pinion.

The pinion bearing fit must now be checked with a torque gauge. This should show 5.20 to 9.55 lb in (6 to 11 kg cm) for used bearings or 9.55 to 20 lb in (11 to 23 kg cm) for new bearings when rotating the pinion. The shim thickness must be adjusted to obtain these values if required.

Finally check the location of the pinion with the dial indicator, retainer SVO.2284 and measuring tool 2393.

Fitting the differential:

Refer to **FIG 8:21**. Lubricate the inside of the adjusting rings SVO.2595 and place them as the differential carrier with the oxidised black ring on the crownwheel side. Place the carrier and the rings in the housing and using the dial indicator, adjust the rings to obtain a tooth flank clearance of .005 to .008 inch (.13 to .20 mm). Tighten the locking screws in the rings.

Fit the brake tool SVO.2597 shown in **FIG 8:22** and then apply marking blue to several teeth around the

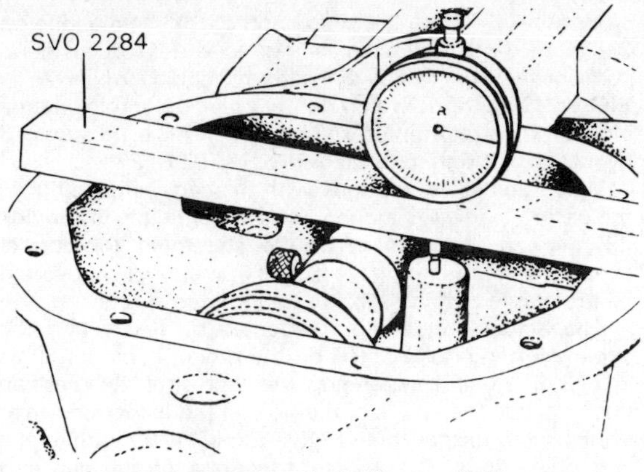

FIG 8:16 Setting the indicator dial to zero

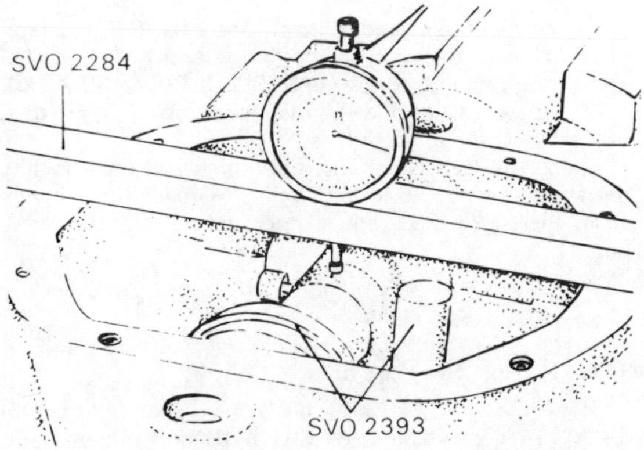

FIG 8:17 Measuring the pinion location

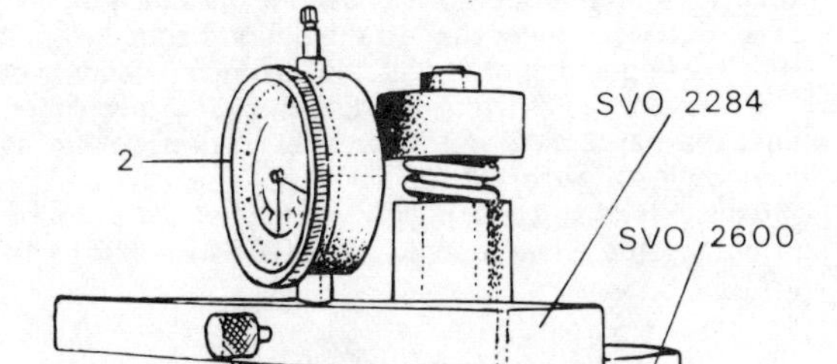

FIG 8:18 Showing method of determining shim thickness

Key to Fig 8:18 1 Adjusting ring 2 Dial indicator 3 Bearing

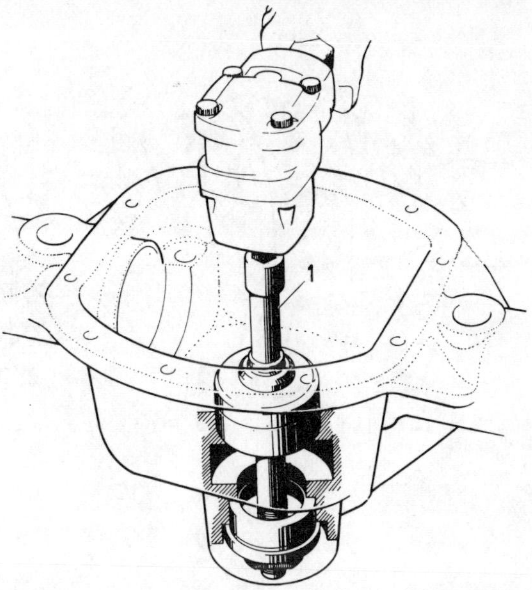

FIG 8:19 Fitting the bearing rings. 1 is press tool SVO 2845

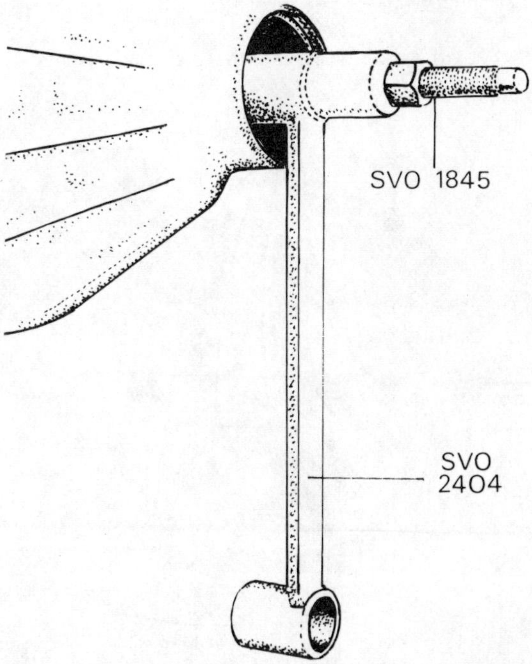

FIG 8:20 Fitting the pinion

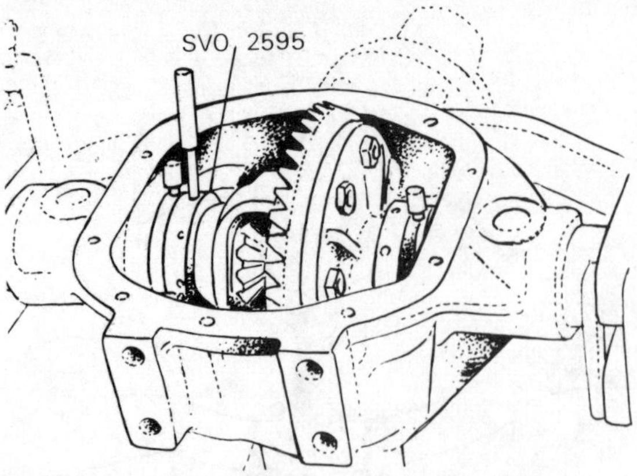

FIG 8:21 Using adjusting rings for fitting the differential gears

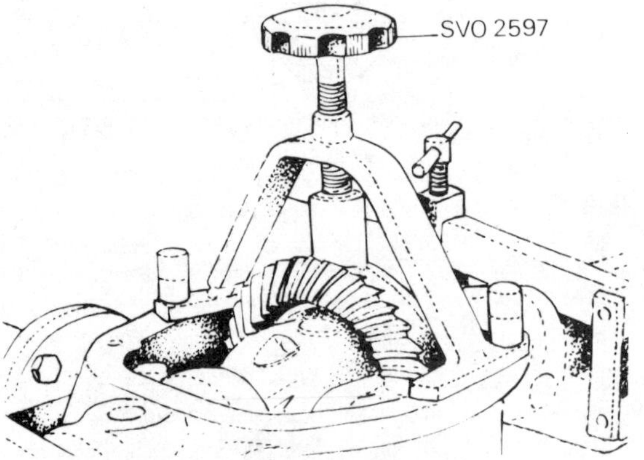

FIG 8:22 Brake tool fitted to differential

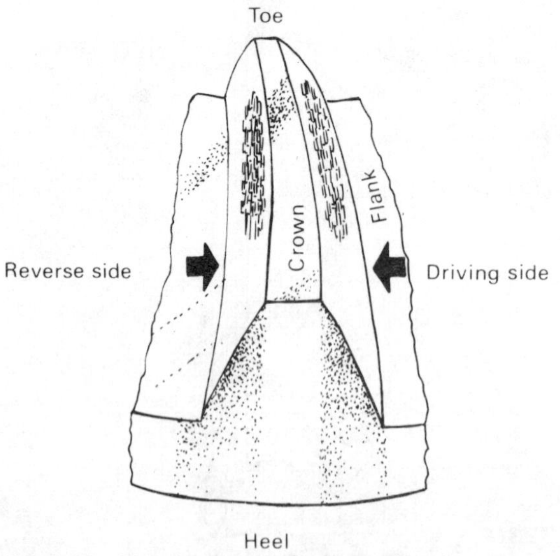

FIG 8:23 Showing pattern for correct tooth contact

crownwheel. Rotate the pinion and check the marking on the teeth. With correct meshing, as should occur if no parts have been fitted, the pattern should appear as in **FIG 8:23**. Patterns which do not coincide in this manner indicate incorrect pinion setting which must be adjusted by means of the shims at 22 and 18 in **FIG 8:23**.

When this has been done with the cage removed from the casing, add .003 inch to each set of shims to provide the preload. Adjustment of the shimming for correct centring and preloading is a skilled operation, and it would be preferable to hand this job to a service station.

The actual preloading is effected by first fitting the expander gauge SVO.2394 on the drive pinion carrier as in **FIG 8:11** and expanding the tool until the pins are flush against the edges of the hole in the carrier and then tightening a further three to five turns. Fit the differential and outer rings, remove the tool then fit the cap and tighten the bolts to a torque of 36 to 50 lb ft (5 to 7 kg m).

With the pinion and differential in position recheck the assembly for correct gear meshing.

Rear axle:

Fit the oil slinger and oil seal. See **FIG 8:8** and refer to **Section 8:6**. Press on the flange and fit the washer and nut, tightening to 200 to 220 lb ft (28 to 30 kg m).

Fit a new gasket and the inspection cover, tightening the bolts evenly all round.

Install the two halfshafts, tightening the bolts for the thrust washers to 36 lb ft (5 kg m). Grease the bearing.

Fit the brake discs and calipers and finally the brake pipes.

8:10 Fitting the rear axle

Place the axle assembly on a jack with fixture tool SVO.1714 if available (see **FIG 8:9**) and move it into position under the car. Fit the bolts for the support arms and torque rods.

Raise the jack until the anti-sway bar attachment on the axle is level with that on the chassis and secure it. Fit the bolts for the springs and then tighten the nuts for the torque rods and support arms. Secure the brackets and hoses. Fit the propeller shaft to the pinion flange.

Fit the upper mountings of the dampers. Reconnect the handbrake cables in the brackets and to the levers then adjust the handbrake and bleed the braking system as described in **Chapter 11**.

Fit the wheels and their nuts, lower the car to the ground and tighten the wheel nuts to 70 to 100 lb ft (10 to 14 kg m).

8:11 Rear suspension

The component parts of this have been described under the rear axle and comprise in addition to the axle, the coil springs and dampers (see **FIG 8:4**).

Details of the coil springs will be found in **Technical Data.** The dampers are of the double-acting telescopic hydraulic type, and are sealed at the factory. No adjustment is required and none is provided. In the event of trouble the damper should be renewed.

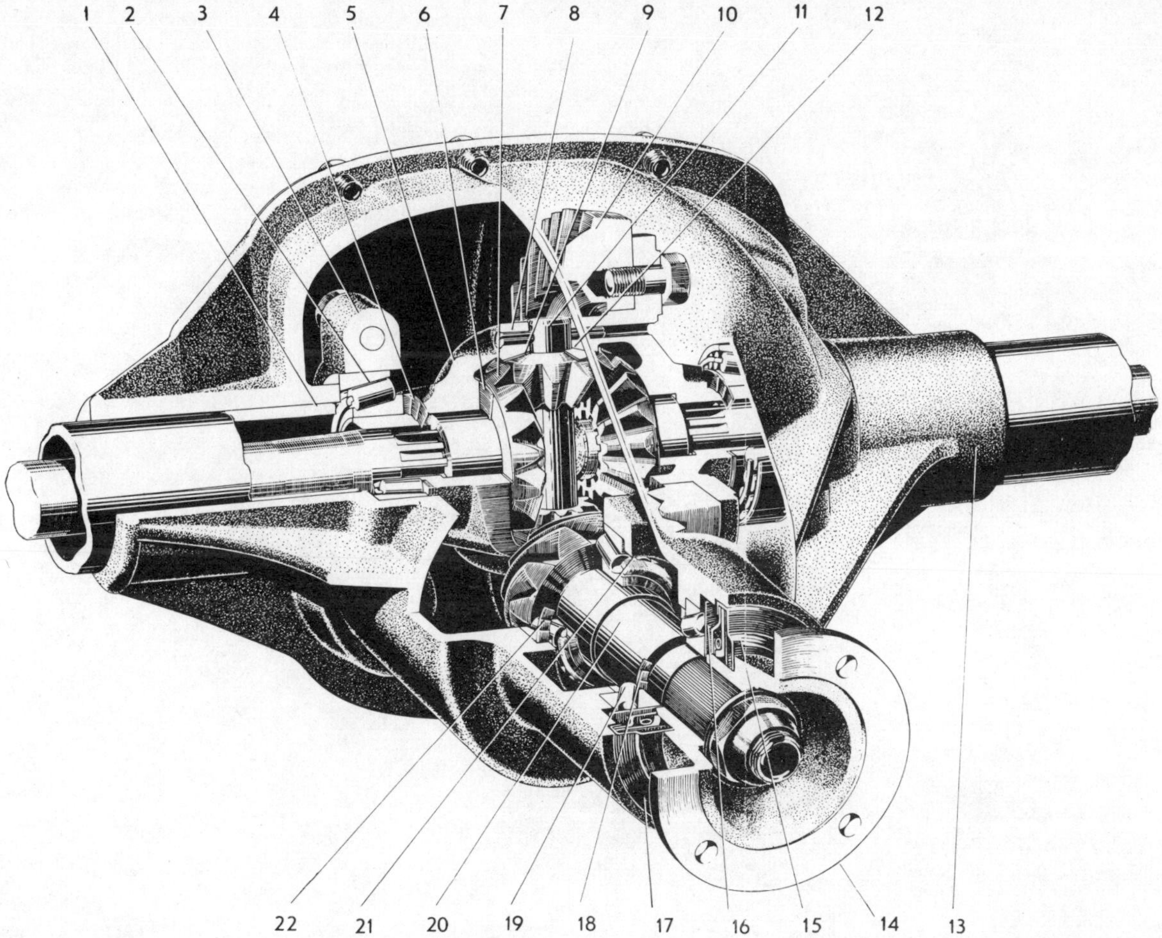

FIG 8:24 Cut-away view of the final drive assembly

Key to Fig 8:24 1 Tubular shaft 2 Differential carrier bearing 3 Bearing cap 4 Shims 5 Differential carrier 6 Thrust washer 7 Differential side gear 8 Lockpin 9 Differential pinion 10 Crownwheel 11 Shaft 12 Thrust washer 13 Rear axle casing 14 Flange 15 Dust coverplate 16 Oil slinger 17 Oil seal 18 Shims 19 Front pinion bearing 20 Pinion 21 Rear pinion bearing 22 Shims

8:12 Fault diagnosis

(a) Noisy axle

1 Insufficient oil
2 Worn bearings
3 Worn gears
4 Incorrect adjustment

(b) Excessive backlash

1 Worn gears of bearings
2 Worn axle shaft splines
3 Worn universal joints
4 Loose or broken wheel studs

(c) Vibration

1 Propeller shaft out of balance
2 Dampers loose
3 Spring seating cups worn
4 Wheels out of balance
5 Loose coupling nuts or bolts
6 Defective centre support bearing

(d) 'Settling' or 'bottoming' of suspension

1 Weak springs
2 Weak or broken damper
3 Defective or broken bump stops

(e) Rattles

1 Loose dampers
2 Broken spring
3 Loose damper attachment
4 Worn or broken bushes

CHAPTER 9

FRONT SUSPENSION AND HUBS

9:1 Description of front suspension

The front suspension comprises a conventional arrangement of wishbone type swinging arms and independent coil springs, hydraulic shock absorbers and a stabilizer bar. The upper and lower arms support the steering knuckles in ball joints permanently lubricated for life, the joints being housed in cups which are a press fit into the ends of the swinging arms.

The complete suspension and front hub assemblies are supported on a front axle member secured to the chassis crossmember by bolts. It is therefore possible to lower the complete front suspension assembly on the axle member by disconnecting only the hydraulic brake connections, the stabilizer attachments and the joints to the steering box pitman arm and relay lever. The stabilizer is secured to the front end of the chassis sidemembers by rubber bushed brackets while the steering box and relay arm are attached to the two sidemembers. The member also provides front engine support (see **FIG 9:1**).

At each end of the front axle member are substantial tower structures providing the housing for the coil spring and shock absorbers and acting as the support member for the upper wishbone shaft. The lower wishbone shaft passes through the axle member terminating in compressed 'live' rubber bushes in the wishbone arms. The upper wishbone shaft, also pivoting in rubber bushes at the arms, is bolted to the tower structure through shims providing the camber and castor adjustment.

Each coil spring is located between the lower wishbone and the upper tower structure and encircles the shock absorber bolted between the lower arm and upper mount.

The wheels are mounted on stub axles integral with the knuckle arms through taper roller bearing hubs which also support the brake disc. The brakes are of the hydraulically operated disc pattern, details of which are given in **Chapter 11**.

9:2 Routine maintenance

The suspension is designed for the minimum of maintenance and the only servicing that is required is to repack the wheel hub bearings with grease every 12,000 miles. The design of hub housing is such that even with double this mileage, lubrication should be adequate but a general overhaul of wheel bearings is advisable at these intervals and part of the overhaul procedure is to remove the old grease and repack after inspection and adjustment and to renew the grease and oil seals.

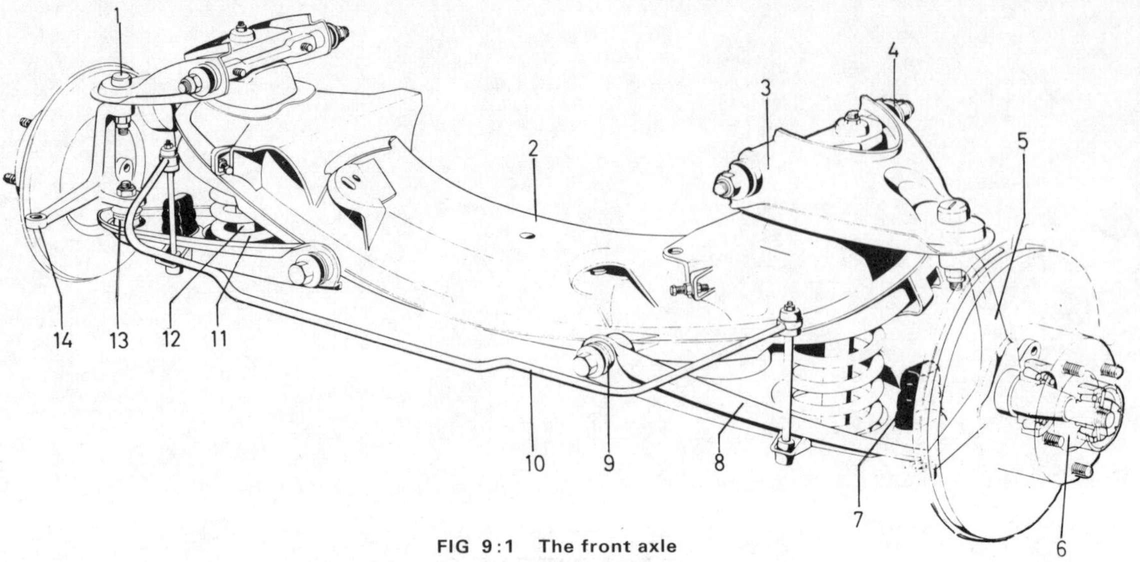

FIG 9:1 **The front axle**

Key to Fig 9:1 1 Upper ball joint 2 Front axle member 3 Upper control arm 4 Upper control arm bush 5 Steering knuckle 6 Hub 7 Rubber buffer 8 Lower control arm 9 Lower control arm bush 10 Stabilizer 11 Spring 12 Shock absorber 13 Lower ball joint 14 Steering arm

Ball joints are lubricated for life and providing that the protective plastic sleeves are undamaged, no attention is needed. Inspection for split or deformed sleeves is however part of regular general inspection. Worn or seized ball joints must of course be replaced by new ones.

9:3 Removing front end complete

Using suitable lifting gear, raise the engine until the weight is taken off the front engine mounting. Remove the hub caps and loosen the front wheel nuts. Jack up the front end of the car and remove the road wheels.

Disconnect the steering rods from the steering arms with tool SVO.2294 as in **FIG 9:2**. Remove the bolts attaching the stabilizer bar.

Refer to **FIG 9:3** and remove the brake hoses from the unions at the support member (items 1, 2, 3 and 4).

Remove the lower nuts for the front engine mountings. Remove the bolts securing the front axle member, then lower and remove the front end.

Instructions for the removal and servicing of the various component parts will be given under their respective headings.

Refitting:

Fit the guide pins in the front holes of the front axle member, then place a jack under the front end assembly and raise it into position. Fit the rear bolts provided with plastic plugs. Remove the guide pins and fit the front bolts.

Fit the engine mounting bolts and tighten to a torque of 15 to 18 lb ft.

Refit the stabilizer mounting bolts and reconnect the brake hoses, ensuring that they are replaced in their original positions.

Reconnect the steering rods. Bleed the brakes. Refit the wheels and tighten to 70 to 100 lb ft after lowering the car to the ground.

9:4 Dismantling the suspension

Stub axle:

Before the stub axle can be removed it is first necessary to remove the front brake caliper as described in **Chapter 11**, then remove the grease cap using tool SVO.2715, the split pin and castellated nut and pull off the hub with a suitable puller such as SVO.2726. The inner bearing can also be pulled off if required with SVO.2722.

Remove the steering rod from the steering arm as shown earlier in **FIG 9:2**.

Slacken, but do not remove, the ball joint nuts and knock on the axle with a hammer until the ball joint pins are loosened. Raise the lower control arm a little with the jack, then remove the ball joint nuts and take off the stub axle.

Clean and wash all the pieces in white spirit and dry carefully, inspect for wear or damage and renew as necessary.

Pack the bearings by hand with as much of the recommended grade of grease as possible and apply engine oil liberally to the felt rings before fitting.

Place the inner bearing in position in the hub and press in the oil seal. Oil copiously.

Place the stub axle in position and tighten up the ball joint nuts, if necessary holding the joint with a screw vice to prevent it twisting. Fit the steering rod on to the steering arm.

Place the hub on the axle and fit the outer bearing, washer and castellated nut.

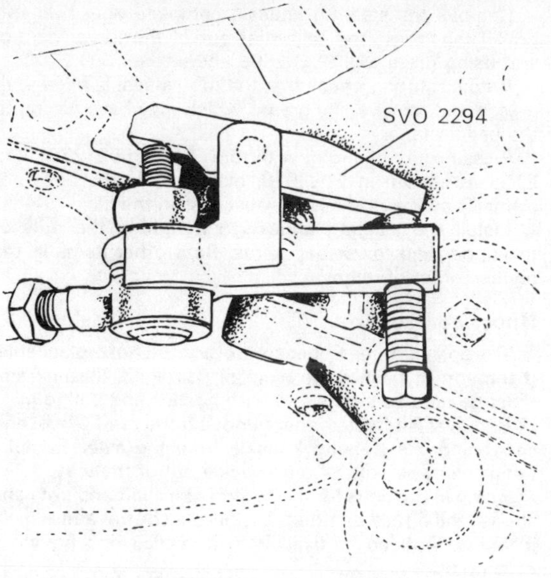

FIG 9:2 Removing the steering rod

Adjust the bearings by spinning the wheel and at the same time tightening the nut to 50 lb ft. Turn the nut back one third of a turn and, if necessary, to the next slot in the nut to coincide with the hole in the stub axle. Check that the wheel turns easily but without any play.

Half fill the cap with grease and replace it. Replace the brake caliper and the road wheel.

Upper ball joint:

After checking that the upper control arm is not in contact with the rubber stop, check to see if the ball joint has any radial clearance. Do not be confused with axial clearance or play in the wheel bearings. If radial clearance is present the joint should be renewed.

Remove the hub cap and slacken the wheel nuts. Jack up the front of the car and remove the wheel.

Slacken the upper ball joint nut and tap with a hammer on the steering knuckle to release the ball joint pin from the axle. Remove the nut and tie up the end of the knuckle out of the way without straining the brake hoses.

Slacken the control arm shaft nuts half a turn, then lift up the arm and press out the ball joint with SVO.2699 and SVO.2701 as shown in **FIG 9:4**.

Before refitting the joint check that the rubber cover is filled with grease.

Press the ball joint into the control arm, making sure that the recess coincides with the longitudinal shaft of the control arm, within ± 8 deg. and that it is a tight fit when in position.

Turn down the control arm and tighten the nuts on the shaft. Tighten the ball joint against the steering knuckle, preventing the pin from rotating by holding it with a screw vice.

Refit the wheel and lower the car to the ground.

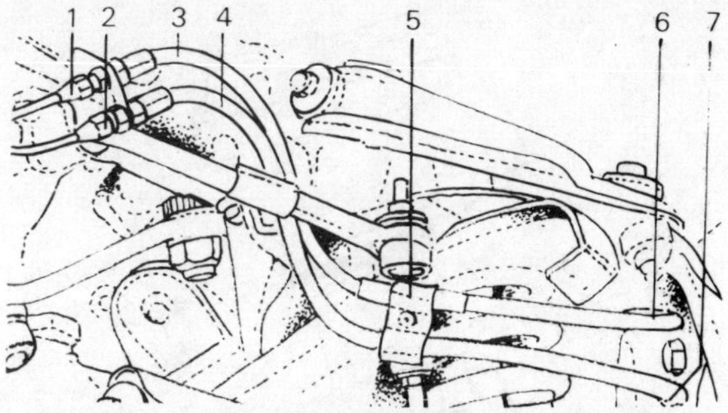

FIG 9:3 Showing front brake hose connections

Key to Fig 9:3 1 Connection for the primary circuit 2 Connection for the secondary circuit 3 Upper brake hose 4 Lower brake hose 5 Clip 6 Connection for lower wheel unit cylinder 7 Connection for upper wheel unit cylinder

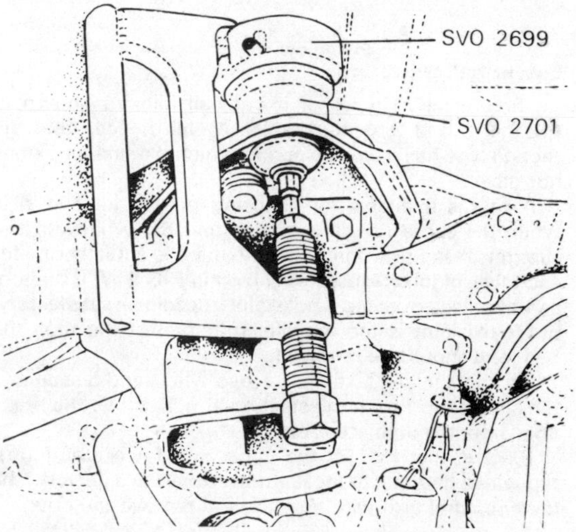

FIG 9:4 Removing the upper wishbone ball joint

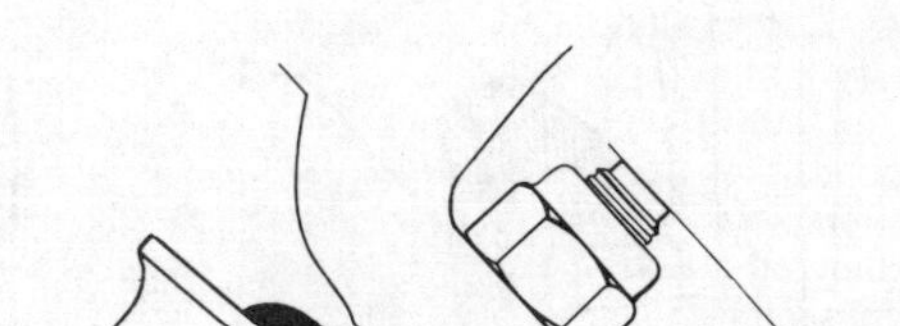

FIG 9:5 Lower ball joint, type 2 (with spring) A= 4.5 inch (113 mm) max.

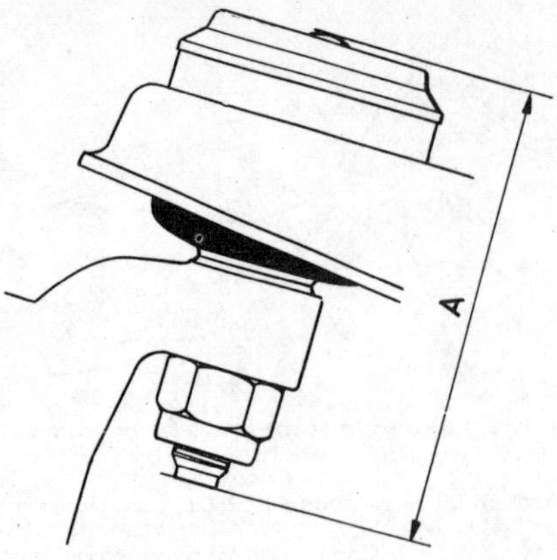

FIG 9:6 Lower ball joint, type 1 (without spring) a=3.91 inch (99.3 mm) max.

Lower ball joint:

There are two types of lower ball joint as shown in **FIGS 9:5** and **9:6** from which it will be seen that the second type has a built-in spring which the first type does not have.

A tool is available for checking on the joint in situ, when the car is normally loaded and the wheels in the straight-ahead position. The tool, there is actually one for each type of joint, is used as shown in **FIG 9:7**. If the tool can be placed over the whole joint, the joint is satisfactory, but if the joint is too long for the span of the tool, the ball joint should be renewed.

Jack up the car, take off the road wheel and disconnect the steering rod from the steering arm. Remove the brake lines from the stabilizer bolt.

Slacken the nuts for the upper and lower ball joints, tap with a hammer to loosen them from the axle, raise the lower control arm with the jack and remove the nuts.

Remove the steering knuckle complete with hub and brake unit. Press the ball joint out of the lower control arm using press tool SVO.2699 and sleeve SVO.2700.

Before refitting check that the rubber seal is filled with grease, but remove any grease which may have run on to the ballpin taper.

Press on the ball joint with tools SVO.2699, 2701 and 2703 as shown in **FIG 9:8**, making sure that it is not slanted and that there is no looseness in the fit.

Install the steering knuckle and tighten the nuts of the upper and lower ball joints. Refit other items in the reverse order of removal.

Upper control arm:

The bushes in the upper control arm are not replaceable. If the arm or bushes are worn or damaged, the link arm must be renewed complete with bushes and ball joint.

Removal is effected after removing the road wheel and separating the steering knuckle from the axle, carefully tying the upper end of the knuckle out of the way.

Remove the bolts for the control arm shaft and note any shims which may be fitted. Lift off the control arm which, it will be noticed, is fixed with a special bolt having a nylon plug.

Replace the control arm in position and loosely fit the bolts. Fit the shims back in their original positions and tighten the shaft nuts to a torque of 40 to 45 lb ft.

Fit the upper ball joint in the steering knuckle and tighten the nut, then refit the remaining items in the reverse order of removal.

Lower control arm (see FIG 9:9):

Jack up the car and remove the appropriate road wheel.

Remove the damper as described later in this chapter then disconnect the steering rod from the steering arm. Loosen the clamp for the brake hoses and remove the stabilizer mounting bolt.

Place the jack under the lower control arm, then slacken the nuts for the ball joints and free the joints from the steering knuckle by tapping with a hammer. Remove the

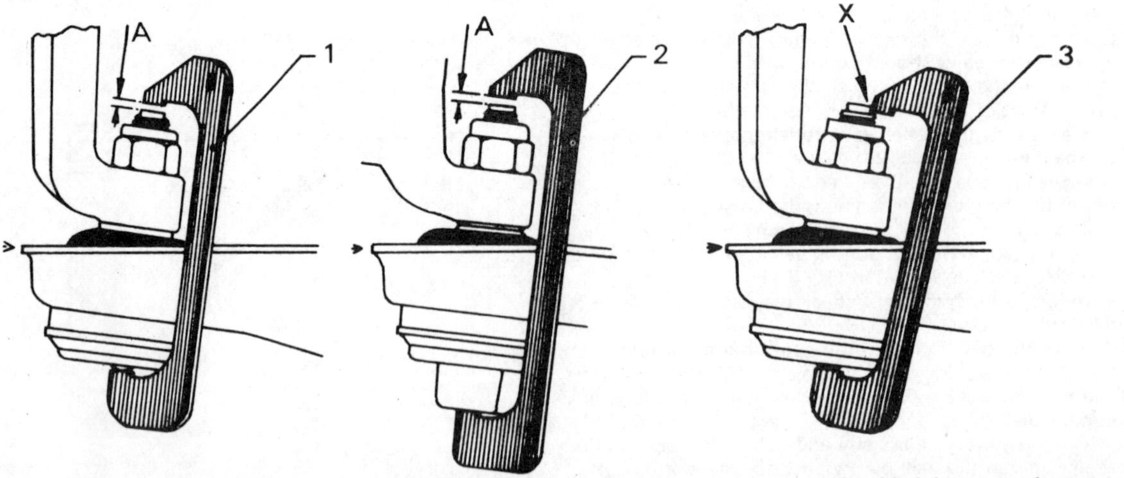

FIG 9:7 Showing the use of the ball joint checking tool, with a clearance at A on a serviceable joint or no clearance at X on a worn joint

Key to Fig 9:7 1 SVO 2967 with ball joint type 1 2 SVO 2968 with ball joint type 2 3 Tool too short with worn joint nuts, lower the jack and take off the front wheel brake unit and place it on one side.

Remove the spring and then take off the nut and remove the control arm shaft. Turn the relay arm and tie-rod to free the shaft for removal and then take off the control arm.

Bushes:

If it is intended to renew the bushes it must be noted that different bushes are supplied for radial or crossply tyres and that the correct type should be obtained.

Hold the press tool SVO.2699 in the vice and, referring to **FIG 9:9** remove the washer 1, rubber ring 2, and spacing ring 3. Press out the bushes using tool SVO.2701 as shown in **FIG 9:10** and using in addition the drift SVO.2904 for bushes used in conjection with crossply tyres or SVO.2905 for radial tyres. The positioning of the tools is clearly shown in the illustration and the bushes are pressed out in the direction towards their flanges.

The bushes are pressed in with the control arm and drift **A** facing in the opposite direction.

Both the bushes should be fitted with the flange facing towards the rear of the car and in the case of a bush for use with radial tyres its recess must also be turned downwards at right angles to the length of the control arm, as seen in **FIG 9:11**.

Refitting lower control arm:

Place the control arm in position together with the spacer ring 3, rubber ring 2 and washers 1, 5 and 7 and fit the control arm shaft 6. Hold the arm horizontal and tighten the nut 8 to a torque of 100 to 130 lb ft.

Fit the spring, then raise the jack and fit the steering knuckle. Tighten the ball joint nuts being careful to see that the pins do not rotate.

Refit the damper and the remaining parts by reversing the removal procedure.

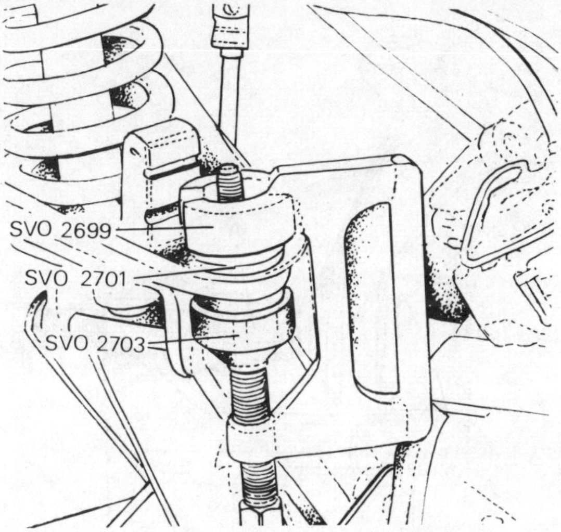

FIG 9:8 Fitting a lower ball joint

9:5 Stabilizer bar

This item, shown at 10 in **FIG 9:1**, is attached to each of the lower control arms through short link rods and rubber bushed mountings and to the chassis sidemembers by rubber bushed brackets. Its function is to make a partial transfer of any deflection of one wheel to the other wheel and so reduce the rolling tendency of the car when on uneven roads or going round bends.

Dismantling is straightforward and apart from damage or corrosion it should not need any attention other than to the rubber bushes which may deteriorate or wear oval around the bar.

FIG 9:9 Lower control arm

Key to Fig 9:9 1 Washer 2 Rubber ring 3 Spacer ring 4 Bush 5 Washer 6 Control arm shaft 7 Washer 8 Nut

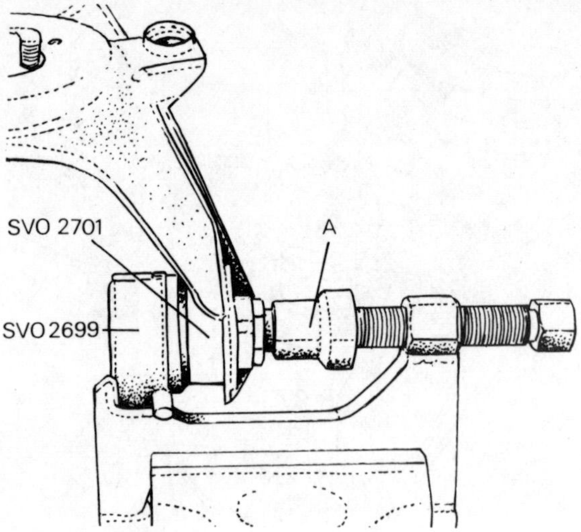

FIG 9:10 Removing a rubber bush from lower control arm. Tool A is SVO 2904 for bushes used with cross-ply tyres or SVO 2905 for radial tyres

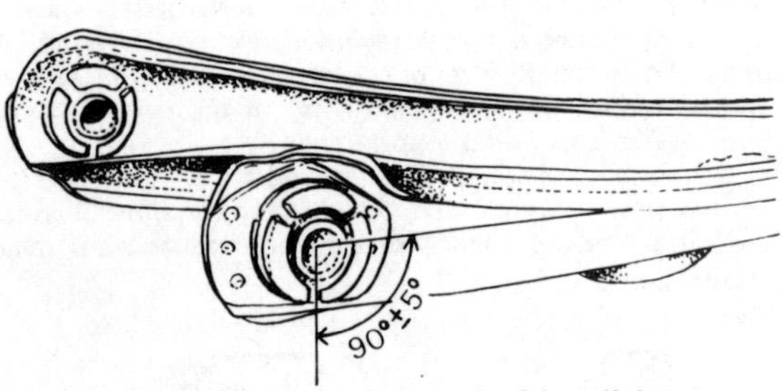

FIG 9:11 Fitting bushes used with radial tyres

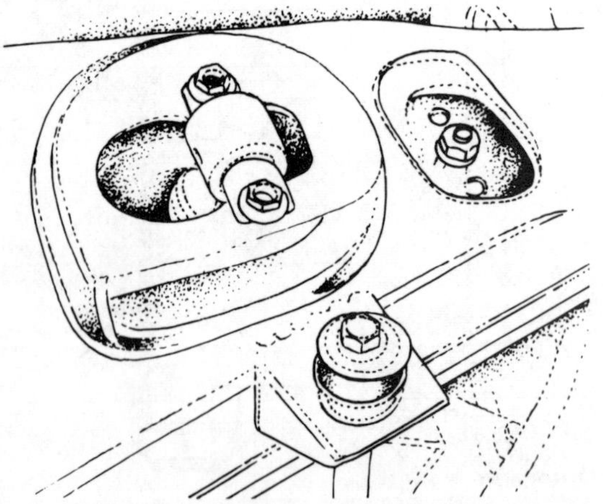

FIG 9:12 Front damper lower attachment

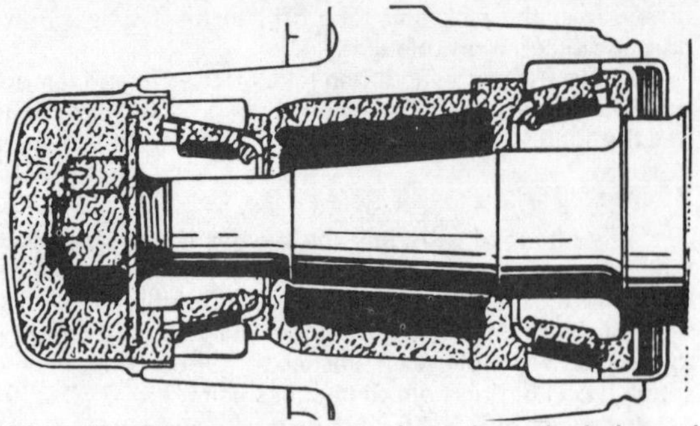

FIG 9:13 Diagrammatic section through hub and bearings

When refitting the bar there should be no loading on it when the car is standing level. To check this, raise the car until the wheels are just clear of the ground and slacken the bracket nuts so that the bar is fairly free in the rubber mounts. Adjust the rod lengths so that each wheel is clear of the ground by the same amount. Lower the car to the ground and tighten the rubber bushes.

9:6 Dampers

The hydraulic, double-acting, telescopic dampers are factory sealed. They require no maintenance and cannot be serviced. Accurate checking of the dampers efficiency can only be carried out with special equipment.

A rough check on the dampers operation can be made by removing it from the car and securely holding the bottom attachment in a vice. If the damper is then pulled out and compressed it may be possible to judge from the resistance offered whether it is working. A firm resistance should be felt throughout each stroke and intermittent or no resistance indicates a fault and the unit should be exchanged. It may be noted that the resistance when being extended should be three times as great as that felt when being compressed.

If the damper does not function satisfactorily in each direction or if the fixed rubber bushes are damaged, it should be renewed or exchanged.

Remove the nut from the top mounting spindle, also the curved washer and the rubber bush.

Remove the two lower attachment bolts (see **FIG 9:12**) and drop the damper down through the extended part of the aperture.

Refitting is the reverse of the above, noting that the top nut is tightened until it makes firm contact with the spacing sleeve.

9:7 Front wheel hubs and bearings

A diagrammatic section through the wheel hubs is shown in **FIG 9:13**. The inner race rings of the two taper roller bearings are a press fit on to the stub axle, while the outer race rings are a press fit into the wheel hub housing, overlapping the inner seating by an amount sufficient to require a suitable drift for removal.

Servicing of the hubs was mentioned in **Section 9:4** under 'Stub axle', but instructions for dealing with the bearing rings were not given.

The inner bearing ring is removed with drift SVO.2724 as shown in **FIG 9:14** and the outer bearing ring with drift SVO.2725, both using the standard handle SVO.1801.

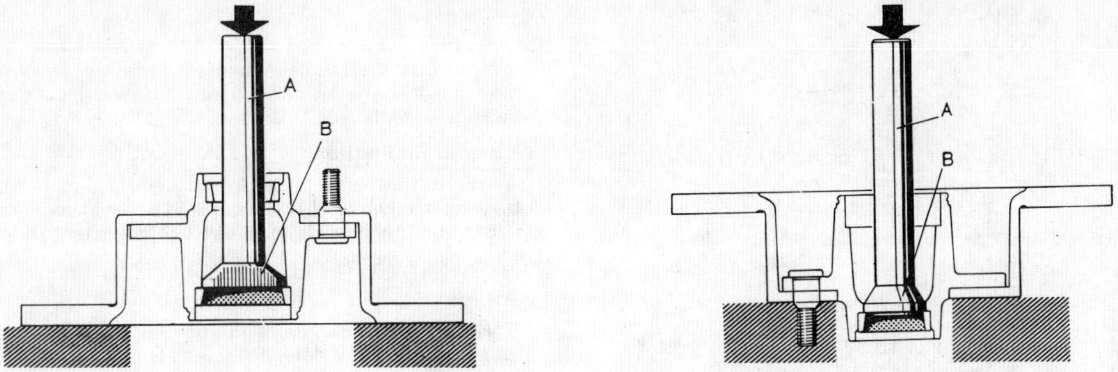

FIG 9:14 **Removing the bearing rings. On left, the inner ring with tools: A=SVO 1801, B=SVO 2724. On right, the outer ring with tools A=SVO 1801, B=SVO 2725**

After cleaning the hub components, brake disc and grease cap, the new bearing rings are pressed in with the tools shown in **FIG 9:15**.

Grease the bearings by packing in as much as there is room for between the roller retainer and the inner ring. Apply grease also to the outer sides of the bearings and on the outer rings pressed into the hub. The recess in the hub is filled with grease all round up to the smallest diameter of the outer ring of the outer bearing as may be seen in **FIG 9:13**.

Refer to **Section 9:4** for fitting and adjusting the bearings.

9:8 Front springs

As already mentioned coil springs are used and can be seen in **FIG 9:1**. The upper end of the spring is seated in a housing formed in the front axle member and the lower end in the bottom of the lower control arm.

Removal:

Jack up the car and remove the road wheel. Remove the damper as described in **Section 9:6**.

Disconnect the steering rod from the steering arm. Loosen the clamp for the brake hoses. Remove the lower attachment for the stabilizer bar.

Place a jack under the lower control arm, lift a little and loosen the nuts for the ball joints. Loosen the joints by tapping with a hammer, then remove the nuts and lower the jack slightly. Remove the steering knuckle and brake unit, then lower the jack fully and remove the spring.

Fitting:

Place the rubber spacer and spring in position and with the jack placed immediately under the spring lift up the lower control arm and fit the steering knuckle.

Tighten the ball joints at the steering knuckle and secure the stabilizer bar in position.

Check the lower rubber bush and lower washer on the upper damper attachment, place it in position and complete its fitting.

Turn the road wheels to the ahead position (with the lower arm unloaded) and firmly clamp the brake hoses. Fit the wheel and lower the car.

FIG 9:15 **Installing the bearing rings. On left, the inner ring with tools: A=SVO 1801, B=SVO 2723. On right, the outer ring with tools A=SVO 1801, B=SVO 2724**

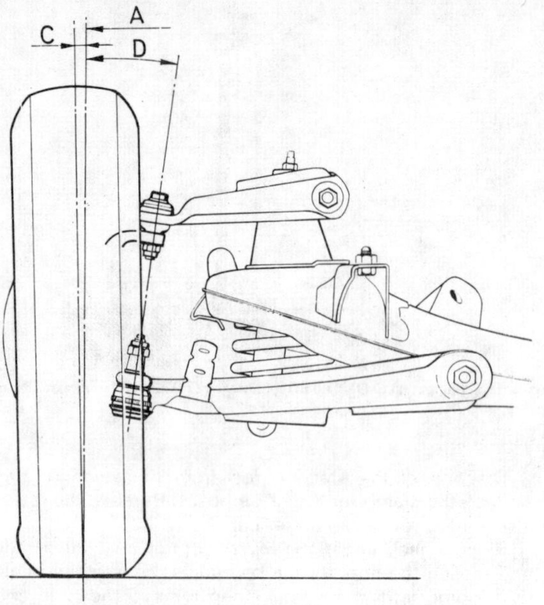

FIG 9:16 Camber angle and kingpin inclination

Key to Fig 9:16 **A** Vertical line **B** Camber **C** Kingpin inclination

9:9 Wheels and tyres

The wheels fitted as standard to these cars are of the ventilated pressed steel disc pattern, the size designation being 5.5J x 15L. The tyres recommended for use on these rims are 165.SR.15 or 165.HR.15. The tyres are tubeless in each instance.

It has been mentioned earlier that either radial or cross-ply tyres may be used and under certain circumstances it is permitted to use both on the same car. The one combination permitted is cross-ply on the front wheels and radial on the rear wheels. **Never the reverse, and never mix the two types of tyre on the same axle.** In view of the possible confusion arising with a spare tyre it is obviously preferable to have all tyres of the same type apart from the driving advantages of this selection.

9:10 Steering geometry

In order to obtain good handling and steering characteristics and a minimum of tyre wear, the front wheels must conform to certain predetermined settings known as the wheel angles or steering geometry. These angles are: castor, camber, kingpin inclination, toe-out and toe-in.

These angles do not require adjustment in normal use and the first three can be set only by a fully equipped service station. Toe-in, or wheel alignment, is preferably adjusted by a service station, but can be set at home with satisfactory results.

Castor:

This refers to the longitudinal inclination (backwards or forwards) of the kingpin or in the case of cars without a kingpin a line through the centre of the ball joints.

Castor has a great effect on the straight running of the front wheels.

Camber:

This is the inclination of the wheel itself outwards or inwards from the vertical. Camber is called positive when the top of the wheel is inclined outwards and negative if it inclines inwards (see **FIG 9:16**).

Kingpin inclination:

This is the angle between the vertical and the line between the centre of the two ball joints as shown in the illustration, and assists in the self-centring tendency of the steering.

Toe-out:

When driving round a bend, the two front wheels are running on circles of different radii, so to prevent excessive tyre wear the inner wheel is turned to a greater extent than the outer wheel. This is a design feature and is not adjustable.

Toe-in:

This is the difference in the distance between the two front wheels measured at hub height at the front and rear of the wheels when in the straightahead position. In the present case this dimension is $\frac{1}{8}$ inch (2 to 5 mm).

To make this adjustment, stand the car, with a normal load and tyres correctly inflated, on a level surface and measure the distance between the inner rims at the front of the wheels and at wheel centre height. Chalk mark the reference points.

Roll the car forward by one half a revolution of the wheels so that the chalk marks are now at the rear of the wheels. Measure the distance between the two marks and confirm that it is $\frac{1}{8}$ inch greater than the first.

Should an adjustment be necessary it is made by slackening the locknuts on the tie rod and turning the rod in the required direction. The distance between the front of the wheels is reduced, i.e. toe-in is increased, by turning the tie rod in the normal direction of rotation of the wheels.

9:11 Fault diagnosis

(a) Wheel wobble

1 Worn hub bearings
2 Broken or weak springs
3 Uneven tyre wear
4 Loose wheel fixings
5 Worn or loose linkage

(b) 'Bottoming' of suspension

1 Check 2 in (a)
2 Rebound rubbers worn or missing
3 Faulty dampers

(c) Heavy steering

1 Binding or damaged ball joints
2 Wrong steering geometry
3 Neglected lubrication

(d) Excessive tyre wear

1 Check 4 and 5 in (a) and 2 in (c)
2 Incorrect inflation

(e) Rattles

1 Check 2 and 5 in (a)
2 Worn rubber bushes
3 Damper or stabilizer mountings loose

CHAPTER 10

THE STEERING GEAR

10:1 Description

On early cars in this series a conventional pattern of recirculating ball type of steering box was used in conjunction with a transverse tie rod and two outer track rods connected to the steering knuckles. This layout is shown in **FIG 10:1** and was only slightly modified when the optional power steering was fitted.

On later cars, when power steering became standard equipment the layout was as shown in **FIG 10:2** in which a different type of steering column assembly also is used.

In both cases steering wheel movement is transmitted from the steering box through a pitman arm and a short track rod to the offside wheel and a central tie rod to a relay lever and track rod on the nearside of the car. The steering box is bolted to the offside chassis member and the relay lever in a similar position on the nearside.

There are two devices incorporated in the steering column assembly for the prevention of injury to the driver in the event of frontal impact. Firstly a rubber coupling and universal joint at the lower end of the column and secondly a sliding portion which permits axial compression of the assembly under heavy pressure.

A steering wheel lock is provided in conjunction with the ignition switch whereby the steering is prevented from turning when the ignition key is removed.

The servo or power assisted steering is of ZF manufacture which comprises in addition to the steering box a pump mounted on the lefthand side of the engine and driven by a belt and an oil reservoir with filter which should be checked at intervals of 6000 miles.

10:2 Steering wheel

Early type:

Remove the securing screws for the two parts of the direction indicator housing and lift it off. Remove the screws on the horn ring, lift it up and pull out the electrical connections.

Remove the steering wheel nut and with the wheels in the straightahead position pull off the steering wheel.

Refitting is a reversal of the above, noting that the required torque on the steering wheel nut is 20 to 30 lb ft.

Later type:

Remove the screw for the upper part of the direction indicator housing and lift it off. Bend loose the central motif pad, disconnect the horn cable, remove four securing screws and lift out the horn ring noting the springs and washers underneath.

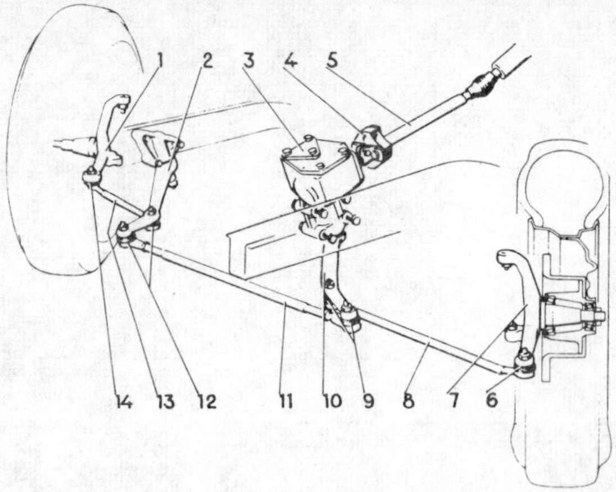

FIG 10:1 Components of early (unassisted) steering gear

Key to Fig 10:1 1 Steering knuckle, right 2 Relay arm 3 Steering box 4 Lower steering column flange 5 Lower steering column section with universal joint 6 Ball joint 7 Steering knuckle, left 8 Steering rod, left 9 Ball joint 10 Pitman arm 11 Tie rod 12 Ball joint 13 Steering rod, right 14 Ball joint

Remove the steering wheel nut and with the wheels in the straight-ahead position, pull off the steering wheel and also the flange for the direction indicator switch.

Refitting is carried out in the reverse order to the above

10:3 Steering wheel lock

In order to render the engine proof against tampering a steering lock is provided, built integrally with the ignition switch. It is mounted on the steering column as shown in **FIG 10:3** by means of two shear bolts and to the dashboard with two screws.

To remove the steering wheel lock it is necessary first to remove the steering wheel as described in **Section 10:2** then disconnect the battery and take off the lower part of the direction indicator switch housing. Remove also the direction indicator switch assembly.

Disconnect the starter contact from the lock. The direction indicator switch and starter contact may be left hanging on their cables.

Make alignment marks on the lock and the steering column jacket then remove the two shear bolts either by drilling out and using a bolt extractor or with a hammer and punch.

When refitting the lock place it in position without tightening the bolts, then fit the starter contact and the direction indicator switch.

Set the road wheels to the straight-ahead position and fit the steering wheel and the horn components. Reconnect the battery and test all the appropriate services before tightening and shearing the securing bolts.

10:4 Renewing the steering column bearings

Early type:

The early type of steering column assembly is shown in **FIG 10:4** and if only the upper bearing 11 is to be renewed, it can be made accessible by removing the steering wheel, spring 13 and seat 12. If the other bearings are to be renewed, it will be necessary to separate the steering column from the sleeve 6. It may also be necessary to release the upper column jacket 8 and the locknut 7.

When reassembling, tighten the nut 7 to 20 to 36 lb ft and then lock the nut by driving the edge into one of the slits.

If it is necessary to remove the lower jacket 4, the rivet 5 will have to be drilled out and a new KN5 x 32 mm rivet used when reassembling.

Later type (see FIG 10:5):

On the later type of steering column the upper bearing can be renewed separately, but if the lower bearing is damaged the complete steering column shaft must be replaced.

Upper bearing (see FIG 10:6):

Remove the steering wheel as described in **Section 10:2**, and the lower part of the direction indicator switch cowling. Detach the switch from the steering column, and also its attachment from the tube.

Pull out the spring 3 and seat 2 then remove the bearing 1.

Grease the new bearing well before fitting and replace the remaining parts in the reverse order.

Removing steering column:

Disconnect the battery and remove the screws between the lower section of the column and the rubber coupling. Remove the steering wheel and the lower portion of the direction indicator switch cowling.

Remove the direction indicator switch, its mounting and the starter contact. There is no need to disconnect the electric cables.

Remove the panel under the dash and then the lower steering column mounting. Remove the screws in the upper column mounting, using a drill and an extractor.

Pull out the steering column complete with jacket and bearing forwards. If the steering lock has to be transferred to the new journalling the screws must be extracted by drilling and the use of an extractor screw.

Refitting

Position the steering column with the jacket and a rubber seal on the jacket. Fit the lower section of the column to the rubber coupling.

Fit the upper and lower jacket mountings but do not yet tighten the bolts. Fit the steering lock, the starter contact and the direction indicator switch.

Turn the front wheels to the straight-ahead position and fit the steering wheel, tightening to 20 to 30 lb ft.

Fit the lower part of the indicator switch housing, then adjust the steering column tube so that the correct distance is obtained between the dash and the switch housing.

Fit the horn components and check the operation, check also the steering column lock. Now tighten the steering column tube attachments and also the shear bolts for the steering lock. Refit the remaining parts in reverse order of dismantling.

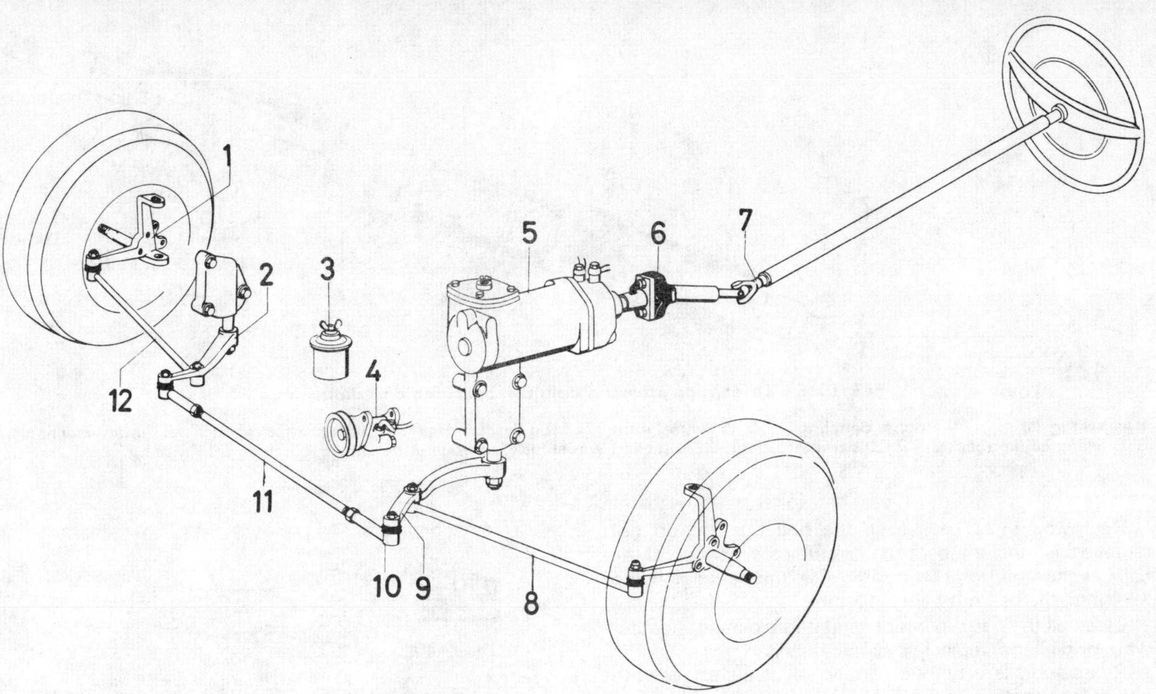

FIG 10:2 Later type power steering layout

Key to Fig 10:2 1 Steering knuckle 2 Relay arm 3 Container, servo steering 4 Pump 5 Steering box 6 Rubber coupling 7 Steering column 8 Steering rod, left 9 Pitman arm 10 Ball joint 11 Tie rod 12 Steering rod, right

10:5 Servicing the steering box (unassisted)

A sectional view of the early manual type of steering box is given in **FIG 10:7**.

To remove the box from the car, jack up the front end, remove the pitman arm locknut and pull off the pitman arm. This will be done most easily if the wheels are turned fully to the right and tool SVO.2849 employed.

Slacken the steering shaft clamping bolt remove the four mounting bolts and pull the steering box out forwards.

Remove the stop plate 8, spacer, spring guide 6 and springs 7, then carefully take off the steering box cover 12 from the guide pins.

Turn the ball nut to the end position and remove the pitman arm shaft and the nut guide (see **FIG 10:8**). From the side of the box remove the steering cam cover 14 with retainer 15 and shims 13 and then pull out the steering cam with the bearing and screw off the ball nut at the same time.

There are 10 balls for the lower ballbearing, and after lifting off the upper bearing another 13 balls will be disclosed. Collect these also.

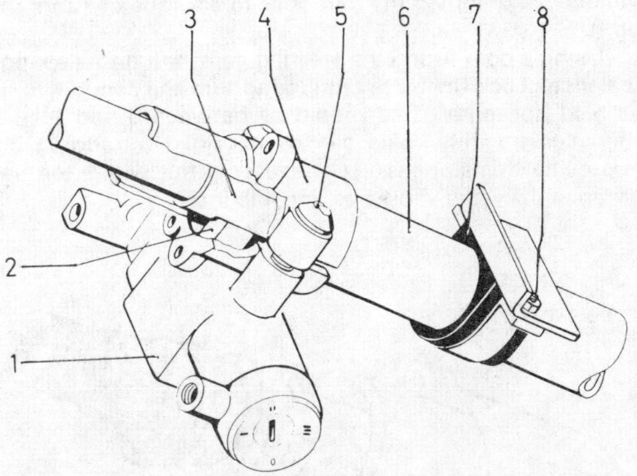

FIG 10:3 The steering wheel lock and ignition switch

Key to Fig 10:3 1 Steering wheel lock 2 Lockpin 3 Lock sleeve 4 Cover 5 Shear-off bolt 6 Steering column jacket 7 Attachment 8 Shear-off bolt

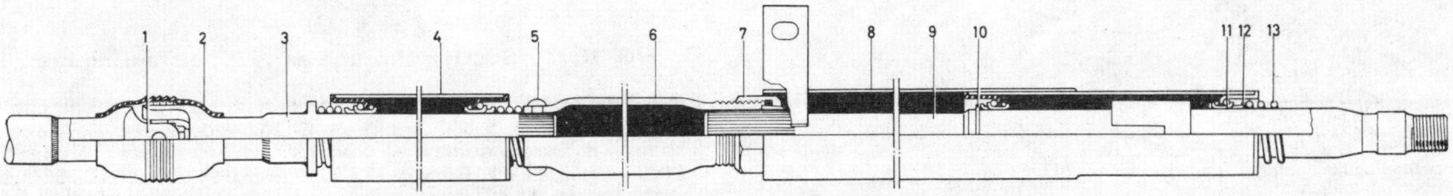

FIG 10:4 Cutaway view of early steering column

Key to Fig 10:4 1 Universal joint 2 Rubber seal 3 Lower steering column section 4 Lower steering column jacket 5 Rivet 6 Sleeve 7 Nut 8 Upper steering column jacket 9 Upper steering column section 10 Ring 11 Bearing 12 Seat 13 Spring

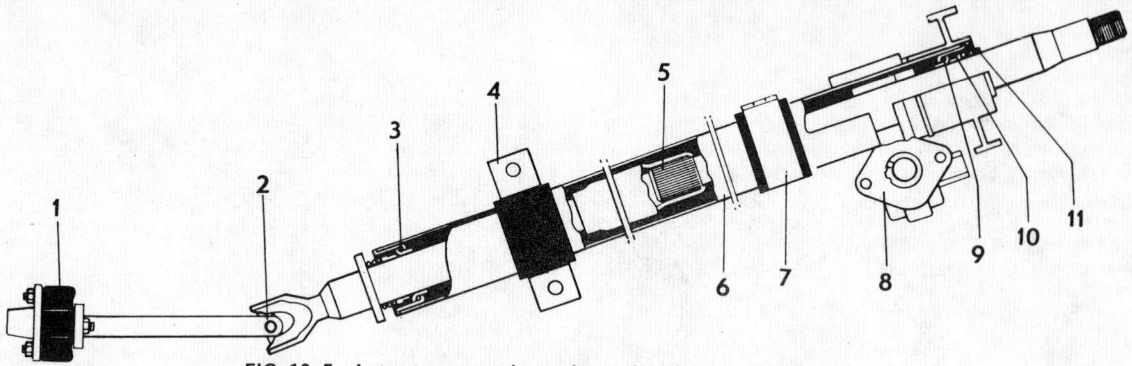

FIG 10:5 Later type steering column, bearings and mountings

Key to Fig 10:5 1 Rubber coupling 2 Universal joint 3 Lower bearing 4 Lower attachment 5 Safety mechanism 6 Steering column jacket 7 Upper attachment 8 Steering wheel lock 9 Upper bearing 10 Seat 11 Spring

Remove the 27 balls from the ball nut but do not remove the transfer tube. Note carefully the location of the balls as they are not all the same size, the bearings being 7.14 mm, the ball nut balls 7.93 mm.

Clean all the parts in white spirit and examine them for wear or damage, replacing as necessary.

Reassembly is very much a reversal of the above with particular attention to the following points.

When replacing the loose balls into position it will be helpful to hold them in place with some bearing grease.

When fitting the oil seal 16 into the cover 14, the lip must face inwards. Fit the gaskets, shims, cover and retainer, and tighten the four bolts to a torque of 12 to 15 lb ft.

Using a cord round the steering camshaft and a spring balance check the force required to turn the cam when it is held horizontal. This should be between 6 and 11 lb. If necessary, this value can be obtained by adding or removing shims or gaskets. If checking this with a torque wrench the value should be 2 to 4 lb inch.

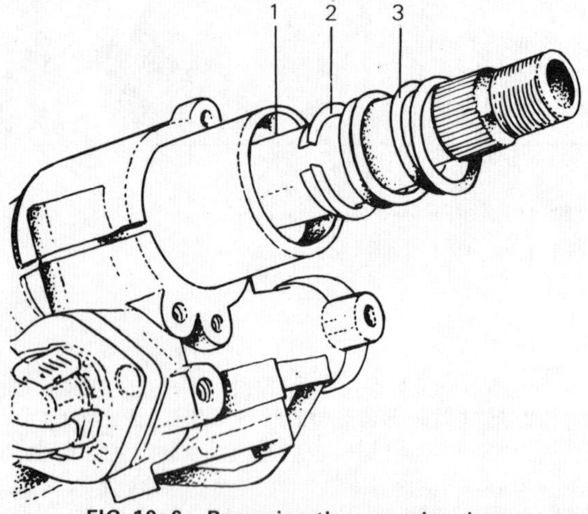

FIG 10:6 Removing the upper bearing

Key to Fig 10:6 1 Bearing 2 Seat 3 Spring

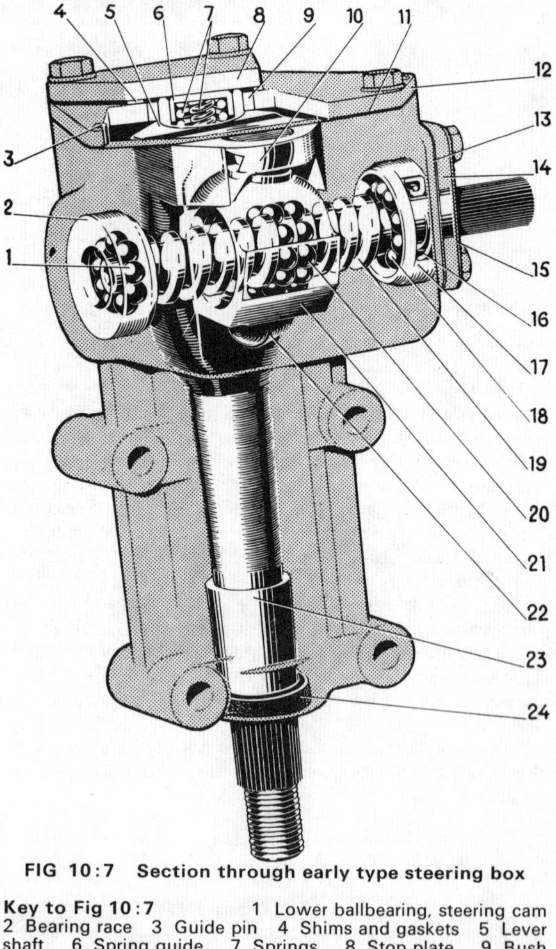

FIG 10:7 Section through early type steering box

Key to Fig 10:7 1 Lower ballbearing, steering cam 2 Bearing race 3 Guide pin 4 Shims and gaskets 5 Lever shaft 6 Spring guide 7 Springs 8 Stop plate 9 Bush 10 Nut guide 11 Gasket 12 Steering box cover 13 Shims and gaskets 14 Steering cam cover 15 Retainer 16 Oil seal 17 Bearing race 18 Upper steering cam bearing 19 Steering cam 20 Balls 21 Ball nut 22 Recirculating ball tube 23 Bush 24 Oil seal

After fitting the gasket 11 and the cover 12, tighten the two bolts to 12 to 15 lb ft, then place the spring guide in position without the springs 7. Fit the paper and steel shims as well as the stop plate 8, and start to tighten the three bolts to a torque of 12 to 15 lb ft, checking that there is always some axial play on the pitman arm shaft, otherwise the balls may be damaged through overtightening.

Measure the axial play after the bolts have been tightened then reduce the total shim thickness to give a preloading of .001 to .003 inch. If, for example, the measured play is .002 inch, and one of the shims measures .005 inch, replace this shim with one measuring .002 inch. This will reduce the play by .003 inch and produce instead a preload of .001 inch.

When the correct clearance has been obtained, remove the stop plate and the spring guide, fit the springs and replace the guide, shims and plate. Fill the box with hypoid oil up to the filling hole level when held in the installed position.

Turn the steering gear into the central position and check that the steering wheel is also in the straight-ahead position then fit the box into position and locate on the flange. Fit the mounting bolts and the clamp bolts.

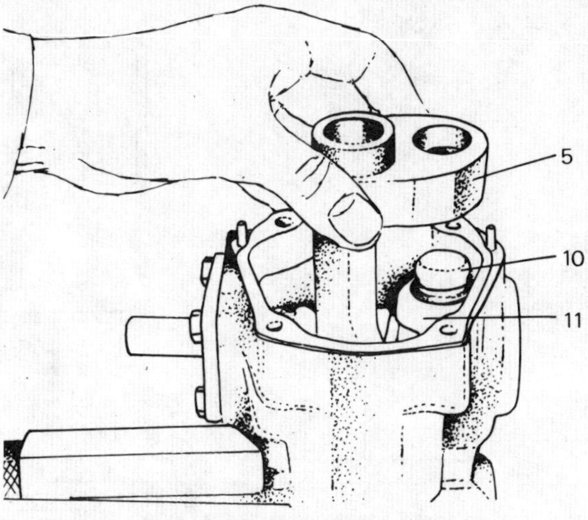

FIG 10:8 Removing pitman arm shaft

Key to Fig 10:8 5 Pitman arm shaft 10 Nut guide 11 Ball nut

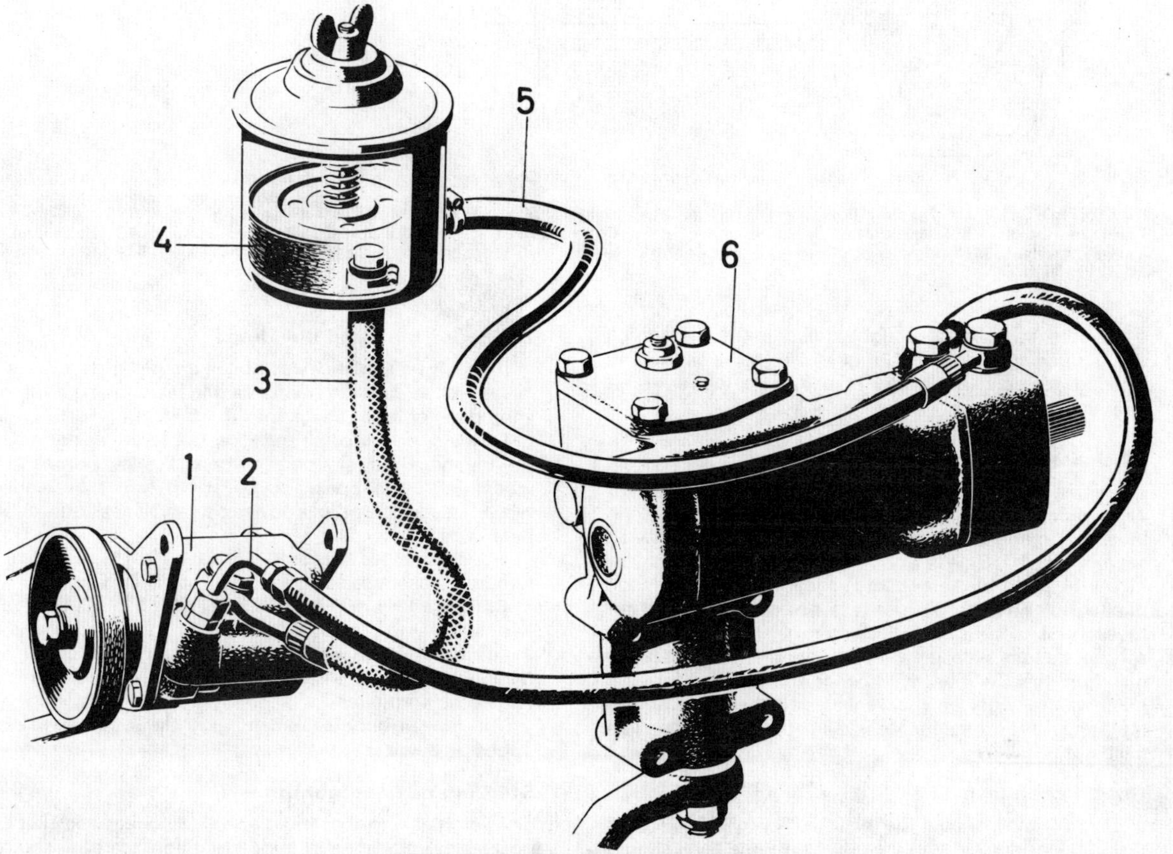

FIG 10:9 Power steering components

Key to Fig 10:9 1 Servo pump 2 Delivery oil line 3 Pump suction line 4 Oil container with filter 5 Return oil line 6 Steering box

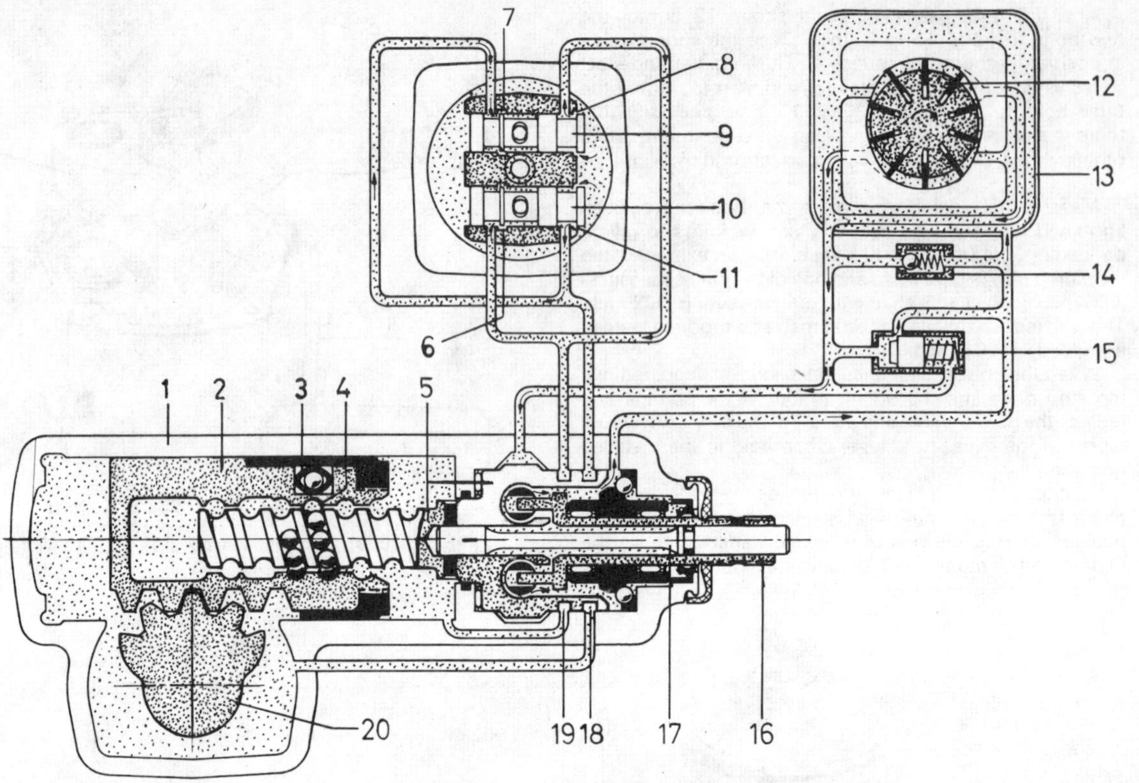

FIG 10:10 Schematic diagram of power steering in neutral position

Key to Fig 10:10 1 Steering box 2 Piston 3 Recirculating tube, ball nut 4 Balls 5 Steering cam 6 Return groove 7 Return groove 8 Intake port 9 Control valve 10 Control valve 11 Intake port 12 Servo pump 13 Oil container 14 Safety valve 15 Flow control valve 16 Control spindle 17 Torsion rod 18 Annular groove 19 Annular groove 20 Lever shaft

Aim the road wheels straight-ahead and fit the pitman arm, tightening the nut to 125 to 145 lb ft. Check that the steering gear can be turned from lock to lock without interference.

10:6 Servicing the servo steering gear

This is a recirculating cam and ball nut type gear of ZF manufacture, the main components being the steering box, servo pump and oil container with filter which may be seen in **FIG 10:9**.

The function of the system is shown in the schematic diagram of **FIG 10:10**, but it is not recommended for these items to be dismantled, other than by authorised service stations with the proper equipment. Instructions given in this Section will be confined, therefore, to maintenance work on the vehicle and the removal and refitting of the components if ever this should become necessary.

Checking oil level:

The oil level should be checked every 6000 miles (10,000 km). Firstly with the engine off, the level should be about $\frac{1}{4}$ inch above the level mark, then with the engine running it should fall to the maximum mark as shown on the inside of the reservoir.

Filling with oil and bleeding:

If for any reason, the oil has been drained off, the system is refilled as follows, remembering that drained off oil should never be put back into the system.

Fill with oil up to the mark on the reservoir then start the engine. Gradually pour oil in as the level drops and when the level appears to be stable turn the steering wheel steadily from lock to lock a few times. Add oil as necessary.

Open the bleed screw (11 in **FIG 10:11**), about one turn and close it as soon as the oil starts flowing out.

Continue to turn the wheel until the oil in the reservoir is practically free of air bubbles, then stop the engine. If the oil level rises to more than $\frac{1}{4}$ inch above the level mark it suggests that there is still air in the system and bleeding should be continued.

The few air bubbles remaining in the system will disappear in service.

Steering box and pump test:

After checking that the oil level is correct and that all hoses and unions are in good condition, start the engine and warm up. Connect up the test instrument SVO.2864 to the delivery line of the steering box as shown in **FIG 10:12**. The inlet hose of the instrument is connected to the

The inlet hose of the instrument is connected to the banjo nipple with SVO.2865 and the outlet to the steering box with SVO.2866. The operating lever of the instrument should be in the open position (to the left).

With the engine idling move the operating lever for a maximum of 10 seconds to the closed position and read off the maximum pressure on the gauge. This should be at least 953 lb/sq inch. If it is less than this, examine the pump and drive as follows:

Check tension and condition of the belt, renewing if necessary.

Clean and remove the pump control valve (see **FIG 10:13**), check for free movement and that the hole is not blocked. If necessary fit a new valve and if this does not rectify the fault fit a new pump.

With the engine idling and the instrument lever open, turn the steering wheel fully to the right. Increase the pressure on the wheel to about 22 pounds for about 5 seconds and read the gauge. Repeat to the lefthand side. If the pressure indicated is below the previously determined pressure for the pump, then the servo steering is faulty and if no external leakage is evident, the box must be replaced.

Checking mechanical operation:

After checking all joints, linkages and attachments, adjusting or renewing as necessary, adjust the pressure points between the piston of the steering box and the pitman arm shaft as follows:

1 Remove the locknut for the pitman arm and remove the pitman arm. This will be assisted by turning the wheels fully to the right.
2 Set the steering box in its central position and slacken the nut for the adjusting screw 8.
3 Turn the adjusting screw 9 clockwise until a light resistance is felt when the flange is turned to left or
4 Tighten the locknut and check that as the steering wheel is turned past the central position a slight increase in the resistance is felt.
5 Turn the road wheels straightahead and fit the pitman arm, tightening to 125 to 145 lb ft.

Steering box:

Jack up the front of the car. Drain the oil out of the drain plug 2 by starting the engine and allowing it to idle till the oil has emptied (about 10 seconds) and give the steering wheel a few turns.

Pull off the pitman arm, then disconnect the oil pipes 5 and 10 in **FIG 10:11**. Slacken the clamp bolt 6. Remove the mounting bolts 1 and pull the steering box forwards.

To refit, centralize the controls and line up any alignment marks. Fit the steering box spindle in the flange of the lower steering column section.

Fit the mounting bolts and the clamp bolt, checking that the distance between the steering box housing and the lower flange is .28 $\pm$.20 inch (7 $\pm$5 mm).

Connect the oil lines, noting that the longer delivery line runs in a curve backwards and should be clamped.

Fit the pitman arm, fill with oil and bleed.

Servo pump (see FIG 10:14):

Before starting to remove the pump, clean round the unions, then disconnect the suction line 5 and collect any oil that may run out.

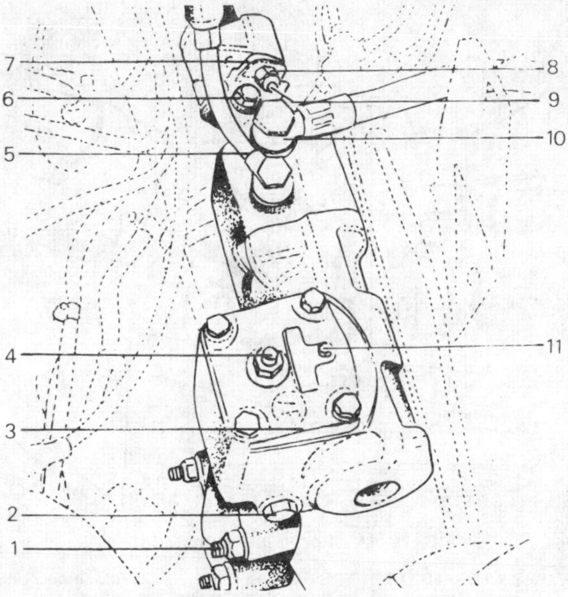

FIG 10:11 Power steering box installed

Key to Fig 10:11 1 Bolt 2 Drain plug 3 Steering box 4 Adjusting screw 5 Delivery line (early prod) 6 Clamping bolt 7 Flange 8 Nut 9 Screw 10 Return line 11 Bleeder screw

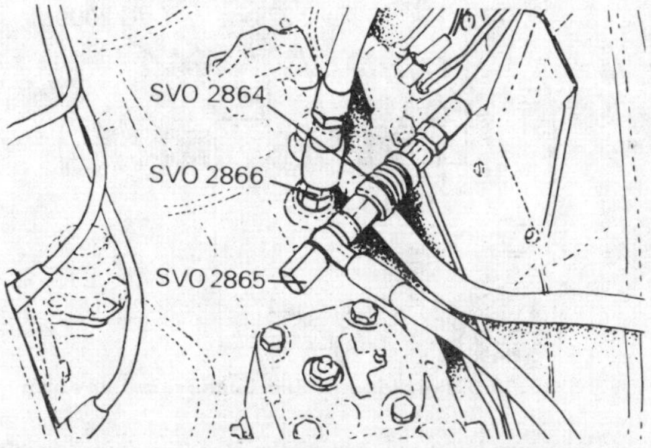

FIG 10:12 Connections for pressure testing

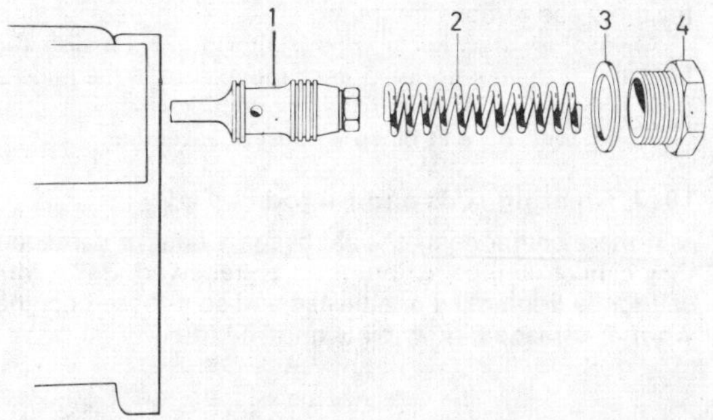

FIG 10:13 Components of the control valve

Key to Fig 10:13 1 Piston 2 Spring 3 Washer 4 Plug

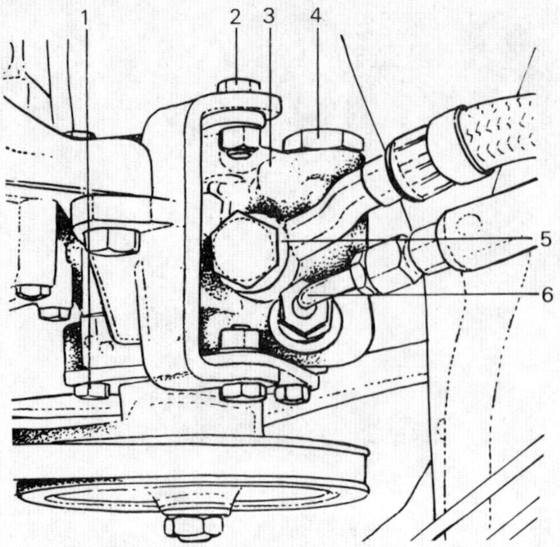

FIG 10:14 Servo pump installation

Key to Fig 10:14 1 Tension bolt 2 Attaching bolt 3 Servo pump 4 Plug for control valve 5 Suction line 6 Delivery line

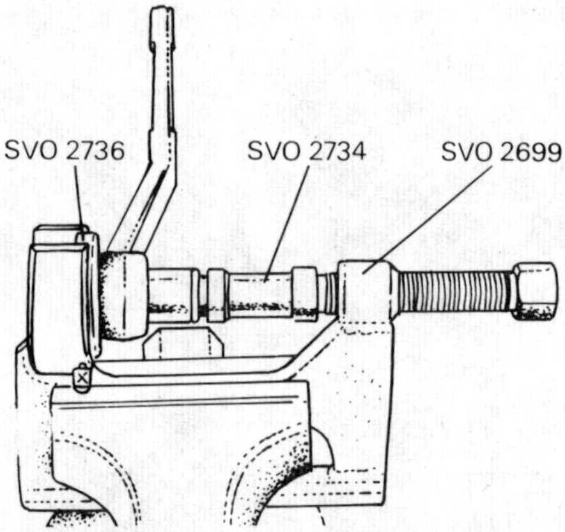

FIG 10:15 Removing rubber bush from relay arm

Disconnect the delivery line 6 and unscrew the tensioning bolt 1 and attachment bolts 2.

Ensure that all unions are protected from dirt, then unscrew and remove the pump.

Always use new seals when refitting and tension the belt so that there is about $\frac{3}{16}$ inch movement in the middle then tighten the bolts and the connections.

Fill up with oil and bleed as described earlier.

10:7 Steering rods and tie rod

If these components should become bent or damaged they cannot be repaired but must be renewed. Ball joints cannot be dismantled or adjusted and so if these become worn or damaged, new joints must be fitted.

The ball joints on the tie rod can be replaced individually. Take out the splitpins and remove the castellated nuts. Loosen the joint with a clamp then remove the locknut on the rod and unscrew the ball joint. If the number of turns taken to unscrew the joint is counted the fitting and adjustment of the new joint will be simplified.

Steering rod ball joints are made integrally with the steering rod and so rod and joint are renewed as one piece. To ensure correct installation, steering rods are marked L and R (left-right) at their outer ends, and the marked end should always be fitted to the steering knuckle.

When fitting the ball joint to the steering knuckle, the ballpin should be turned so that the splitpin hole is transverse to the axis of the steering rod. Do not forget to check the toe-in after replacing any of these components.

10:8 Relay arm

A complete unit is easily removed after jacking up the front of the car and disconnecting the steering rod, tie rod ball joints. Three mounting bolts have to be removed and the relay arm unit lifted away.

Relay arm bush:

Having removed the relay arm, secure press tool SVO. 2699 in a vice as shown in **FIG 10:15** and press the old bush out with tool SVO.2736 and drift SVO.2734.

Press the new bush into position and refit the relay arm with washer and nut which is tightened to 50 to 60 lb ft.

Fit the steering rod in the inner hole on the relay arm and the tie rod. The Nyloc nuts are tightened to 25 to 30 lb ft.

10:9 Fault diagnosis

(a) Wheel wobble

1 Unbalanced wheels and tyres
2 Loose ball joint connections
3 Excessive wear in steering linkage
4 Broken or weak front springs
5 Worn hub bearings

(b) Wander

1 Check 2 and 3 in (a)
2 Uneven tyre pressures
3 Ineffective dampers

(c) Heavy steering

1 Tyres underinflated
2 Incorrect geometry
3 Seized bearing in column or box
4 Low fluid level
5 Steering box incorrectly adjusted
6 Air in system
7 Pump drive slippery
8 Faulty pump or hoses

CHAPTER 11

THE BRAKING SYSTEM

11 :1 Description

The main braking system on the Volvo 160 Series is hydraulic, controlled by the foot pedal and operating on discs on all four wheels, the braking effort applied by the pedal being amplified by a vacuum servo unit connected directly to the pedal. The other brake system, the parking brake, is operated by the handbrake lever and works on separate drum brakes integral with the rear wheel discs through a mechanical linkage.

The layout of this Volvo system is a little different from most others in that the tandem master cylinder on the servo unit distributes the braking effort equally between two circuits each of which applies the brakes on both front wheels and one rear wheel. Each front brake caliper embodies duplicate opposing brake cylinder pairs, one of which is coupled to the rear offside wheel and the other to the circuit for the rear nearside wheel. A balance valve in the circuit provides the driver with a visual warning should either of the two circuits fail for any reason, in which case the available braking effort will be reduced by only 25 per cent.

A diagrammatic view of the system is given in **FIG 11 :1**, which applies to all cars in the range, although there may be some slight detail differences in the various models.

11 :2 Maintenance

A regular check should be made on the level in the fluid reservoir to see that it does not fall below the 'Min' mark and topping up if necessary. The level should drop only very slowly as the brake pads wear and any sudden loss or rapid fall in the level should be investigated at once and the fault rectified.

The fluid recommended for use in these systems must meet the requirements of specification SAE.J.1703, but fluids labelled DOT.3 or DOT.4 may also be used.

The brake pads should be checked for wear at intervals of 6000 miles (10,000 km) and renewed when worn down to a thickness of $\frac{1}{8}$ inch (3 mm). On no account should they be permitted to wear below $\frac{1}{16}$ inch (1.5 mm).

At 36,000 miles (60,000 km), or every third year, the rubber seals in the system should be renewed and also the air filter for the servo unit, although this may require changing more frequently if the vehicle is operated under very dusty conditions.

11 :3 Wheel brake units

Front:

A front wheel caliper is shown in **FIG 11 :2**. As already mentioned it incorporates two pairs of cylinders and

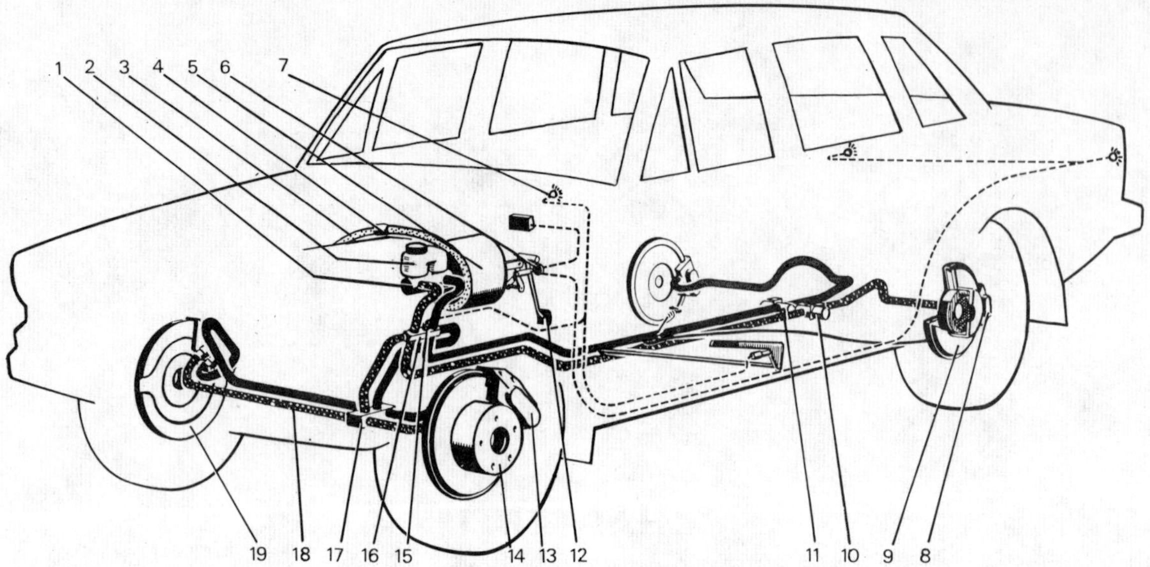

FIG 11:1 Layout of the hydraulic brake system

Key to Fig 11:1 1 Tandem master cylinder 2 Brake fluid container 3 Vacuum line 4 Check valve 5 Servo brake cylinder 6 Brake switch 7 Warning lamp 8 Rear brake caliper 9 Brake disc with drum 10 Brake valve, secondary circuit 11 Brake valve, primary circuit 12 Brake pedal 13 Front brake caliper 14 Brake disc 15 Warning switch 16 Warning valve 17 6-branch union (double 3-branch union) 18 Brake pipe 19 Coverplate

pistons operating on a common pair of brake pads. In normal use the braking effort is balanced between the four pistons, but in the event of a line failure only the lower or upper pair of pistons will be effective and the pressure will be applied to one half of the pads which are manufactured with a central flexible division to permit such asymmetric application.

Rear:

In a rear wheel caliper unit there is only one pair of pistons as will be seen from **FIG 11:3**, otherwise their construction and operation is similar.

The lower cylinders of the front wheel units are coupled with the righthand rear wheel unit to the primary chamber of the master cylinder, while the upper cylinders and the lefthand rear unit are coupled to the secondary chamber.

11:4 Renewing brake pads

As stated earlier, these should be renewed when about $\frac{1}{8}$ inch of the lining remains. The procedure is as follows:

Remove the hub caps and loosen the wheel nuts. Jack up the car, remove the wheel nuts and take off the wheel.

Tap out the upper guide pin with with a suitable drift, remove the tensioning spring and then tap out the lower guide pin.

Pull out the pads, noting that if they are to be refitted they should be marked to ensure that they are returned to their original positions.

Carefully clean out any dust from the spaces occupied by the pads and replace any rubber dust covers which may be damaged. At the same time check that dirt has not entered and damaged the cylinder bore and that the friction area of the disc is not excessively scored.

To make room for the new pads it will be necessary to push the pistons back into their bores and this will cause the fluid level to rise in the reservoir. To prevent overflowing it may be necessary to syphon off a quantity of fluid.

On rear brake calipers it is important to see that the pistons are correctly located to avoid brake squeal. The piston recess should incline 20 deg. relative to the lower guide area on the caliper, and this can be checked with the template SVO.2919 as shown in **FIG 11:4**. There is a ± 2 deg. tolerance, that is to say, that when the template is placed against one recess the distance to the other (dimension A) may be up to a maximum of .04 inch (1 mm).

Fit the new pads (see **FIG 11:5**), then position one guide pin and tap it gently home. Fit a new tensioning spring and press it inwards while fitting the second guide pin. Check that the pads can move freely.

After fitting the pads, operate the brake pedal a few times to check the operation and to bring the pads up against the disc. The system should not require bleeding after this operation.

Refit the wheels and the nuts which should be tightened progressively to 70 to 100 lb ft after the car has been lowered to the ground.

11:5 Dismantling the calipers

Front:

Jack up the front end of the car securely and remove the road wheel. Take steps to reduce fluid spillage and disconnect the hydraulic hoses. These should be carefully identified and reference to **FIG 9:3** may be of assistance.

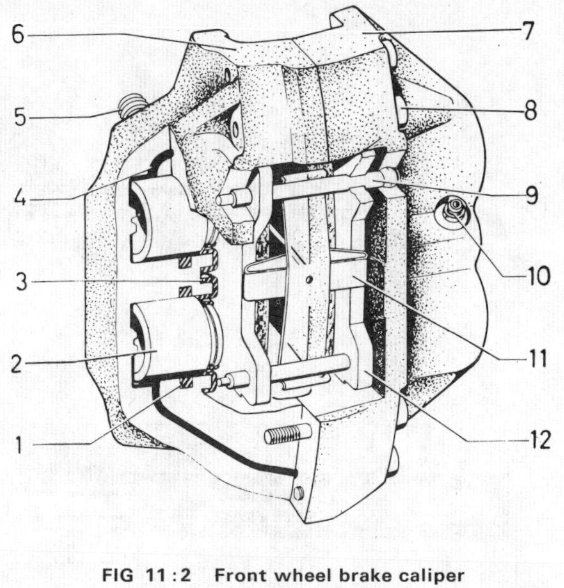

FIG 11 : 2 Front wheel brake caliper

Key to Fig 11 : 2 1 Sealing ring 2 Piston 3 Rubber dust cover 4 Channel 5 Upper bleeder nipple 6 Outer half 7 Inner half 8 Bolt 9 Guide pin 10 Inner bleeder nipple 11 Damping spring 12 Brake pad

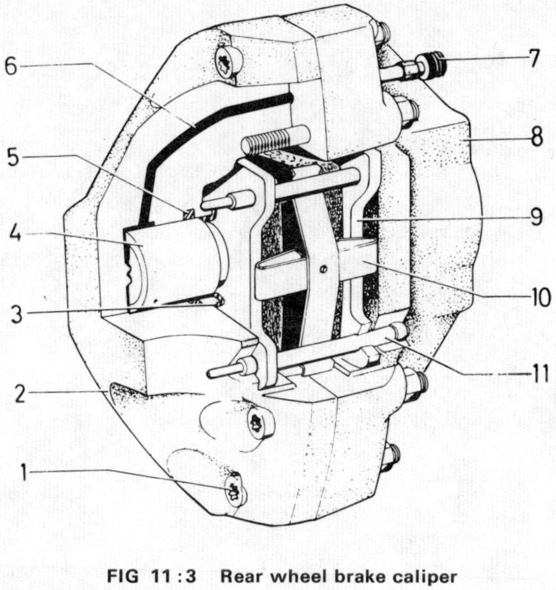

FIG 11 : 3 Rear wheel brake caliper

Key to Fig 11 : 3 1 Bolt 2 Outer half 3 Rubber dust cover 4 Piston 5 Sealing ring 6 Channel 7 Bleeder nipple 8 Inner half 9 Brake pad 10 Damping spring 11 Guide pin

Remove the brake pads, unscrew the two mounting bolts and lift off the caliper unit.

Clean the assembly well before dismantling and cut a wooden plate the size of a brake pad and about 1 inch thick. Insert this wooden separator between the pistons in the caliper and press them out of their bores against the wood by means of compressed air applied to the inlet union. Take out the pistons and lever off the rubber dust covers.

Remove the sealing rings with a blunt tool, taking care not to damage the grooves. Thoroughly clean all the pieces in brake fluid and dry either by means of compressed air or with a lint free cloth.

Obtain new seals and, if necessary, new dust covers in readiness for reassembly. Any other parts which are worn or damaged should also be renewed, but if the cylinder bores are scored or scratched the complete housing should be replaced. Note that under no circumstances should the two halves of the caliper be separated as special equipment is needed for their assembly.

Before reassembling, dip the pieces in clean brake fluid and assemble wet. Fit new oil sealing rings in the cylinders as in **FIG 11 : 6**.

Insert the pistons into the cylinders with the larger end diameter facing inwards, then fit the rubber covers into place on the pistons and the housing and secure with the circlips.

Fit the brake pads and connect the hydraulic lines.

Place the caliper in position and check its location relative to the disc. Axial deviation, measured with a feeler gauge on each side of the disc, must not exceed .01 inch (.25 mm) from side to side. The caliper must also be parallel with the disc. This is measured by the distance between the disc and the upper and lower support nibs on the caliper. The location of the caliper can be adjusted with shims which are available in thicknesses of .008 and .016 inch (.2 and .4 mm). Apply a couple of drops of Locktite before fitting the mounting bolts.

Reconnect the brake hoses and clip, making sure that they are not twisted or strained. Fit the wheels, lower the car to the ground and tighten the wheel nuts (70 to 100 lb ft). Bleed the brake system as described later in this Chapter.

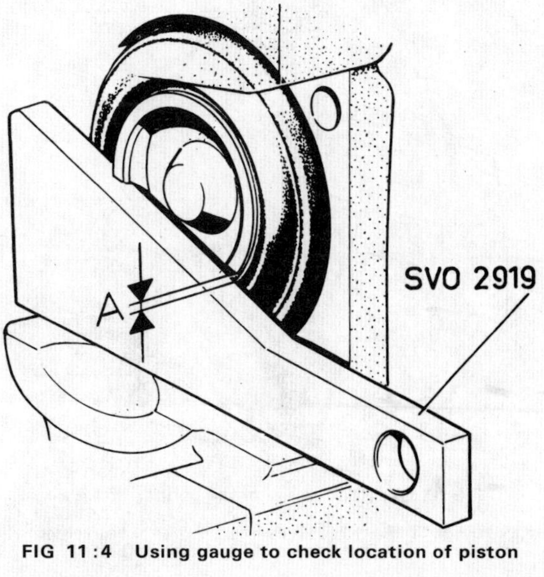

FIG 11 : 4 Using gauge to check location of piston

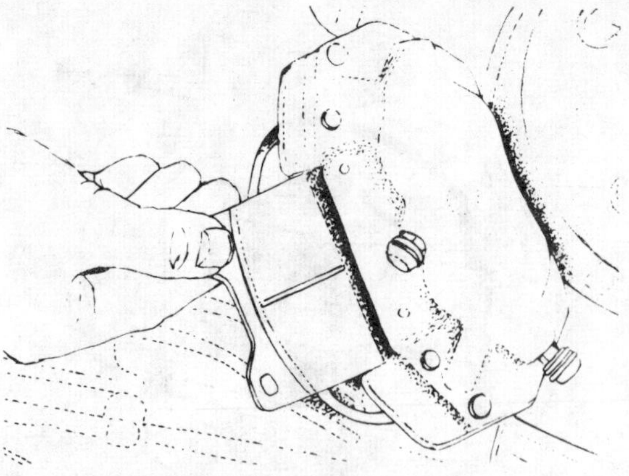

FIG 11:5 Fitting new pads

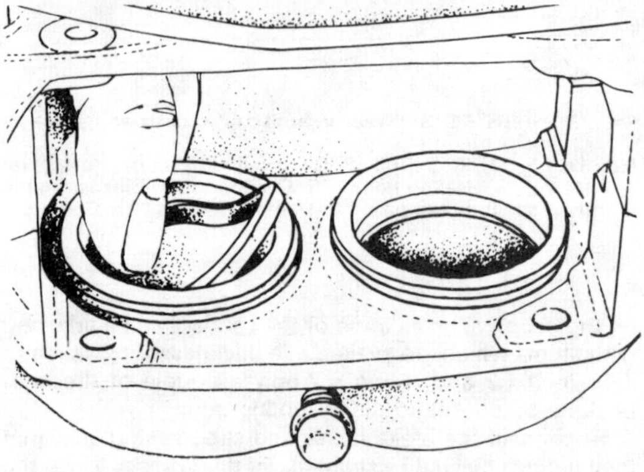

FIG 11:6 Fitting a sealing ring

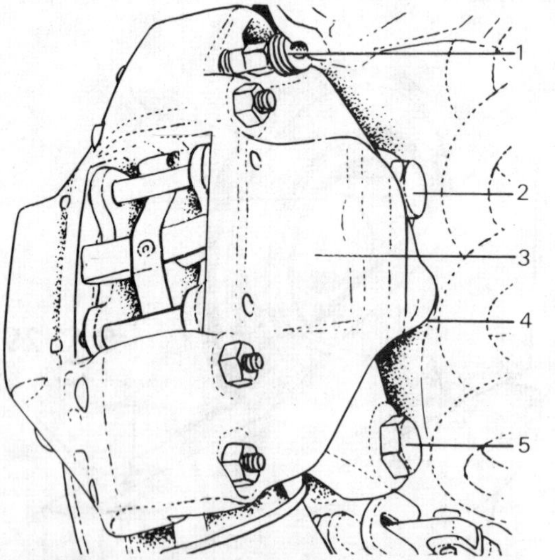

FIG 11:7 Rear wheel brake caliper installed

Key to Fig 11:7 1 Bleed nipple 2 Attaching bolt 3 Caliper 4 Brake line 5 Attaching bolt

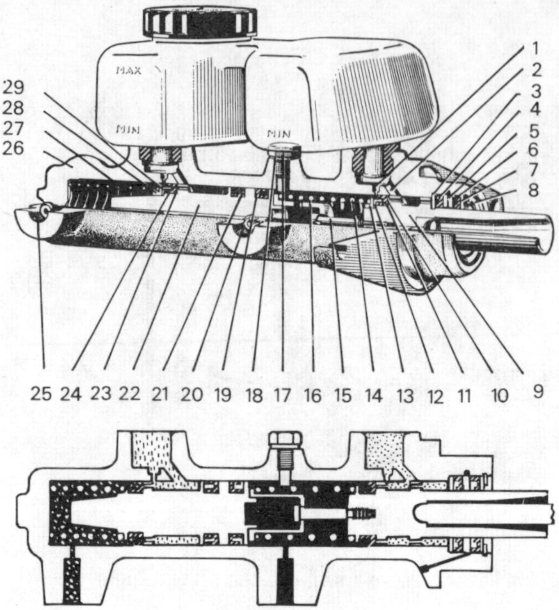

FIG 11:8 The master cylinder

Key to Fig 11:8 1 Equalizing hole 2 Overflow hole 3 Washer 4 Piston seal 5 Washer 6 Piston seal 7 Washer 8 Circlip 9 Primary piston 10 Washer 11 Piston seal 12 Washer 13 Thrust washer 14 Spring 15 Screw 16 Spring retainer 17 Stop screw 18 Seal 19 Piston seal 20 Connection for primary circuit 21 Piston seal 22 Secondary piston 23 Washer 24 Piston seal 25 Connection for secondary circuit 26 Cylinder 27 Spring 28 Thrust washer 29 Washer

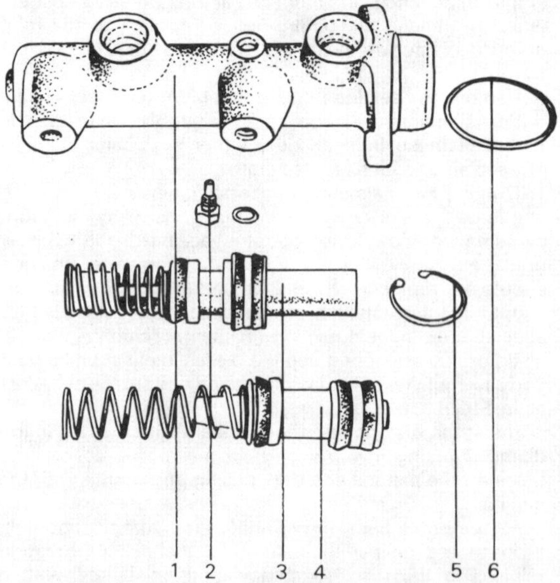

FIG 11:9 Components of master cylinder

Key to Fig 11:9 1 Cylinder housing 2 Stop screw 3 Primary piston 4 Secondary piston 5 Circlip 6 Sealing ring

Rear:

The procedure to be adopted for the rear units is similar to the front. Jack up the car and remove the wheels. release the handbrake. Disconnect the brake line after preparing for fluid escaping and plug the pipe. Remove the two mounting bolts and pull off the caliper to the rear (see **FIG 11 :7**).

Remove the brake pads and also the retaining rings and rubber dust covers. Using a wooden disc inserted between the pistons press out the pistons by means of compressed air, remove them and lever off the rubber covers.

Carefully use a blunt tool to remove the sealing rings and unscrew the bleed nipple.

Reassembly is a reversal of the above, using new seals and rubber covers, and being careful to align the pistons as described in **Section 11 :4**.

11 :6 Brake discs

The brake discs should be examined for wear, alignment and damage. Minor scratches are of little importance, but radial scratches may reduce braking efficiency and increase lining wear. In many cases the disc can be restored by machining, but if this is done care must be taken to see that the disc thickness is not reduced below the minimum permissible. This is .90 inch for front discs and .331 inch for the rear wheel brakes.

Runout should be measured with a dial indicator at the outer perimeter of the disc, after ensuring that the wheel bearings are correctly adjusted and the disc is securely bolted to the hub. Runout limits are .004 inch (.1 mm) front and .006 inch (.15 mm) rear.

Check also that the disc is of uniform thickness over a full revolution. Any variation must not exceed .0012 inch (.03 mm). If any fault is revealed in these tests, a new disc should be fitted.

Remove the caliper and unscrew the mounting nuts and gently tap the disc with a plastic hammer to remove it.

11 :7 The master cylinder

This is mounted on the forward face of the servo unit by two bolts and is of tandem type with two separate reservoirs in one container. A part section view is given in **FIG 11 :8** together with a diagram showing the function of the master cylinder.

Fluid from the two reservoirs feeds into the primary and secondary cylinders and when the brake pedal is depressed the primary piston is forced down its bore and so applies a pressure on the secondary piston as well as the primary braking circuit. Thus the secondary piston transmits the pressure on to the secondary braking circuit and both circuits are similarly and simultaneously pressurized.

In the event of a failure in the primary circuit releasing all the hydraulic pressure, the primary piston will be pressed into direct contact with the secondary piston which will then operate in the normal way and braking will still be available on the two front wheels and one rear wheel.

If a fault occurs in the secondary circuit, the secondary piston will simply be pressed to the end of the cylinder and full braking occur on the primary circuit of two front wheels and the other rear wheel.

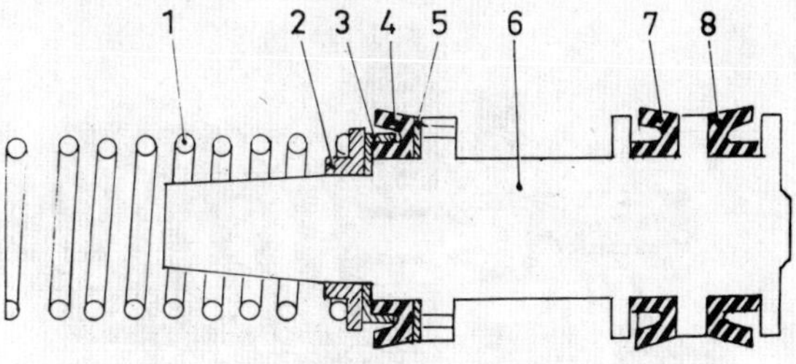

FIG 11 :10 The secondary piston

Key to Fig 11 :10 1 Spring 2 Thrust washer 3 Back-up ring 4 Piston seal 5 Washer 6 Piston 7 Piston seal 8 Piston seal

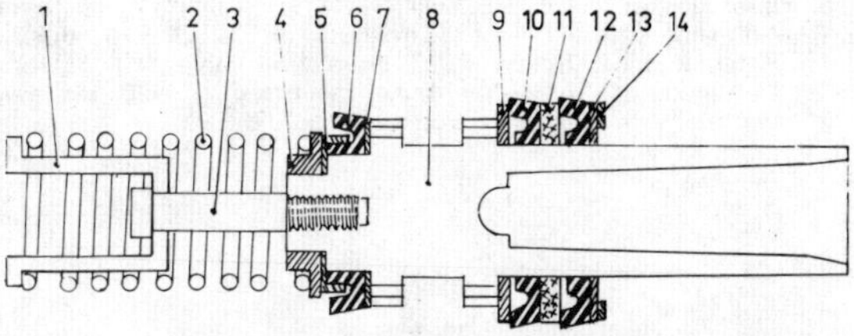

FIG 11 :11 The primary piston

Key to Fig 11 :11 1 Sleeve 2 Spring 3 Screw 4 Thrust washer 5 Back-up ring 6 Piston seal 7 Washer 8 Piston 9 Washer 10 Piston seal 11 Plastic washer 12 Piston seal 13 Washer 14 Circlip

11 :8 Servicing the master cylinder

Before commencing to dismantle the master cylinder the operator is again advised of the necessity for absolute cleanliness when handling any components associated with the hydraulic system.

Taking care to avoid spillage of the fluid, disconnect the supply pipes from the master cylinder and plug them to prevent the entry of any foreign matter.

Remove the two securing nuts and lift off the master cylinder forwards. Empty out the brake fluid.

Hold the flange firmly in a vice and with both hands lift up the reservoir out of the two rubber seals which should then be pulled out of their holes.

Refer to **FIG 11 :9**. Remove the stop screw 2 and the circlip 5 from the primary piston and extract the two pistons.

Carefully clean the parts and examine them for wear or damage. The manufacturers recommend that if wear or deterioration is present new piston assemblies complete should be obtained, but if only rubber seals are being renewed great care must be taken to see that they are fitted in the direction in **FIGS 11 :10** and **11 :11**.

Reassembly:

Fit the washer 5 and seal 4 on the secondary piston and make sure that seals 7 and 8 are correctly located. Fit the lock-up ring 3, thrust washer 2 and spring 1, dip in clean brake fluid and insert into the cylinder, being particularly careful not to turn back or damage the lips of the rubber seals.

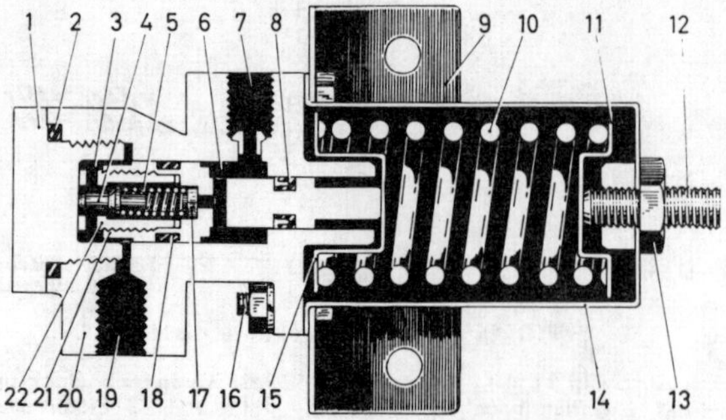

FIG 11:12 Section through brake valve

Key to Fig 11:12 1 Plug 2 O-ring 3 Cylinder 4 Valve 5 Valve spring 6 Cylinder 7 Connection to master cylinder 8 Piston gasket 9 Bracket 10 Spring 11 Retainer 12 Adjusting screw 13 Locknut 14 Spring housing 15 Retainer 16 Screw 17 Equalizing valve 18 O-ring 19 Connection to rear wheel brake cylinders 20 Housing 21 Piston 22 Valve housing

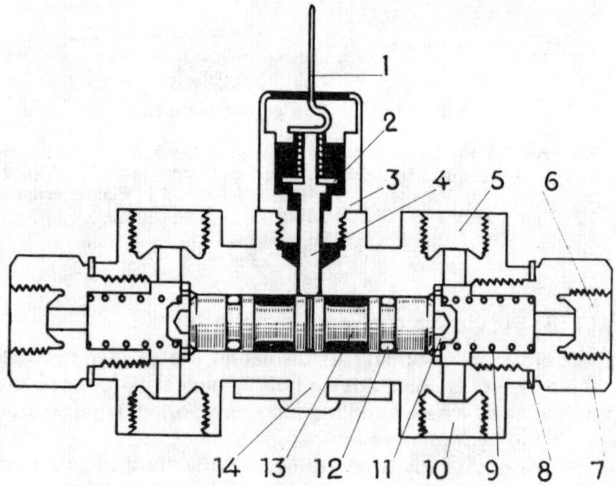

FIG 11:13 Section through warning valve

Key to Fig 11:13 1 Electrical connection 2 Switch washer 3 Switch housing 4 Guide pin 5 Connection, rear wheel brakes 6 Connection, master cylinder 7 End piece 8 Sealing washer 9 Spring 10 Connection, front wheel brakes 11 Thrust washer 12 O-ring 13 Piston 14 Housing

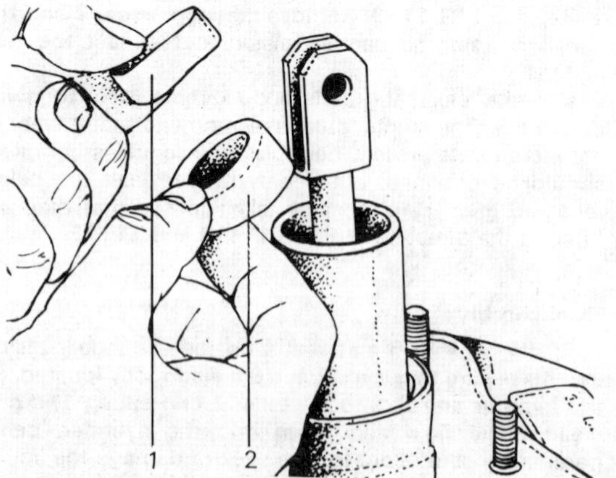

FIG 11:14 Fitting 1 Damper, 2 Air filter to servo unit

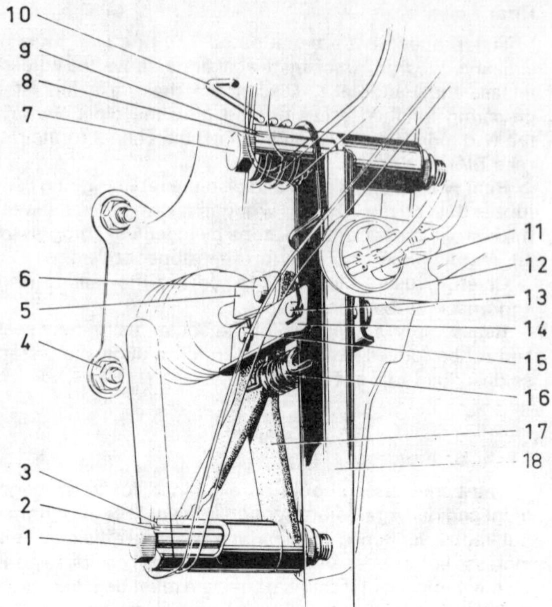

FIG 11:15 Pedal mounting arrangement

Key to Fig 11:15 1 Bolt 2 Bearing sleeve 3 Bush 4 Nut 5 Thrust rod 6 Splitpin bolt 7 Bolt 8 Bearing sleeve 9 Bush 10 Return spring 11 Brake light switch 12 Bracket 13 Splitpin bolt 14 Link 15 Splitpin bolt 16 Spring 17 Link arm 18 Brake pedal

Assemble the components of the primary piston in the same way (noting the different direction of the rubber seals) and push it into the cylinder finally fitting the circlip.

Check that the hole for the stop screw is clear and fit the screw with a new washer, tightening to 3.6 to 5.7 lb ft.

Check the movement of the pistons and see that the through-flow holes are clear. The equalizing hole is checked by pressing the pistons in about .04 inch (1 mm) and inserting a soft copper wire of 22.SWG down through the hole. If the hole is not clear there has been faulty assembly.

Fit the two rubber seals and the fluid reservoir. See that the gasket ring is in position and refit the master cylinder to the servo unit, tightening the nuts to 9 to 11 lb ft. Loosely connect the pipes, press down the pedal and tighten up the unions when fluid free from air flows out. Bleed the system.

11:9 The brake valves

A brake valve, shown in section in **FIG 11:12**, is connected in each of the rear brake supply lines, the purpose of which is to reduce the supply to the brake when the input pressure exceeds 484 lb/sq inch. The higher the pedal pressure the greater the reduction and therefore the larger the difference between the pressures applied to the front and rear brake units. This ensures a suitable distribution of braking force between the two pairs of wheels.

The brake valve is easily removed from the car after disconnecting the metal brake pipe. Slacken the brake hose a quarter of a turn at the valve, remove the mounting bolts and unscrew the valve from the brake hose.

Separate the spring housing from the hydraulic section by removing the four screws 16. Shake out the spring and retainer, but do **not** remove the adjusting screw 12.

Screw out the plug 1 and press out the piston assembly. Clean carefully in brake fluid and inspect. If the interior surfaces are scratched or rusty, replace the complete valve. If a piston seal is being replaced, note that its open end faces the thicker end of the piston.

Dip the piston in brake fluid and refit it into its cylinder, then screw in the plug and sealing ring, tightening to a torque of 70 to 85 lb ft.

Place the retainer 11 in the spring housing 14 as shown in **FIG 11:12**, fit the other retainer 15 in the spring and fit into the housing. Reassemble the spring housing on to the hydraulic section.

Screw the brake valve unit on to the brake hose, place the valve in position and see that there is no strain on the hose. Fit the mounting bolts, connect up the brake pipe, tighten up all connections and bleed the brake system.

11:10 The warning valve

This is fitted between the brake lines from the master cylinder to the six branch union, its purpose being to warn the driver when the pressure difference between the two circuits exceeds about 142 lb/sq inch.

The device is in the form of a letter H (see **FIG 11:13**), with the two arms in series with the two brake circuits and the cross-piece housing a shuttle type valve which, when moved from its central position, actuates an electric switch.

Under normal circumstances with equal pressures in each brake circuit, the piston is held in the position shown in the diagram, but as soon as the pressure in one circuit is caused to drop the piston will be forced to that side of the warning valve, actuate the switch and alert the driver to the failure. It may be noted that the switch pin 4 cannot return to its OFF position until the switch has been removed and the fault rectified.

11:11 The vacuum servo unit

This is a mechanical tandem type servo device located between the brake pedal and the master cylinder by means of which the difference between the low pressure in the manifold and atmospheric is used to supplement the braking pressure exerted by the driver on his pedal.

As there is very little the home operator can do with regard to servicing the unit, a full description will not be necessary. It should suffice to describe the few operations which do not require factory attention.

Check valve:

This is connected in the hose between the engine inlet manifold and the servo unit and its purpose as a non-return valve is to ensure that air is not allowed to flow back to the cylinder and disperse the vacuum present.

The valve is removed by loosening the two retaining clips and refitted in reverse order. Note that the arrows on the valve casing must point away from the servo cylinder and the vacuum hose connection should face downwards.

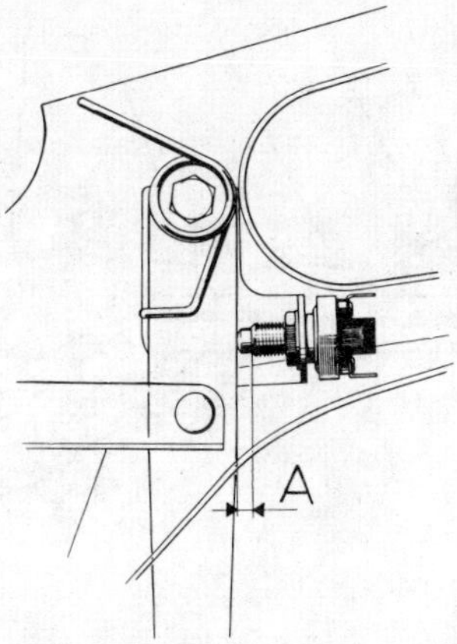

FIG 11:16 Adjusting the brake light switch. A=$\frac{1}{8}$ inch

Renewing air filter:

This item should be renewed every 36,000 miles (60,000 km) or more frequently if the vehicle is operated under very dusty conditions. Refer to **FIG 11:14** and proceed as follows:

Remove the panel under the dashboard and the brake light fuse.

Remove the bracket for the brake light switch (12 in **FIG 11:15**) and also the splitpins and bolts 6 and 13. Lift up the brake pedal and remove the rubber boot over the servo thrust rod.

Remove the protective washer, damper 1 and air filter 2.

When reassembling, note that the slots on the damper and washer should be at 180 deg. to each other. The remaining parts are fitted in the reverse order to dismantling.

Removing the servo unit:

As mentioned earlier, no servicing can be carried out and in the event of a failure in the unit it should be returned to the service agents for attention or replacement.

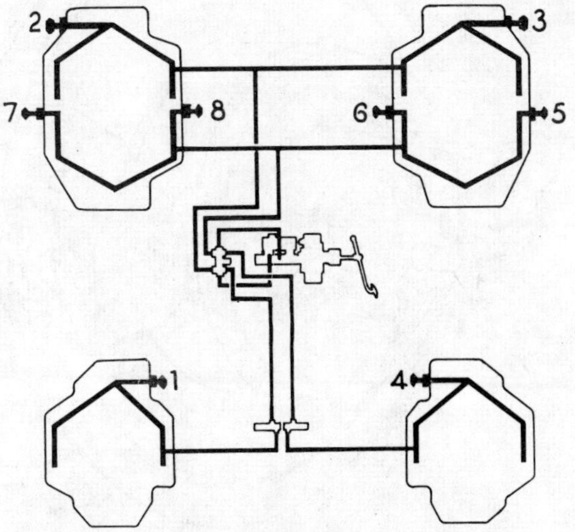

FIG 11:17 Sequence for bleeding the brakes

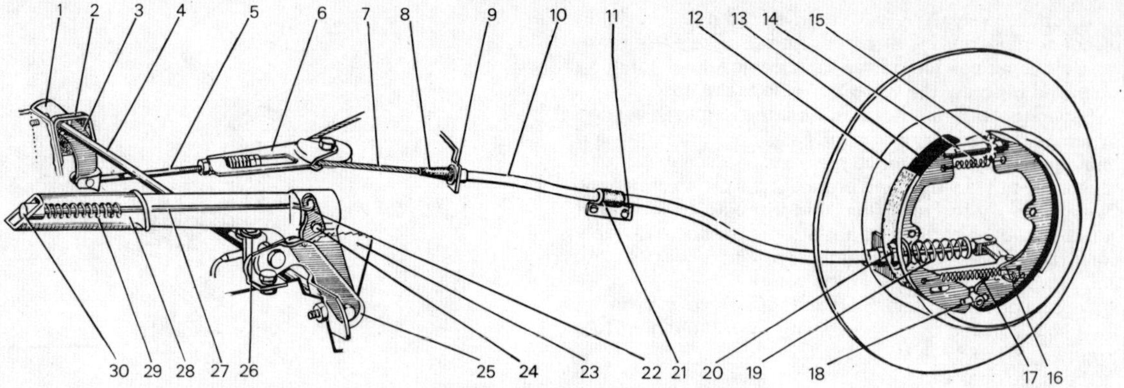

FIG 11:18 The handbrake system

Key to Fig 11:18 1 Inside support attachment 2 Rubber cover 3 Lever 4 Shaft 5 Pull rod 6 Pulley 7 Cable 8 Rubber cover 9 Front attachment 10 Cable sleeve 11 Attachment 12 Brake drum 13 Brake shoe (secondary shoe) 14 Return spring 15 Adjusting device 16 Lever 17 Movable rod 18 Anchor bolt 19 Return spring 20 Rear attachment 21 Rubber cable guide 22 Pawl 23 Ratchet segment 24 Rivet 25 Outside support attachment 26 Warning valve switch 27 Push rod 28 Parking brake 29 Spring 30 Push button

Remove the master cylinder as described in **Section 11:7** and disconnect the vacuum hose.

Disconnect the link arm 14 from the brake pedal and remove the bracket with the clutch pedal stop from the cowl.

Take off the four nuts retaining the servo unit and pull it forwards, disconnecting the fork from the link arm.

When refitting, make sure that the rubber boot is firmly located, then secure the fork to the link arm and push the unit in to line up the mounting bolts. Fit the nuts and their spring washers.

Fit the clutch pedal bracket and secure the link arm to the brake pedal. Fit the vacuum hose with the connection downwards.

Bleed the brake system.

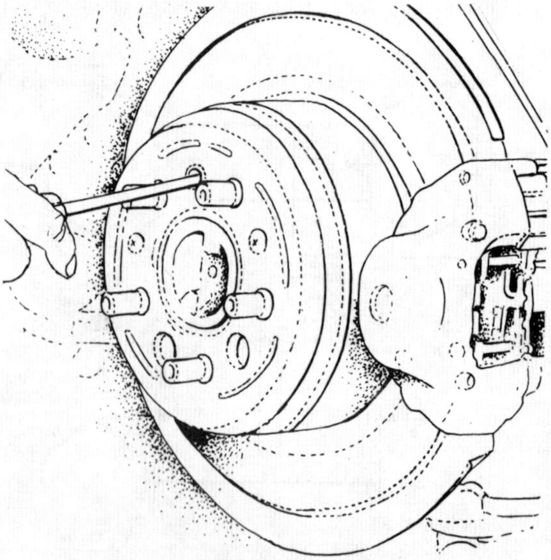

FIG 11:19 Adjusting the handbrake shoes

11:12 The brake pedal

To remove the brake pedal, first take out the panel under the dashboard then remove the bracket for the brake light switch.

Remove the splitpin and bolt 13. Unhook the return spring 10 and the spring 16. Unscrew the nut for the bolt 7 and pull out the bolt. Lift out the pedal.

Fit new pedal bushes 9 and lubricate the bearing sleeves 8 with a little ballbearing grease. Fit the sleeve and the return spring.

Place the pedal in position and fit the bolt 7 and the nut. Hook on the springs and fit the bolt 13 and splitpin. Fit the bracket 12 and adjust the brake light switch 11. Replace the panel.

Bushes:

The bushes 3 and 9 are replaced simply by pressing out the old ones after removing the pedal and the bearing sleeves 2 and 8 and then pressing in the new bushes. If the sleeves are worn, they also should be renewed at this time.

Brake light switch (see FIG 11:16):

Measure the distance **A** between the brass hub on the switch and the brake pedal when the pedal is released. This should be about $\frac{1}{8}$ inch (2 to 6 mm).

To adjust the clearance, slacken the screw for the bracket (12 in **FIG 11:15**), and tighten after adjustment.

11:13 Bleeding the brake system

This is not an item of nominal maintenance, but becomes necessary if air has entered the hydraulic system for any reason such as removal of a part of the system or an excesssive drop in the reservoir fluid level. A sign that air is in the system is a spongy feeling when applying the brakes. If it important that the procedure given should be followed closely.

Check that the brake pedal has a full unhindered movement (about 6 inch), and work it a few times to disperse any residual vacuum in the servo unit.

Ensure that the fluid reservoir is full and note that a check must be mainteained on the level as a quantity of fluid will be used as the operation proceeds.

Remove the electric switch from the warning valve.

Refer to **FIG 11 :17** and note that the bleeding points must be used in the order shown and as follows:

Fit a length of rubber or plastic hose on the first bleed nipple and allow the free end to be submerged in a quantity of clean brake fluid in a clean glass jar. Open the bleed nipple one half turn and slowly press the brake pedal down fully. At the end of the stroke pause and quickly release the pedal.

Repeat this procedure until the fluid being expelled into the jar is quite free of air bubbles then close the bleed nipple at the end of the next down stroke.

Remove the bleed tube and proceed to the other wheels in the order shown. Do not use the fluid expelled in this operation for topping up, although it may be useful after it has stood for at least 24 hours to allow any air bubbles to disperse if it is perfectly clean.

Refit the warning switch and tighten it to 10 to 15 lb ft and connect the cable.

11 :14 The handbrake

The construction of the parking brake system is shown in **FIG 11 :18** from which it will be seen that the movement of the lever, which is mounted on the floor outside the drivers seat is transmitted to the rear wheel units by a linkage of rods and cables.

The wheel units, housed in drums integral with the rear brake discs, are partly self-applying (Duo-Servo) and are adjusted as follows:

Jack up the rear of the car, take off the wheels and release the handbrake.

Turn the drum until the hole coincides with the serrations on the adjusting screw 15 which should then be turned by levering with a screwdriver (move the handle upwards) until the shoes are applied and the drum can no longer be turned easily by hand. Turn the adjuster back by 4 to 5 serrations and check that there is no drag in the normal direction of rotation. If necessary, release the adjuster by 2 to 3 further serrations (see **FIG 11 :19**).

Repeat the above procedure on the other wheel.

Apply the handbrake lever and check that the brakes are fully applied on the 3rd or 4th notch. If they are not, the cable should be tensioned by means of the adjuster shown in **FIG 11 : 20**. This is done by loosening the locknuts 1 and 6 and turning the nut 2 as required. Tighten the locknuts and recheck the settings.

Refit the wheels and lower the car.

11 :15 Rear wheel drum brakes

Dismantling:

Jack up the rear of the car, remove the wheels and release the handbrake.

Disconnect the brake fluid line from the caliper and plug to avoid spillage, then remove the two securing bolts and lift out the caliper.

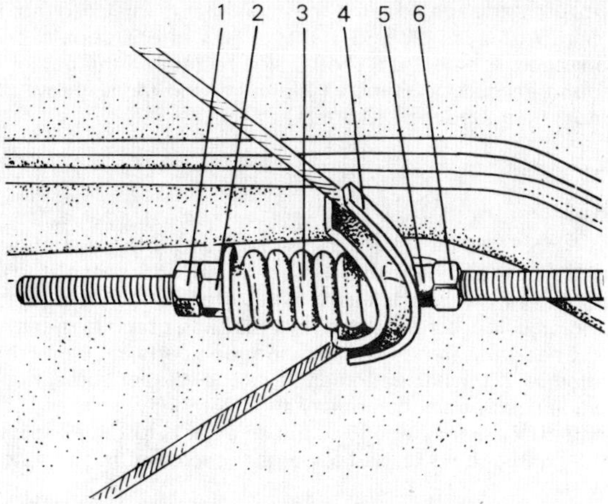

FIG 11 :20 Brake cable adjuster

Key to Fig 11 :20 1 Locknut 2 Adjusting nut 3 Spring 4 Clevis 5 Sleeve 6 Locknut

Remove the securing bolts and lift off the brake drum to expose the internal mechanism as in **FIG 11 :21**.

Remove the two return springs and the adjusting device then ease the shoes out of their retainers.

After cleaning the parts they should be examined and renewed where necessary.

If the brake linings are worn to the extent that the rivets are about to contact the drums new shoes should be obtained. Oil or grease on the linings can vary rarely be satisfactorily removed and if this contamination is present new shoes should be fitted.

The brake drums should be examined for rust spots or scoring and if the condition is not too bad may be cleaned

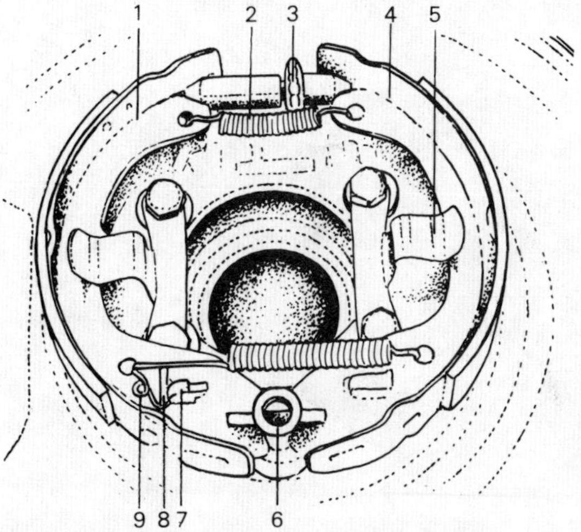

FIG 11 :21 Rear drum brake mechanism

Key to Fig 11 :21 1 Rear brake shoe (primary shoe) 2 Upper return spring 3 Adjusting device 4 Front brake shoe (secondary shoe) 5 Retainer for brake shoe 6 Anchor bolt 7 Lever 8 Washer 9 Spring up, but if this would bring the maximum diameter to more than 7.0 inch (178.33 mm) a new drum should be obtained. A new drum should also be fitted if the out-of-round exceeds .008 inch (.2 mm) or the radial throw is more than .006 inch (.15 mm).

Reassembling:

Before assembly, release the tension on the operating cable by slackening the cable adjuster and coat the six guide lips on the backing plate as well as the lever joint and adjusting screw with a heat resisting graphite grease.

Check that the lever and anchor bolt parts are correctly fitted as in the illustration and that the washer and spring are in position on the primary shoe. Fit the two shoes and note that the shorter end of the adjuster is to the front on the righthand wheel and towards the rear on the lefthand wheel.

Hook on the return springs and fit the drum and securing bolts.

Fit the calipers, together with any shims which may have been included, and bolt up using a smear of Locktite on the threads.

Check the action of the brake pads and adjust the handbrake cable. Bleed the caliper(s) which had been disconnected and refit the road wheels.

11:16 Fault diagnosis

(a) Spongy pedal

1 Air in the system
2 Leak in the system
3 Worn master or wheel cylinders

(b) Brakes grab or pull to one side

1 Distorted disc
2 Wet or oily linings
3 Piston sticking in caliper
4 Loose caliper mounting
5 Uneven tyre pressures
6 Worn steering linkage
7 Servo unit faulty
8 Blocked pipe

(c) Brakes dragging

1 Check 1 and 3 in (b)
2 Master cylinder piston sticking
3 Return spring broken

(d) Lack of servo assistance

1 Air filter blocked
2 Vacuum pipe blocked or broken
3 Non-return valve leaking
4 Faulty servo unit

CHAPTER 12

THE ELECTRICAL SYSTEM

12:1 Description

The electrical system is a conventional 12-volt arrangement with the power being supplied by an alternator and using a negative earth return.

Instructions for servicing most of the items of electrical equipment are given in this chapter and wiring diagrams will be found in the **Appendix** to assist in locating and rectifying faults. It will, however, be appreciated that it may not be always economical to attempt to repair defective equipment when new units are readily available on an exchange basis, particularly as it is so important that accurate and expensive equipment is available for the correct checking and adjustment of the instruments and controls.

Special instructions should be mentioned which are applicable to operations on cars fitted with an alternator and which do not necessarily apply when a DC generator is used.

Particular attention must be paid to ensuring correct polarity when wiring any component in the system.

Never run the alternator with the output leads disconnected. Do not make or break any connections in the charging circuit while the engine is running.

When charging the battery in the car the negative battery lead should be disconnected.

Do not use a boost charger for starting the engine.

Always disconnect the alternator when carrying out any electric welding on the car.

12:2 The battery

The Tudor 6 Ex4F 12-volt battery is of 60-amp/hr capacity and is located on a shelf to the right of the radiator.

Maintenance is a matter of keeping the outside of the battery clean and dry and making a periodical check on the electrolyte level and specific gravity with a hydrometer.

The level should be about $\frac{1}{4}$ inch above the plates and if necessary distilled water should be added. Never add neat acid. If it is ever required to prepare dilute acid for use in the battery, always add the acid to the water and never water to acid as this could cause dangerous spitting to occur.

The indications from the hydrometer readings of the specific gravity are as follows:

For climates below 87° or 27°

Cell fully charged	Specific gravity 1.270 to 1.290
Cell half charged	Specific gravity 1.190 to 1.210
Cell fully discharged	Specific gravity 1.110 to 1.130

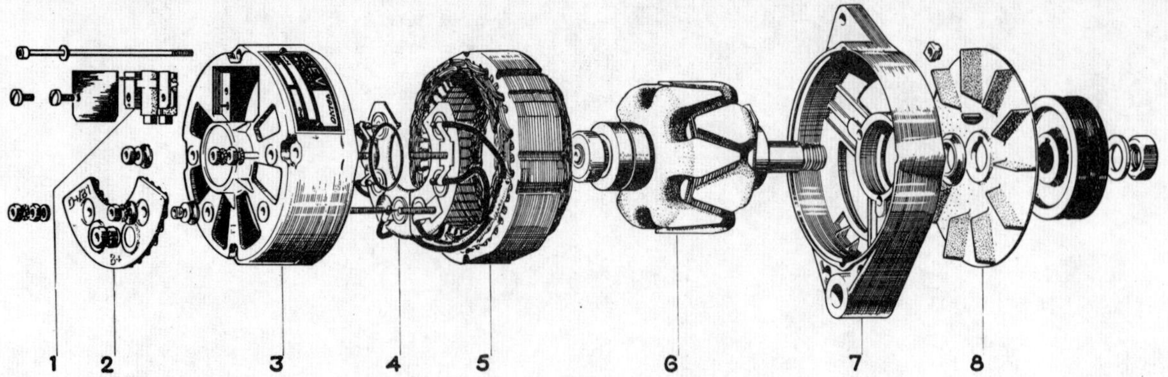

FIG 12:1 **Components of the alternator**

Key to Fig 12:1 1 Brush holder 2 Isolation diodes with holder 3 Slip ring and shield 4 Rectifier (silicon diodes) 5 Stator 6 Rotor 7 Drive end shield 8 Fan

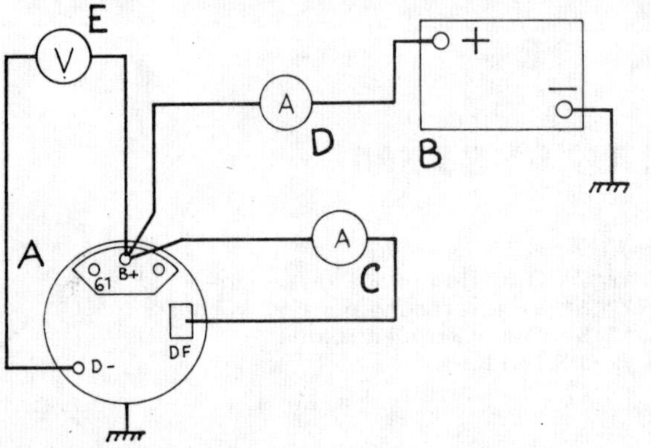

FIG 12:2 Wiring diagram for alternator test circuit

Key to Fig 12:2 **A** Alternator **B** Battery 60 Ah **C** Ammeter 0 to 10 amps **D** Ammeter 0 to 50 amps **E** Voltmeter 0 to 20 volts

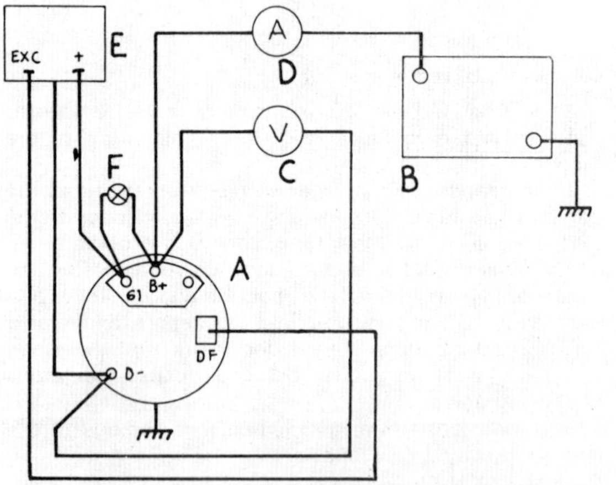

FIG 12:3 Wiring diagram for regulator test circuit

Key to Fig 12:3 **A** Alternator **B** Battery 60 Ah **C** Voltmeter 0 to 20 amps **D** Ammeter 0 to 50 amps **E** Voltage regulator **F** Warning lamp 12 volts 2 watts

These figures assume an electrolyte temperature of 60°F or 16°C. For temperatures in excess of this, add .002 for each 5°F or 3°C rise. Subtract .002 for any corresponding value below.

12:3 The alternator

The S.E.V. Motorola alternator is a three-phase star connected unit, located on the righthand side of the engine and driven by a V-belt from the crankshaft pulley.

The rectifier which consists of six silicon diodes passes current in one direction only, so that the conventional cut-out control can be dispensed with and the only external control is a simple voltage regulator.

Testing:

Before starting any tests on the alternator or regulator in the car, check first on the state of the battery, wiring, connections and terminals. Check also that the fan belt is correctly tensioned. It is also desirable to have a fully charged battery when carrying out these tests.

To check the voltage drop in the wiring:

Start up the engine and switch on the main headlamp beams and measure the voltage between the battery positive terminal and B+ on the alternator. If the voltage drop exceeds .3 volt, there is a fault in the wiring which must be rectified. Then with the same load measure the voltage drop between battery negative and alternator terminal D—. If the drop here exceeds .2-volt, check the battery earth lead, alternator mounting on the engine and the engine/chassis connection.

To check the alternator:

Wire up the circuit shown in **FIG 12:2** and check that the current through the field winding (ammeter C) is 3 to 3.5 amps. If not, check the brush holder and field winding.

Run the engine up to 1500 rev/min, when the alternator should produce at least 48 amps at 14 volts.

Measure the voltage at B+ and 61 with the alternator charging. The first should be more than at 61, otherwise the isolation diode assembly is faulty and should be renewed.

FIG 12:4 Components of the starter motor

Key to Fig 12:4 1 Shift lever 2 Pivot pin 3 Plunger 4 Steel washer 5 Rubber washer 6 Winding 7 Contact plate 8 Terminal for battery lead 9 Connection lead to field 10 Screw 11 Rubber gasket 12 Shims 13 Lock washer 14 Bush 15 Commutator end frame 16 Adjusting washers 17 Brush holder 18 Brush 19 Bush spring 20 Commutator 21 Armature 22 Pole shoe 23 Stator 24 Field winding 25 Drive end frame 26 Roller bearing 27 Pinion 28 Stop ring 29 Snap ring 30 Bush

To check the voltage regulator:

Connect up the circuit shown in **FIG 12:3** and run the engine up to 2500 rev/min for 15 seconds. Note the reading on the voltmeter. With no load this should be 13.1 to 14.4 volts.

With a load of 10 to 15 amps, such as the headlights, the voltage should be the same. If it is outside these limits, the regulator should be exchanged.

Removal and dismantling:

First disconnect the negative lead from the battery and the leads to the alternator, then remove the bolt for the adjusting bar and the alternator mounting bolt. Remove the drive belt and lift the alternator out towards the front.

Refer to **FIG 12:1** for a view of the components of the machine and commence by releasing the two screws securing the brush holder and isolation plate. Pull out the brush holder.

Remove the pulley nut and washer, lift off the pulley, fan key and spacing washer.

Remove the nuts and washers from terminal 61 and from that corresponding on the other side of the isolation diode. Lift off the isolation diode holder.

Mark the two end shields and the stator to assist in reassembly, then remove the four attaching screws.

Remove the stator and slip ring end shield by inserting two screwdrivers in two of the sockets between the stator and drive end shield. Do not allow the screwdrivers to enter more than $\frac{1}{16}$ inch (2 mm) otherwise the stator may be damaged.

Remove the three screws securing the drive end bearing plate to the casing and ease the stator and bearing out of the shield by tapping the end of the shaft on a piece of soft wood.

Remove the retaining nuts and washers and remove the diode holders from the slip ring end shield.

Clean all parts and check the stator windings for continuity.

Check that the slip rings are not worn or burnt, and if necessary clean them with a petrol moistened cloth or, in more severe cases, a very fine glasspaper. Check the rotor windings for continuity and insulation, and if at all faulty the entire rotor assembly.

Check the diodes with a 12-volt battery and test lamp, noting that the lamp should light in one direction only. If it lights in both directions or not at all the diode is faulty and the complete assembly must be renewed.

FIG 12:5 Lubricating the starter motor

Key to Fig 12:5 1 Smear grease on insulating washers, shaft end, adjusting washers and lockwashers 2 Soak bush in oil for 1 hour 3 Grease well in rotor thread and shift lever groove 4 Smear grease on armature shaft 5 Soak bush in oil for 1 hour 6 Grease lever joints and solenoid core

Reassembling:

Fit the stator and the diode holders in the slip ring end shield, not forgetting the insulating washers for the positive diode holder, and fit the nuts and washers on the negative diode holder screws.

Press the rotor into the drive end shield and fit the three screws for the drive end bearing plate. Fit the rotor and stator assemblies together.

Fit and tighten the retaining screws to 2 to 2.2 lb ft.

Fit the isolation diode after fitting the plastic tube and insulating washers on the mounting screws. Screw up the nuts and washers and then fit the brush holder.

Fit the spacer, key, fan, pulley, washer and nut, tightening to 29 lb ft. If possible test the alternator before before mounting in the car.

Refitting to the engine is a reverse of the removal procedure, noting that when tensioning the fan belt to give a movement of about $\frac{1}{2}$ inch the leverage must be applied only to the drive end shield.

12:4 The starter motor

The Bosch starter is mounted on the flywheel housing on the lefthand side of the engine and is of the pre-engaged type, that is to say that the drive pinion is engaged with the flywheel ring gear before the starting current is switched on. A roller clutch drive in the pinion assembly enables the pinion to freewheel when the engine starts to prevent over-speeding the starter motor. The internal layout can be seen in the cut-away view of **FIG 12:4**.

When the ignition switch is turned to energize the solenoid, the armature is pulled in and the engaging arm moves the pinion into mesh with the flywheel ring gear. At the end of the stroke the main contacts are closed and the motor is energised and rotates the pinion.

Servicing for the starter motor is minimal and consists of keeping it clean and the connections tight. Brushes should be examined for wear at about 12,000 mile intervals.

Removing and dismantling:

As mentioned earlier, in the event of failure in the starter, the most economical course is probably to remove

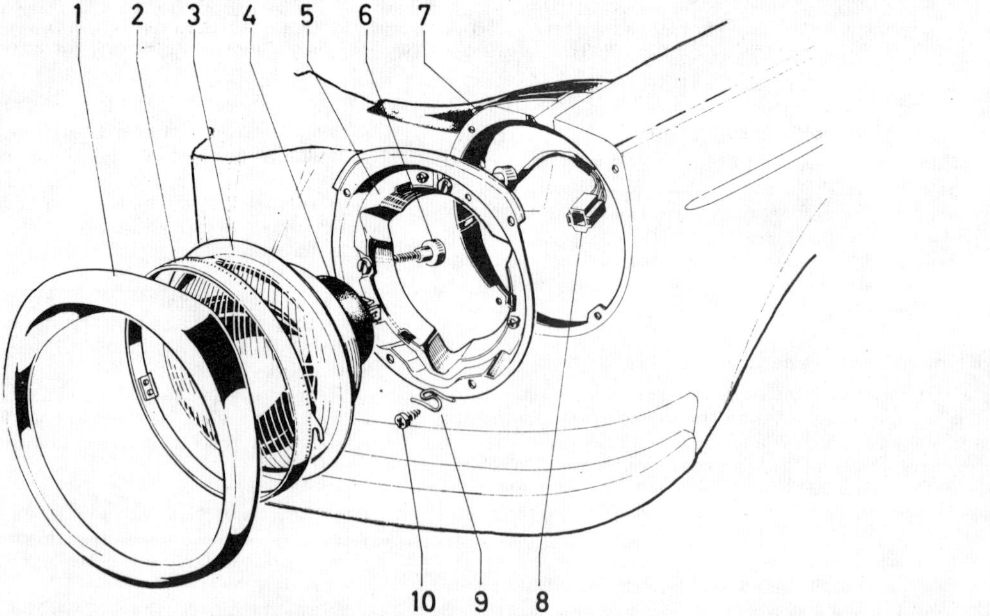

FIG 12:6 Components of headlight

Key to Fig 12:6 1 Outer rim 2 Inner rim 3 Headlight insert 4 Rubber cover 5 Holder unit 6 Adjusting screw 7 Plastic cover 8 Connector 9 Spring wire holder 10 Attaching screw it and fit a new or exchange reconditioned unit. For the owner who wishes to dismantle his starter the procedure is as follows:

Disconnect the battery and the leads from the starter. Unscrew the two mounting bolts and lift it off.

Remove the small cover on the end of the shaft and take off the U-shaped and circular adjusting washers. Remove the two bolts securing the commutator bearing end frame and lift it off.

Lift up the brushes and their holders, and remove the bridge from the armature shaft. The negative brushes will be removed with the bridge, but the positive brushes will remain in the field winding.

Unscrew the nut holding the field terminal connection to the solenoid and the screws securing the solenoid. Remove the solenoid.

Remove the drive end bracket and the armature from the stator and then take off the metal and rubber sealing washers. Take out the screw carrying the shift or operating lever, then lift out the armature together with the pinion and lever from the bracket.

Knock back the stop washer and remove the circlip from the armature shaft. Remove the stop washer and pull off the pinion.

Clean all the parts and examine for any excessive wear or damage. Replace any brushes which have worn to less than $\frac{9}{16}$ inch (14 mm). The bushes are self-lubricating and are easily removed if necessary, but before fitting a new bush it should be immersed in a light oil for at least one hour.

Reassembling:

Lubricate all joints and rubbing surfaces (including the bushes) before assembling as follows (see **FIG 12:5**):

Fit the pinion onto the armature shaft together with the washer and circlip. Fit the engaging lever on the pinion and then place the armature in the drive end frame. Insert the engaging lever screw.

Fit the metal and rubber washers in the drive end bracket and place the stator in position.

Connect the end of the engaging lever to the solenoid operating rod and secure the solenoid. Fit the steel and fibre washers on the armature shaft, place the brush bridge in position and fit the brushes.

Fit the commutator bearing frame and secure the two through-bolts.

The adjusting washers and circlip are now fitted on the shaft end and the end play adjusted by means of a selection of washers to give a clearance of between .002 and .012 inch (.05 to .3 mm). Secure the small cover over the end of the shaft.

12:5 The headlights

Adjustment:

This must be done to conform with local regulations, and is best carried out at a service station with the necessary optical equipment. If necessary, an acceptable setting can be made by aiming the beams at a wall and setting them parallel to each other and to the road surface by means of the two adjusting screws at the rear of the lamp unit. The upper screw is used for vertical adjustment and the screw on the side is for the lateral setting.

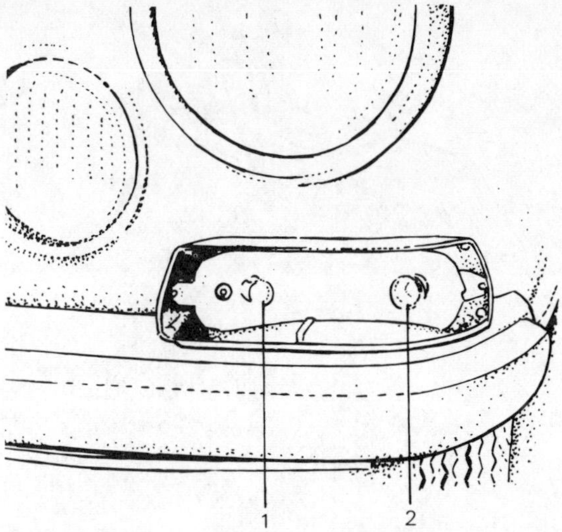

FIG 12:7 Parking and direction indicator lights with glass removed

Key to Fig 12:7 1 Parking light 2 Direction indicator flasher

Bulb replacement (see FIG 12:6):

From underneath the bonnet remove the retaining screw and lift away the plastic cover 7 over the back of the headlight. Pull out the connector 8. Remove the rubber cover 4 and release the retaining spring, then pull out the bulb holder with bulb.

Fit the new bulb in the holder and push into position making sure that the bulb holder fits securely into the socket in the insert 3.

Replace the spring, rubber cover and the connector. Before fitting the plastic cover check the lamp adjustment as described above.

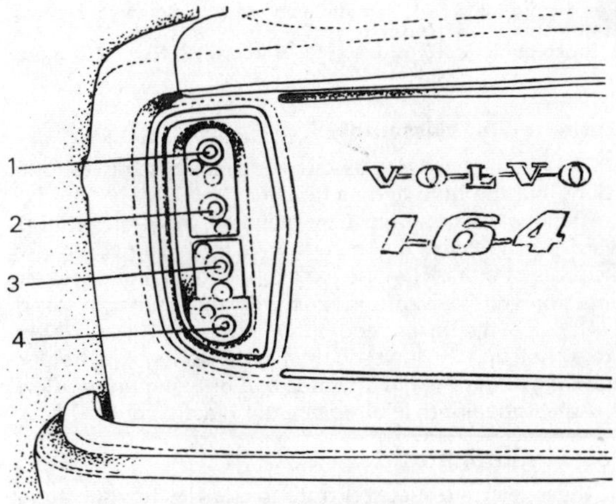

FIG 12:8 Rear lamp cluster with glass removed

Key to Fig 12:8 1 Direction indicator flasher 2 Reversing light 3 Stoplight 4 Rear light

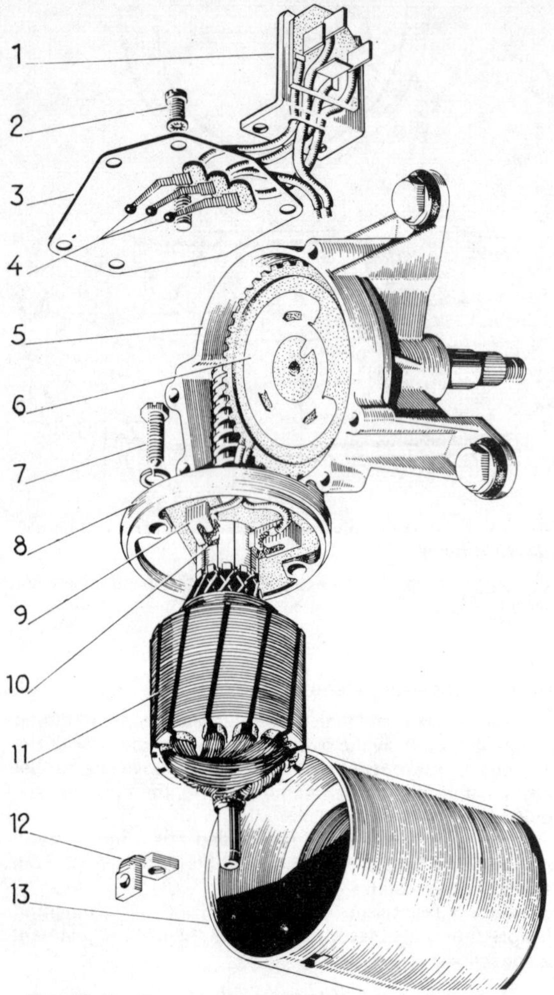

FIG 12:9 Components of windscreen wiper motor

Key to Fig 12:9 1 Terminal contact 2 Screw 3 Cover 4 Contacts 5 Housing 6 Gear 7 Screw 8 End 9 Brush holder 10 Brush 11 Rotor 12 Nut 13 Stator

Reflector/lens assembly:

The headlight insert, as this is called, is removed after taking out the bulb and its holder.

Remove the outer rim 1 by pulling it forwards and upwards, then release the three screws for the inner rim 2 by a couple of turns. Turn the rim slightly in an anticlockwise direction and lift it off together with the headlight insert.

Replace the insert and inner ring and fit the outer rim by hooking the lower section in the spring wire holders and then lifting the rim upwards and hooking on securely.

Adjust the lights and replace the plastic cover.

Fog or spotlights:

These also are reached from inside the bonnet under the plastic cover. The bulb is removed, after disconnecting the cable, by squeezing the holder together and pulling straight out.

When fitting the new bulb make sure it is fitted correctly and the bosses on the socket will only go fully home in one position.

Lamp adjustment can be carried out by slackening the nut holding the lamp.

12:6 Lamps

Parking and direction indicators:

These are shown in **FIG 12:7** with the front glass removed. This is retained, together with its sealing strip, by two screws.

Rear lights:

The location of the bulbs in the rear light cluster is shown in **FIG 12:8**. The glass cover for these is also retained by two screws.

The glass cover for the number plate light is held in place by one screw.

12:7 Direction indicator system

The switch for this is mounted on the steering column, and to gain access it is necessary first to remove the plastic cowling. One screw holds the upper section of this and three screws are used to retain the lower portion. Note that if an overdrive is fitted, the overdrive switch bracket must be removed before the direction indicator switch can be released.

The four direction indicator flashers are also used for the hazard warning system when the switch for this function on the instrument panel is switched on. The flasher relay unit is mounted on the hazard warning switch.

12:8 Windscreen wiper and washer

A self-parking two-speed motor is controlled by a dashboard mounted switch and connected to the wiper blades by means of link arms.

To remove the wiper unit:

Disconnect the battery and remove the wiper arms. Take off the panel under the dashboard, remove the heater switch and take out the combined instrument cluster (see **Section 12:9**).

Remove the intermediate defroster nozzle and hoses then detach the wiper motor.

Disconnect the control cables for the heater, the earthing cables and remove the fusebox. Remove the choke control. Release the screws securing the wiper frame and carefully lift it out.

Wiper motor (see FIG 12:9):

Take off the nut from the drive shaft and gently tap off the crankarm.

Remove the five retaining screws 2 and bend the cover 3 away, then press out the plastic gearwheel 6. Remove the two screws 7 and pull out the stator 13. Further dismantling can be carried out as required.

Reassembly is carried out in the reverse order, noting that end play of the gearwheel can be adjusted by means of the screw in the cover.

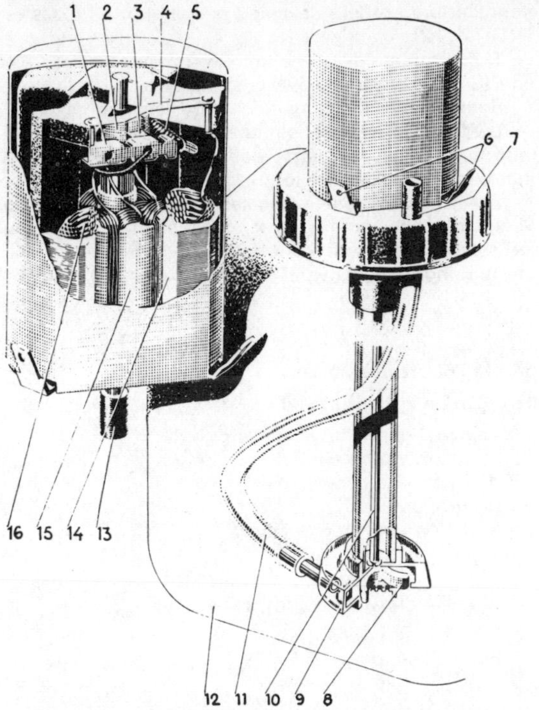

FIG 12:10 Cutaway view of windscreen washer

Key to Fig 12:10 1 Brush holder 2 Commutator 3 Brush 4 Thermal fusing 5 Spring 6 Connection tags 7 Water outle 8 Pump impeller 9 Pump housing 10 Shaft 11 Hose 12 Container 13 Flange 14 Stator 15 Rotor 16 Field winding

Windscreen washer (see FIG 12:10):

Two types of windscreen washers are used and are located on the lefthand wheel arch. In each case an electric motor mounted in the cover of the water container drives a centrifugal type pump through an extension shaft.

In the event of a fault developing in the washer it is recommended that it is taken to a service station for repair or replacement.

12:9 The instrument panel

This is a combined instrument assembly shown in **FIG 12:11** and consists of a speedometer with odometer and and trip, a voltage stabilized temperature gauge and fuel gauge, warning lamps and rheostat controlled instrument lighting, the four latter items are mounted on a common baseplate below the speedometer.

Removal:

First remove the panel below the dashboard by taking out the two securing screws on either side and then pulling the upper section of the panel to the rear to free it from the clips in the dashboard and loosen it from the bonnet release mechanism.

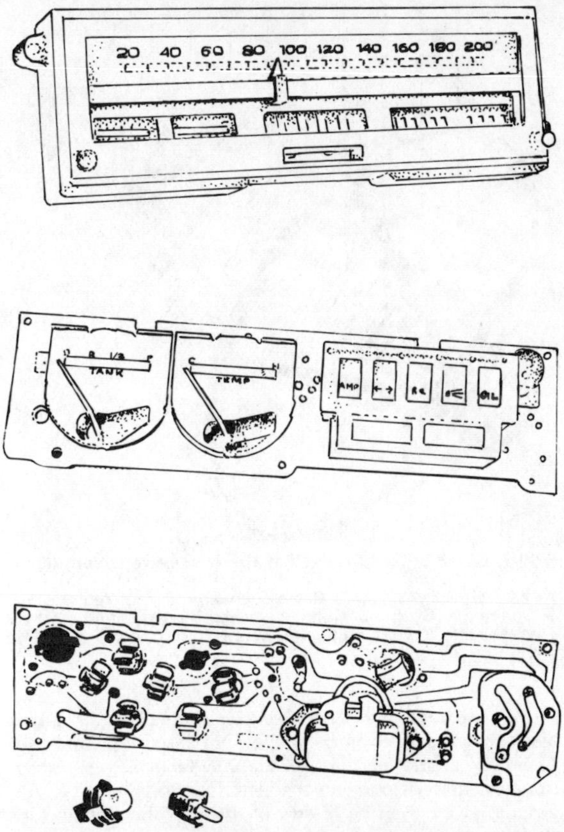

FIG 12:11 The combined instrument assembly, showing (top) front side (centre) mounting plate with instrument and warning lamps (bottom) reverse side

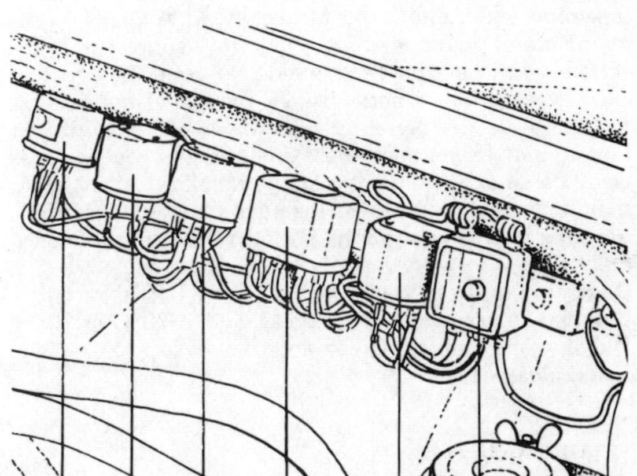

FIG 12:12 Showing location of control relays

Key to Fig 12:12 1 Foglight relay 2 Reversing light relay (or start relay for vehicles with automatic transmission) 3 Main relay 4 Step relay for dipped/full beam switching 5 Horn relay 6 Fusebox for foglights and fuel pump

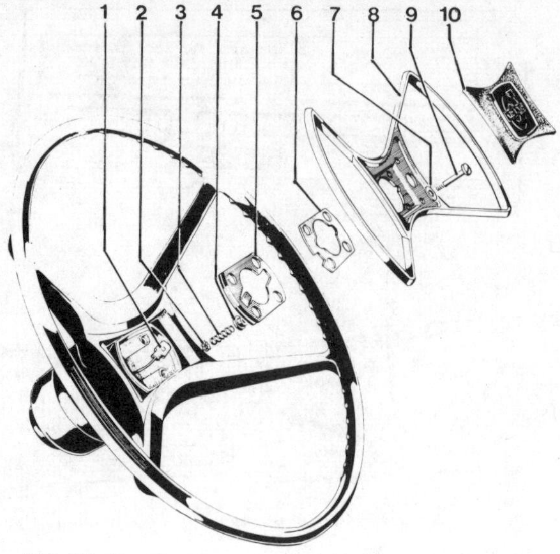

FIG 12:13 Components of the horn ring assembly

Key to Fig 12:13 1 Cable connector 2 Tab washer 3 Spring 4 Bush 5 Contact washer 6 Insulating washer 7 Washer 8 Horn ring 9 Screw 10 Shock guard

Remove the heater controls and the speedometer cable, also the flange nuts on the instrument assembly. Turn the assembly a quarter turn so that its reverse side faces upwards then disconnect the electrical connections. The assembly can then be lifted out through the opening in the panel.

The lamps on the instrument panel are mounted in holders which have to be turned anticlockwise to remove. The bulbs are released by pulling straight out.

Both the fuel gauge and the temperature gauge are non-repairable and if faulty, must be renewed. A check on the temperature gauge can be made by submerging the sender unit in a suitable container in water heated to a known temperature and observe the panel gauge. The following are the correct values for checking purposes, but do not forget that these instruments receive their electrical supply from the voltage stabilizer at 5.1 volts that to connect them across the full battery voltage would not only give false readings but also damage the instrument.

Beginning of green sector (at C)	40°C or 105°F
Dividing line between green areas	70°C or 105°F
Dividing line between green and red areas	100°C or 212°F

12:10 The horns

Two horns are fitted, one high frequency and one low frequency, and they are fitted on the support irons for the front bumper. It is not advisable to interfere with the adjustment of the horns which in normal use give very little trouble. Most faults in the horn operation can be traced to loose mountings or connections. The horn is operated by a ring mounted inside the steering wheel through a relay situated on the lefthand wheel arch together with other relays and a small box of fuses (see **FIG 12:12**).

The components of the horn ring assembly are shown in **FIG 12:13** and removal is as follows:

Remove the shock guard 10 by levering off with a screwdriver, then take out the four retaining screws 9 and disconnect the supply cable 1. When lifting off the horn ring take care not to lose any of the smaller pieces.

The screws 9 are also used to adjust the pressure required on the horn ring to actuate the horns. They should be set so that a signal is obtained with a light pressure on the ring irrespective of where the pressure is applied.

12:11 Fault diagnosis

(a) Battery discharged

1 Terminal connections loose or dirty
2 Shorts in wiring circuits
3 Alternator not charging
4 Control unit faulty
5 Battery internally defective

(b) Insufficient charging rate

1 Check 1 and 4 in (a)
2 Fan belt slipping

(c) Battery does not hold charge

1 Low electrolyte level
2 Plates sulphated
3 Electrolyte leaking from cracked case
4 Battery plate separators defective

(d) Alternator output low or nil

1 Drive belt broken or slipping
2 Faulty control unit
3 Worn bearings, loose polepieces
4 Slip ring worn, burned or shorted
5 Rotor shaft bent or worn
6 Brushes sticking, springs weak or broken
7 Rotor windings broken or shorted

(e) Starter lacks power or does not operate

1 Battery discharged
2 Loose connections
3 Starter pinion jammed
4 Starter switch faulty
5 Solenoid faulty
6 Brushes worn or sticking
7 Commutator worn or dirty
8 Motor shaft bent
9 Engine abnormally stiff

(f) Starter runs but does not turn engine

1 Defective roller clutch
2 Broken teeth on pinion or flywheel gear
3 Low battery voltage

(g) Lamps inoperative or erratic

1 Battery discharged
2 Loose connections to lamp or battery
3 Earth connections faulty
4 Switch gear faulty or dirty
5 Fuse blown

(h) Wiper motor sluggish

1 Faulty armature
2 Commutator dirty
3 Brushes worn or sticking, weak springs
4 Stiff linkages
5 Lack of lubrication

(j) Wiper motor runs but does not drive

1 Gearbox worn or broken
2 Broken linkage
3 Motor gearbox worn or broken

(k) Gauges do not register

1 Wiring broken
2 Voltage stabilizer faulty
3 Transmitters faulty

CHAPTER 13

THE BODYWORK

13:1 Body maintenance

The body structure is made up from a series of pressed steel sections joined together by welding. Damage to any section too great to permit of local rectification can be dealt with by replacing the section and welding it into position. As this is a process entailing, in many cases, realignment of the chassis or its assembly in a special jig, the work should not be attempted by the owner/mechanic but placed with a Volvo repair agent who is in possession of the necessary jigs and tools.

The enamel finish is of a durable nature and will last many years if kept reasonably clean by regular washing and polishing. Do not attempt to wipe road dust from the body with a dry cloth or its high finish will be impaired by fine scratches. Always wash the dirt and dust away by copious flushing with water from a jet or hose. Use a soft sponge or soft brush to loosen the dirt while under the flow of water. Dry off with a chamois leather and finally polish with a soft cloth.

The protective film of wax should be renewed from time to time. There are two good indications of wax surface deterioration. The first is when water sprayed onto the surface tends to wet it evenly all over. Water should run off or at least stand on the surface in separate globules if the wax is in good condition. The second is the 'feel' of the surface when polishing after drying. If the clean duster slips easily over the surface with no effort, the film is there. If there is the slightest feel or drag, either the film has deteriorated and you are down to the enamel or the film is contaminated by ingrained dirt and must be removed.

Renovation is in two stages; the removal of the old film with its ingrained dirt and the replacement by a new wax surface. Many excellent proprietary cleaners and waxes are available and can be used with safety so long as the instructions are followed. The separate compounds are to be favoured but the polishing can be a long and arduous task which, however, pays good dividends. Combined cleaners and polishers are an acceptable second best.

Most products are now based on silicone waxes and not be allowed to contaminate the windscreen. The water-repellent film it leaves behind makes the use of the wind-screen wiper inefficienct in preserving clean vision when light rain is falling. The film is difficult to remove and, in any case, prevention is better than cure. To remove, use non-abrasive scouring powders, with plenty of water, or metal polish.

Tar can be removed by the use of a little butter on a soft cloth, finishing off with an application of wax. Bird droppings should be removed as soon as possible. Wipe

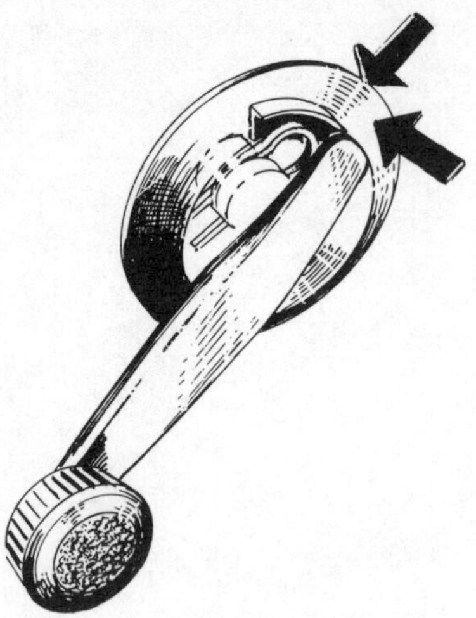

FIG 13:1 Removing a winding handle

off with a very wet cloth applied with a rotary motion and little pressure until all is clear. Renew the wax. Most bird droppings have constituents which eat through the wax and affect the colour of the enamel beneath leaving a lighter coloured area.

Clean the upholstery and imitation leather panels or trim with a wet cloth and soap or soap liquid. Allow to stand for a few moments, wipe clean with a damp cloth and finish off with a dry one. Do not use spirit cleaners or ammonia or soda in any form. On very dirty upholstery, the use of a soft scrubbing brush is permissible to get dirt from cracks and crevices. Do not allow stains to remain for long or their removal may prove to be impossible.

Brush out the interior regularly and use a vacuum cleaner, if possible, to extract dirt from the corners on the floor and from the upholstery.

13:2 Removing door trims

Remove the armrest in the front door by taking out the plastic plugs with a small screwdriver and removing the retaining screws located inside. Turn the plastic ring at

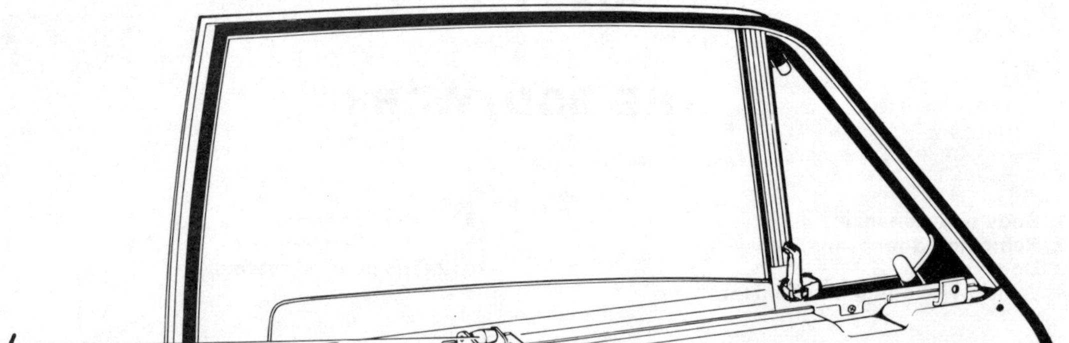

FIG 13:2 The front door with trim removed

Key to Fig 13:2 1 Screws for door lock 2 Lock cylinder attaching screws 3 Screws for window channel 4 Window support roller the front of the armrest several turns to the left, push the armrest forward to disengage the front hook and lift off.

The armrest on the rear door is removed by taking out the plastic plugs and undoing the retaining screws.

Remove the window winding handle by pressing in the circular escutcheon both towards the upholstery and towards the handle as shown in **FIG 13:1**. This releases the spring clip and enables the handle to be pulled off. When refitting make sure that the spring clip has its open end towards the handle as shown in the illustration.

Take out the screws at the top edge of the door trim panel and then lever the panel away by inserting a screwdriver under the panel edges.

13:3 Door locks

Front:

First remove the door trim panel and then remove the lock cylinder by taking out the securing screw fitted in the rear edge of the door (item 2 in **FIG 13:2**).

Release and pull out the locking pull rod (see **FIG 13:3**) and release the inner door opening pushrod. Unlock the outer handle pull rod.

Undo the two screws for the rear window guide on the rear edge of the door (3 in **FIG 13:2**) and the three screws for the door lock 1. The lock can now be eased out by carefully levering the window guide channel forwards.

Rear:

Remove the trim panel and then release the locking pull rod (8 in **FIG 13:4**).

Release the inner door opener pushrod and the outer handle pull rod, then wind the window down so that its lower edge comes level with the upper edge of the door lock.

Remove the weatherstrip for the door frame, unscrew the retaining screws and lift off the door frame.

Remove the retaining screws on the rear edge of the door and lift out the door lock.

Outer handle, front:

Wind up the window to the fully closed position and remove the inner door handle and trim panel as already described. Then adjust the window so that the hole in the winding rail is opposite the foremost of the two screws (7 in **FIG 13:3**) and take out the screw.

Wind down the window to expose the rear screw 7 and take this out also. Unhook the return spring 8 and lift out the handle and cover together.

Refit in the reverse order and if necessary adjust the length of the pull rod 9 to obtain correct operation.

Outer handle, rear:

Close the window and remove the inner handle and trim panel. Unhook the return spring 7.

Take out the two screws 6 securing the cover and lift out the handle and cover together.

When refitting, first place the handle in position and locate the pull rod 3 in the lifting arm, then fit the retaining screws 6.

Check now to see that there is a clearance at **A** of approximately .04 inch (1 mm) between the pull rod eyelet and the pin in the rock lever. Fit the return spring and check that the lock functions correctly before replacing the trim.

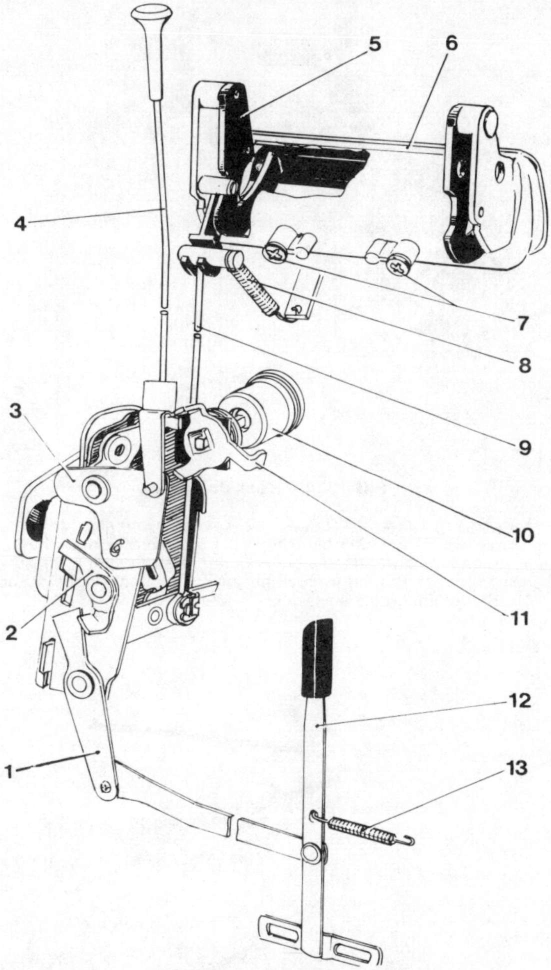

FIG 13:3 Front door lock

Key to Fig 13:3 1 Lever 2 Lever 3 Lever 4 Pull rod for lock button 5 Outer handle 6 Cover for outer handle 7 Screws for outer handle cover 8 Return spring for outer handle 9 Pull rod for outer handle 10 Lock cylinder 11 Lock device 12 Inner door opener 13 Return spring for inner door opener

13:4 Window winding mechanism

The door frame must first be removed by winding the window down and removing the trim panel. Unscrew the screws for the bracket of the lower mounting of the front guide channel and remove.

Remove the sealing strip running round the door frame, then take out the attaching screw on the front and rear edge and lift the door frame straight up and away.

Remove the window guide roller from the upper edge of the door panel and then remove the locking springs and washers between the slide rail and the lifting arms. These springs can best be removed by pressing them right in and then releasing them and pulling off. Take great care at this point that the window glass does not fall down in the door as it can easily be damaged during this operation.

Withdraw the window from the pins in the winder and then lift it straight up and out.

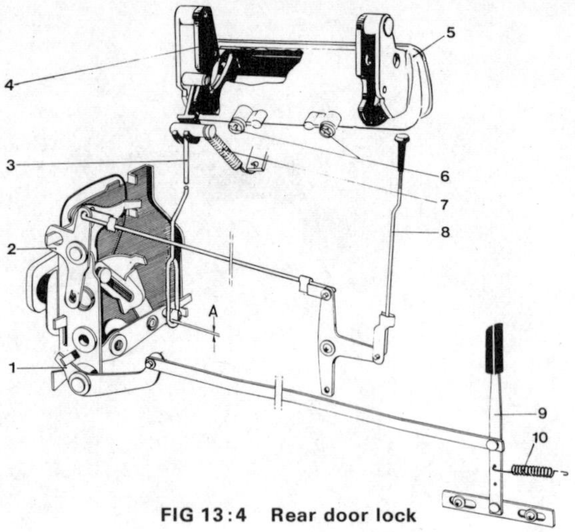

FIG 13:4 Rear door lock

Key to Fig 13:4 1 Lever 2 Lever 3 Pullrod for outer handle 4 Outer handle 5 Cover for outer handle 6 Screws for outer handle cover 7 Return spring for outer handle 8 Pullrod for lock button 9 Inner door opener 10 Return spring for inner door opener

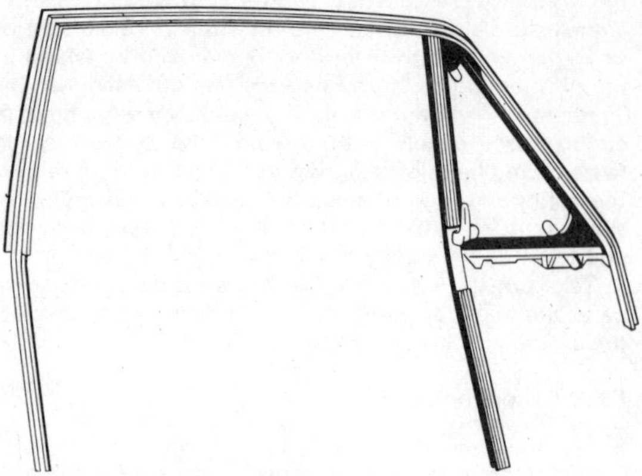

FIG 13:5 The door frame

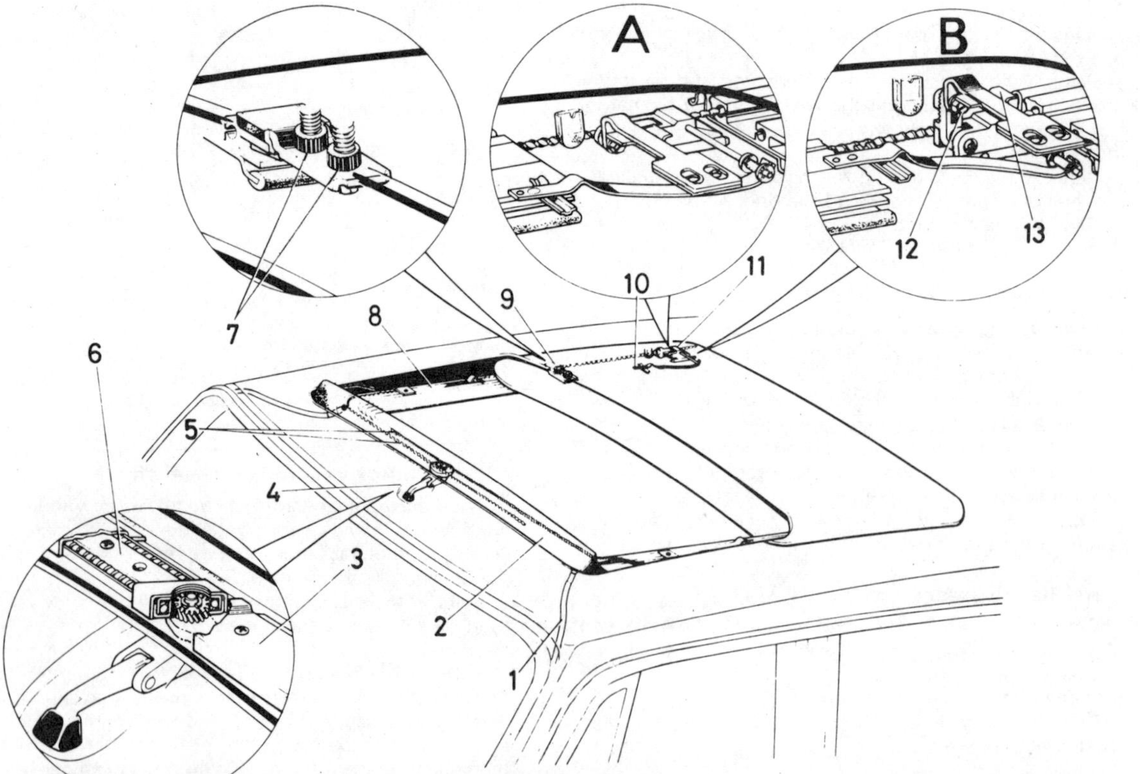

FIG 13:6 The sun roof

Key to Fig 13:6 **A** Rear attachment when roof is open **B** Rear attachment when roof is closed 1 Drain hose 2 Wind deflector 3 Covering strip 4 Crank housing with crank 5 Cables 6 Front guide rail 7 Front adjustment 8 Intermediate piece 9 Front attachment 10 Blade spring 11 Rear attachment 12 Rear adjustment 13 Reinforcing plate

Ventilation windows:

First remove the door frame as described above, then remove the grooved strip from the front channel of the winding window and undo the screws holding the plate under the ventilation window. Undo the screws on the opposite side and remove the plate.

When the rubber strip has been eased out of its groove all round the ventilation window the window can be taken out (see **FIG 13:5**).

13:5 The sun roof

This is shown in **FIG 13:6**, and normally requires no attention other than a little lubrication on the moving parts. After a long period of use it may be necessary to replace the operating cables and the sealing strips.

Removing the cables:

Open the sun roof and release the clips securing the front end of the roof upholstery. Push the fabric back to leave an opening.

Crank the roof forwards and slacken the screws at the four attachments 9 and 11, bend the blade springs 10 to one side and remove the reinforcing plates 13 at the rear attachment points. Lift off the roof.

Remove the wind deflector 2. Remove the intermediate pieces 8, covering strip 3 and the holders above the drive. Release the front guide rails 6 and pull out the cables 5.

Fitting cables:

First fit the cables so that the sun roof attachments come opposite each other and at the rear end of the roof opening. Screw the front guide rails firmly in place.

Fit the intermediate pieces, holders and covering strip. Refit the wind deflector.

Screw the roof on securely and replace the leaf springs.

Wind the roof forwards to the fully closed position and check that it is level with the car roof panels. If vertical adjustment is necessary, this is done by means of the adjusters at the front and rear attachments. Note that the lifting devices should be vertical when the roof is closed.

Unscrew the crank and gear housing 4 and turn the crank to the stop position while the gear housing is removed. Refit, and note that the crank should now be towards the front of the car with the sun roof completely closed.

Replace the fabric trim and check the operation of the roof.

Sealing strips:

The sun roof must be removed in order to replace the insulating and sealing strips attached to it, but the insulating strip around the roof opening can be replaced simply by cranking the sun roof back to its fully open position.

13:6 The windscreen

Before commencing to remove a windscreen or the remains of a broken screen, always place a covering sheet over the bonnet (hood) and the driving compartment of the car, particularly the ventilation apertures, to avoid damage from pieces of glass or other items which may cause scratches in the course of the operation. Remove the wiper arms.

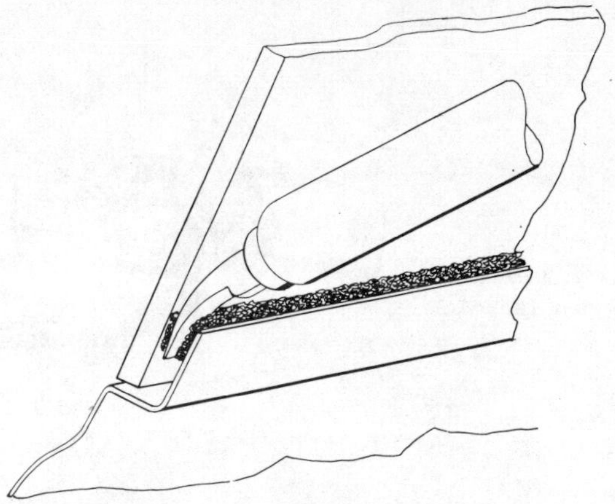

FIG 13:7 Removing the windscreen

The moulding round the windscreen is removed by inserting a steel putty knife between the glass and the moulding and levering free from the retaining clips.

Unscrew the inner covering strips and rear-view mirror.

Cut the glass loose with a warm soldering iron (see **FIG 13:7**). Insert the point of the iron between the glass and the body from inside the car and move the soldering iron all round the screen to cut the sealing strip. The glass can now be pushed out by hand and any remaining sealer cut off with a knife. Clean all traces of jointing from the body and replace any defective clips after injecting sealing compound into the holes.

Fitting a windscreen:

Having cleaned both surfaces where the jointing tape is to lie with methyl-acetate, coat the clips with sealer 686275 to form a smooth surface for the butyl tape to cover.

Spread the adhesive on the clean surfaces of the glass and body about $\frac{3}{4}$ inch (20 mm) wide measured from the outer edge. Two coats may be given to ensure complete coverage.

Fit the two spacers on the lower edge of the opening between the second and third clip from each corner pillar.

Apply the butyl tape between 10 and 60 minutes after applying the adhesive. Roll the tape round the entire opening, with the protective paper on, making the joint opposite one of the screen pillars and cutting the two ends at an angle. Remove the protective paper immediately before fitting the glass.

Two men are required with a glass lifter for fitting the windscreen, and as very little adjusting can be done, it should be very carefully fitted in the opening before being pressed against the tape. Do not allow the glass to lie against a clip.

Press the glass into position with its outer surface 1 ± 1.5 mm ($.04 \pm .06$ inch) from the outer edge of the body. Any tape squeezed beyond the edge of the glass on the inside can be cut off with a warm knife.

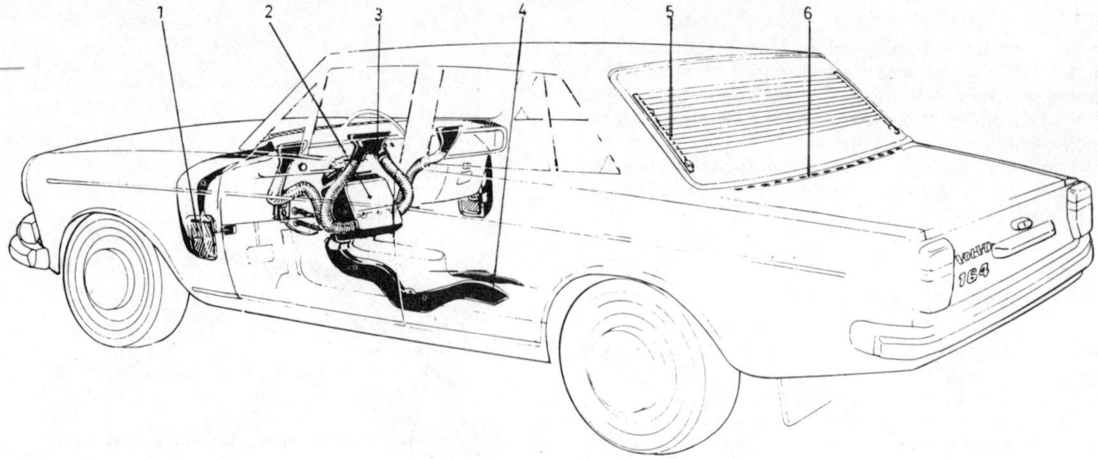

FIG 13:8 The heater system

Key to Fig 13:8 1 Fresh air intake 2 Car heater 3 Windshield defroster 4 Air ducting to rear seat area 5 Electrically heated rear window 6 Air extractor vents

Fit the moulding by pressing it between the body frame and the clips as follows: Fit the lower moulding with a corner joint on and then a side moulding also with a corner on. Finally fit the remaining moulding together with corners on to the body frame.

Fit the inner cover strips and rear view mirror. Fit the windscreen wiper arms.

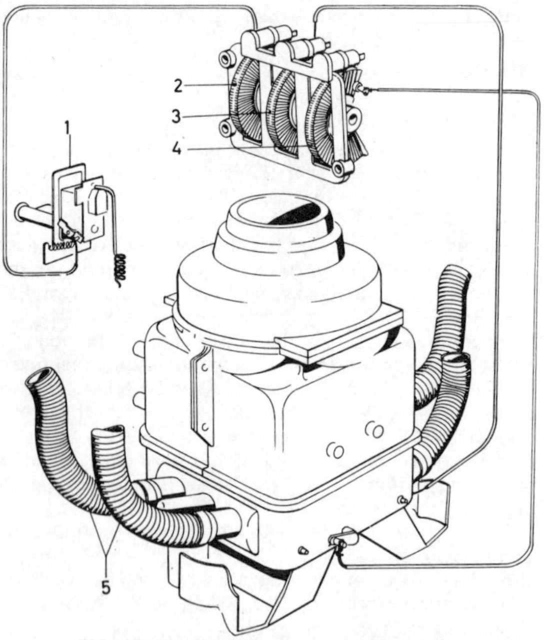

FIG 13:9 The heater unit and controls

Key to Fig 13:9 1 Heat control valve 2 Heater control 3 Defroster control 4 Heater control, floor 5 Hoses to defroster nozzles

The rear window and quarterlights:

These are held in shaped rubber mounting strips which are accessible after removing the metal mouldings. The rubber strip can be released by running a putty knife moistened in synthetic washing solution round the edges.

Before fitting a new glass make sure that all traces of sealant are removed, or for best results fit a new rubber strip.

13:7 The heating system

This provides a combination of fresh and heated air which can be directed to the desired area of the car interior by means of various controls after passing through the cellular system of the heater unit. Ventilation is further improved by air extractor vents at the base of the rear window.

The temperature of the heated air is regulated by means of a heat control valve which is designed to maintain the heated air at a predetermined and constant temperature by means of a built-in thermostat.

The heated rear window, rated at 150-watt, is controlled by a switch on the dashboard through a relay (see Wiring Diagram) which cuts off the supply when the ignition is switched off. The layout of the heating system is shown in **FIG 13:8**.

Removing heater unit:

Drain the cooling system and disconnect the battery. Remove the hoses to the control valve (see **FIG 13:9**).

Remove the panel below the dashboard by undoing two screws one on the left cowl side and the other beside the glove box. Pull the upper part of the panel to the rear to free it from the clips in the dashboard and free the panel from the bonnet release control. Remove the mat on the transmission tunnel. Remove the defroster and control wires, the switch for the fan and disconnect the cable to the fan motor.

Remove the two screws holding the fuse box to the heater, take out the control valve and loosen the upper hose to the heater unit. Care must be taken not to damage the control valve and the fine copper tube to the heater unit.

Plug the water outlets on the heater, release the earthing cables from the righthand bracket and the draining hose, then remove the four securing screws and carefully lift out the heater and control valve.

The heater unit is refitted by reversing the removal procedure.

Heater controls:

These may be seen in **FIG 13:9** and the control unit is attached to the dashboard with three nuts. To remove, first remove the panel below the dashboard and then release the wires on the heater unit and control valve.

The lamps for lighting the controls are removed by pulling them straight out of their holders. Remove the three retaining nuts and lift out the control unit.

APPENDIX

TECHNICAL DATA

(Dimensions are in inches unless otherwise stated)

ENGINE

Number of cylinders	6
Firing order	1–5–3–6–2–4
Bore	3.501 (88.92 mm)
Stroke	3.15 (80 mm)
Capacity	2980 cc
Weight with gearbox	530 lb (241 kg)
Type	B.30.A, B.30.E and B.30.F
Compression ratio	9.3:1, 10:1 and 8.7:1
Output (DIN) bhp at rev/min	130/5000, 160/5500 and 145/5500
Cylinder block material	Special alloy cast iron
Bore, standard	3.501 (88.92 mm)
oversize	3.531 (89.68 mm)
Pistons	
Material	Light-alloy
Weight	17.75 ±.18 oz
Permissible deviation	.35 oz
Height, total	2.79
Gudgeon pin to crown	1.81
Clearance	.0016 to .0024
Piston rings	
Number	2 compression, 1 scraper
Height, Compression	.078
Scraper	.186
Clearance in groove	.0016 to .0028
Gudgeon pin	
Type	Floating
Fit, in rod	Close-running fit
in piston	Push-fit
Diameter, standard	.866
oversize	.868
Crankshaft	
End float	.0019 to .0054
Main bearing clearance	.0011 to .0033
Big-end clearance	.0012 to .0028
Main journal diameter	2.4981 to 2.4986
undersizes	.01, .02
Big-end bearing diameter	2.1299 to 2.1304
undersizes	.01, .02
Flywheel	
Permissible runout	.002 at 5.9 diameter
Camshaft	
Identification	C
Number of bearings	4
Clearance	.0008 to .0030
End float	.0008 to .0024
Valve clearance for camshaft setting	.057 (cold)
Inlet valve then opens at	0 deg. TDC

Valves

Inlet

Head diameter B.30.A	1.654
B.30.E and B.30.F	1.732
Stem diameter	.3132 to .3138
Face angle	44.5 deg.
Seat angle	45 deg.
Clearance (hot and cold)	.020 to .022

Exhaust

Head diameter	1.378
Stem diameter	.3120 to .3126

Valve guides

Length inlet	2.047
exhaust	2.323
Bore	.320 to .321
Height	.689

Valve springs

Unloaded length B.30.A	1.77
At 145 lb	1.20
Unloaded length B.30.E and B.30.F	1.81
At 180 lb	1.18

FUEL SYSTEM

B.30.A

Carburetter

Type	Zenith/Stromberg 175CD-2SE (2)
Choke	1.63
Needle	BI BE
CO test	2.5 per cent
Idling speed	800 rev/min synrhomesh 700 rev/min Automatic

B.30.E and B.30.F

Fuel injection

Type	Bosch electronic

COOLING SYSTEM

Type	Sealed
Capacity	12.4 litres (11 Imp. pint)
Thermostat, type	Wax
identification	82 deg.
begins to open at	177 to 182°F (81 to 83°C)
fully open at	914°F (90°C)
Radiator cap pressure	10 lb/sq inch

IGNITION SYSTEM

B.30.A

Timing at 600 to 800 rev/min	10 deg. BTDC
Distributor, type	Bosch JFUR6
direction	Anticlockwise
Plugs, type	Bosch W200.T.35
gap	.028 to .032

B.30.E, B.30.F

Timing at 600 to 800 rev/min	10 deg. BTDC
Distributor, type	Bosch JFURX6
Plugs type,	225.T.35 (B.30.E) 200.T.35 (B.30.F)

CLUTCH

Type	Diaphragm, single dry plate
Diameter B.30.A	9
B.30.E and B.30.F	$9\frac{1}{2}$
Release lever play	.08 to .12 (right steer)
	.16 to .20 (left steer)

GEARBOXES

Ratios	
1st	3.54:1
2nd	2.12:1
3rd	1.34:1
4th	1:1
Reverse	3.54:1
Overdrive	.797:1
Lubricant	Engine oil SAE.30 or 20W40
Capacity	1.1 pints (.6 litres)
Capacity with overdrive	2.5 pints (1.4 litres)
Automatic transmission	
Type	Borg-Warner 35
Identification B.30.A	323
B.30.E and B.30.F	319
Normal stall speed B.30.A	2100 rev/min
B.30.E	2300 rev/min
B.30.F	2200 rev/min
Fluid type	Automatic transmission fluid F
Capacity	14 pints (8.2 litres)

FRONT SUSPENSION

Type	Helical spring
Turns	6.5
Dampers	Double-acting hydraulic telescopic
Length free	13.39

REAR SUSPENSION

Type	Helical spring
Turns	8.9
Dampers	Double-acting hydraulic telescopic
Length free	17.44

STEERING

Type	ZF, ball and nut with servo or Burman, cam and ball nut, manual
Castor angle	0 to +1 deg.
Camber angle	0 to +.5 deg.
Kingpin inclination	7.5 deg.
Toe-in, early cars	0 to .16
later cars	.08 to .20
Oil type	ATF type A
Capacity	2.1 pints (1.2 litre)

BRAKING SYSTEM

Type	Hydraulic, disc front and rear
Disc diameter, front	10.7
rear	11.6
runout	.004 maximum
Parking brake	Drum at rear, cable operated
Diameter	7.0
Radial throw	.006 maximum
Out of round	.008 maximum

ELECTRICAL SYSTEM

Battery	
Type	Tudor 6.ex.4F
Polarity	Negative earth
Voltage	12-volt
Capacity	60.AL
Alternator	
Type	SEV Motorola 14-volt 26642 or 14-volt 34833
Output	420-watt or 770-watt
Brushes minimum length	.20
Regulator type	SEV Motorola 14-volt 33544
Starter motor	
Type	Bosch GF.12V.1.PS
Direction	Clockwise
Rotor end float	.002 to .012
Pinion to ring gear	.047 to .173

TORQUE WRENCH SETTINGS

Values are in lb ft unless otherwise stated

Cylinder head	65
Main bearing	87 to 94
Big-end bearings	38 to 42
Flywheel	36 to 40
Camshaft nut	94 to 108
Crankshaft pulley bolt	51 to 58
Oil filter nipple	32 to 40
Sump bolts	6 to 8
Manifold nuts	13 to 16
Alternator bolt ($\frac{1}{2}$ inch)	50 to 60
Torque converter drive plate	25 to 30
Converter housing	8 to 13
Oil fan	8 to 13
Centre support	10 to 18
Pressure joint	4 to 5
Pump strainer	1.7 to 2.5
Brakeband adjustment	30 to 40
Inhibitor switch locknut	4 to 6
Coupling flange	35 to 50
Oil cooler connection	5 to 7
Propeller shaft flange	200 to 220
Upper control arm shaft	40 to 50
Pitman arm nut	125 to 145
Tie rod locknut	55 to 65
Caliper mounting front	65 to 70
Caliper mounting rear	45 to 50
Wheel nuts	70 to 100
Brake hoses	12 to 15
Brake pipes	8 to 11

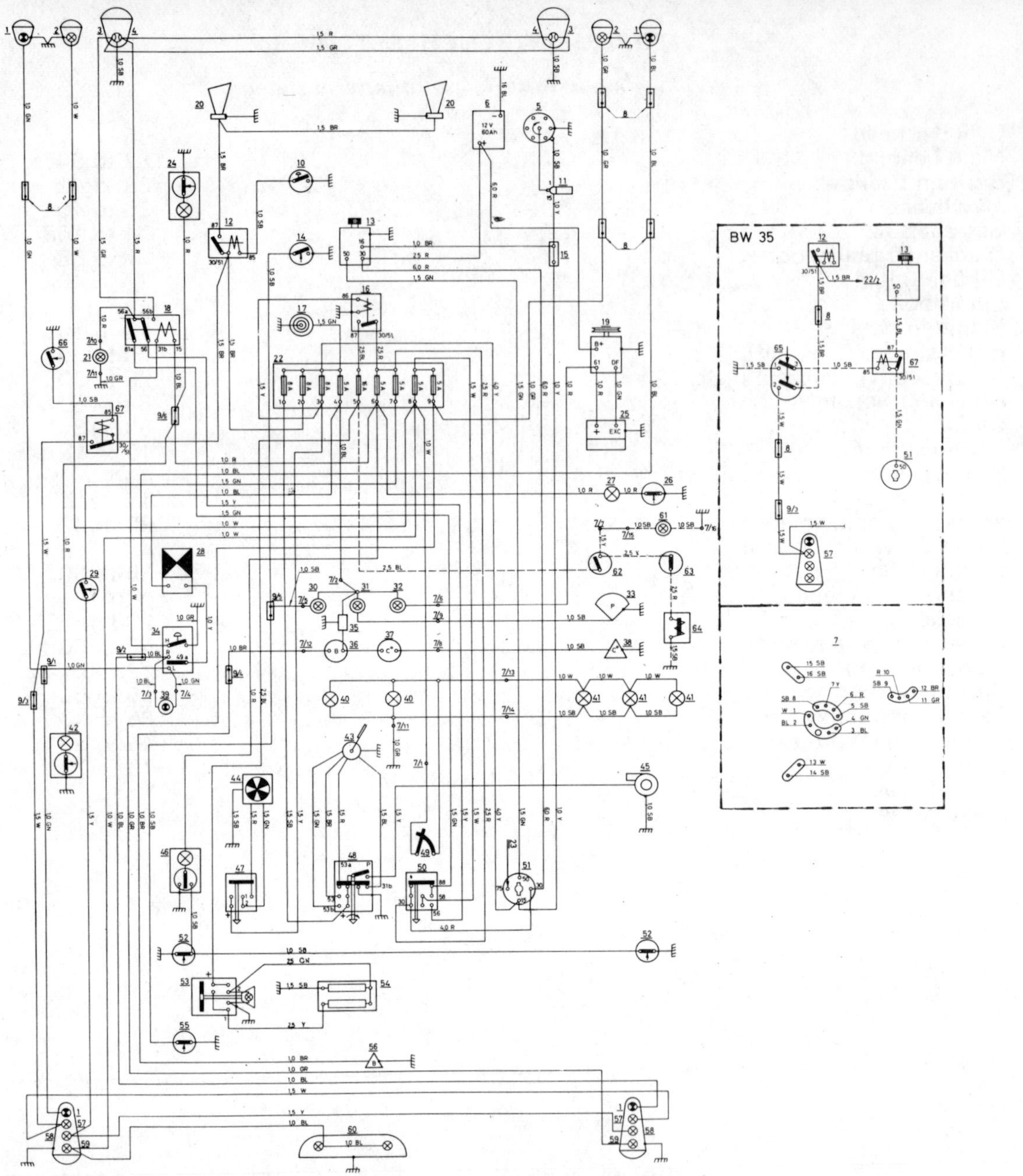

FIG 14:1 Wiring diagram for Volvo 164 (1968-70)

Key to Fig 14:1 1 Direction indicator flashers 2 Parking light 3 Headlight dipped beam 4 Headlight main beam 5 Distributor firing order 6 Battery 7 Conn. at instrument 8 Junction 9 Part of 6-pole conn. unit 10 Horn ring 11 Ignition coil 12 Relay for horn 13 Starter motor 14 Brake warning contact 15 Resistor 16 Relay for heated rear window 17 Cigarette lighter 18 Dipper relay for main and dipped beams and headlight flasher 19 AC generator 20 Horn 21 Mainbeam control lamp 22 Fusebox 23 Radio connection 24 Engine comp. lighting 25 Charging control unit 26 Switch glove comp. lighting 27 Glove compartment lighting 28 Flasher unit 29 Brake contact 30 Brake control lamp 31 Oil pressure control lamp 32 Charging control lamp 33 Oil pressure tell-tale 34 Switch for headlight signalling and flashers 35 Voltage regulator 36 Fuel gauge 37 Temperature gauge 38 Temperature gauge sensitive head 39 Flashers control lamp 40 Instrument lighting 41 Heater control lighting 42 Luggage comp. light 43 Windscreen wipers 44 Heater 45 Windscreen washers 46 Interior lamp 46 Interior lamp 47 Switch for heater 48 Switch for windscreen wipers and washer 49 Instrument lighting rheostat 50 Light switch 51 Ignition switch 52 Door contact 53. Switch heat, rear window 54 Heated rear window 55 Switch for handbrake control 56 Fuel gauge tank unit 57 Reversing light 58 Brake stoplight 59 Tail light 60 Number plate lighting 61 Overdrive control lamp 62 Switch for overdrive 63 Switch for overdrive on gearbox 64 Solenoid for overdrive 65 Switch on gearbox BM 35 66 Switch for reversing light only for M400 and M410 67 Relay for reversing light on M400, M410 and starter relay on BW 35

Key to Cable Colour Code: **SB**=Black **W**=White **Y**=Yellow **GN**=Green **GR**=Grey **BL**=Blue **R**=Red **BR**=Brown

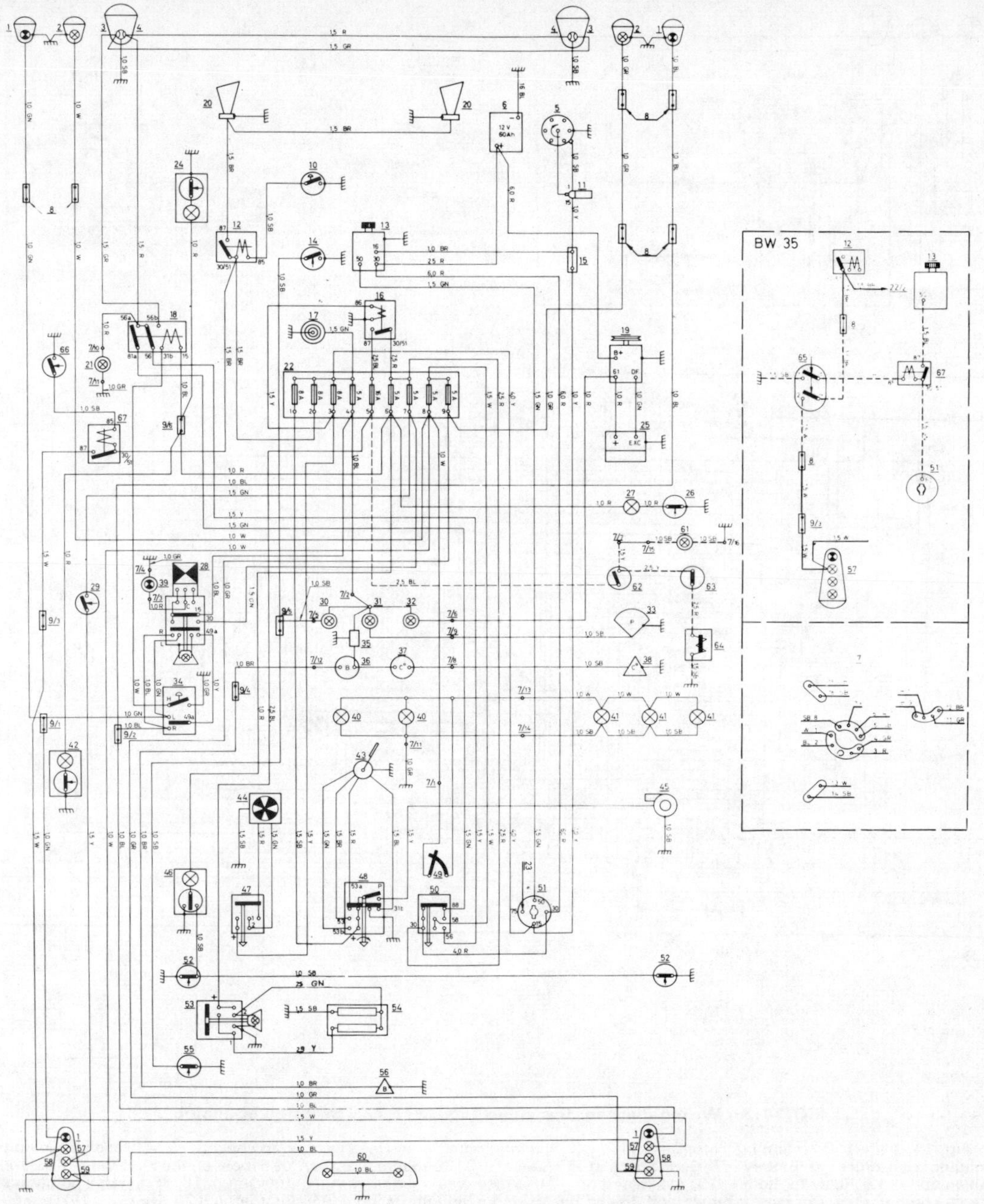

FIG 14 : 2   **Wiring diagram for Volvo 164 (1968-70) USA**

Key to Fig 14 : 2   1 Direction indicator flashers   2 Parking light   3 Headlight dipped beam   4 Headlight main beam   5 Distributor firing order   6 Battery   7 Connection at junction   8 Junction   9 Part of 6-pole connection unit   10 Horn ring   11 Ignition coil   12 Relay for horn   13 Starter motor   14 Caution contact   15 Resistor   16 Relay for heated rear window   17 Cigarette lighter   18 Dipper relay for main and dipped beams and headlight flasher   19 AC generator   20 Horn   21 Main beam control lamp   22 Fusebox   23 Radio connection   24 Engine compartment lighting   25 Charging control unit   26 Switch glove compartment lighting   27 Glove compartment lighting   28 Warning flashers   29 Brake contact   30 Brake control lamp   31 Oil pressure control lamp   32 Charging control lamp   33 Oil pressure telltale   34 Switch for headlight/signalling and flashers   35 Voltage regulator   36 Fuel gauge   37 Temperature gauge   38 Temperature gauge sensitive head   39 Flashers control lamp   40 Instrument lighting   41 Heater control lighting   42 Luggage compartment light   43 Windscreen wipers   44 Heater   45 Windscreen washers   46 Interior lamp   47 Switch for heater   48 Switch for windscreen wipers and washer   48 Instrument lighting rheostat   50 Light switch   51 Ignition switch   52 Door contact   53 Switch heat, rear window   54 Heated rear window   55 Switch for handbrake control   56 Fuel gauge tank unit   57 Reversing light   58 Brake stoplight   59 Tail light   60 Number plate lighting   61 Overdrive control lamp   62 Switch for overdrive   63 Switch for overdrive on gearbox   64 Solenoid for overdrive   65 Switch on gearbox BW.35   66 Switch for reversing light only for M.400 and M.410   67 Relay for reversing light on M.400, M.410 and starter relay on BW.35

Key to Cable Colour Code: **SB**=Black   **W**=White   **Y**=Yellow   **GN**=Green   **GR**=Grey   **BL**=Blue   **R** Red   **BR**=Brown

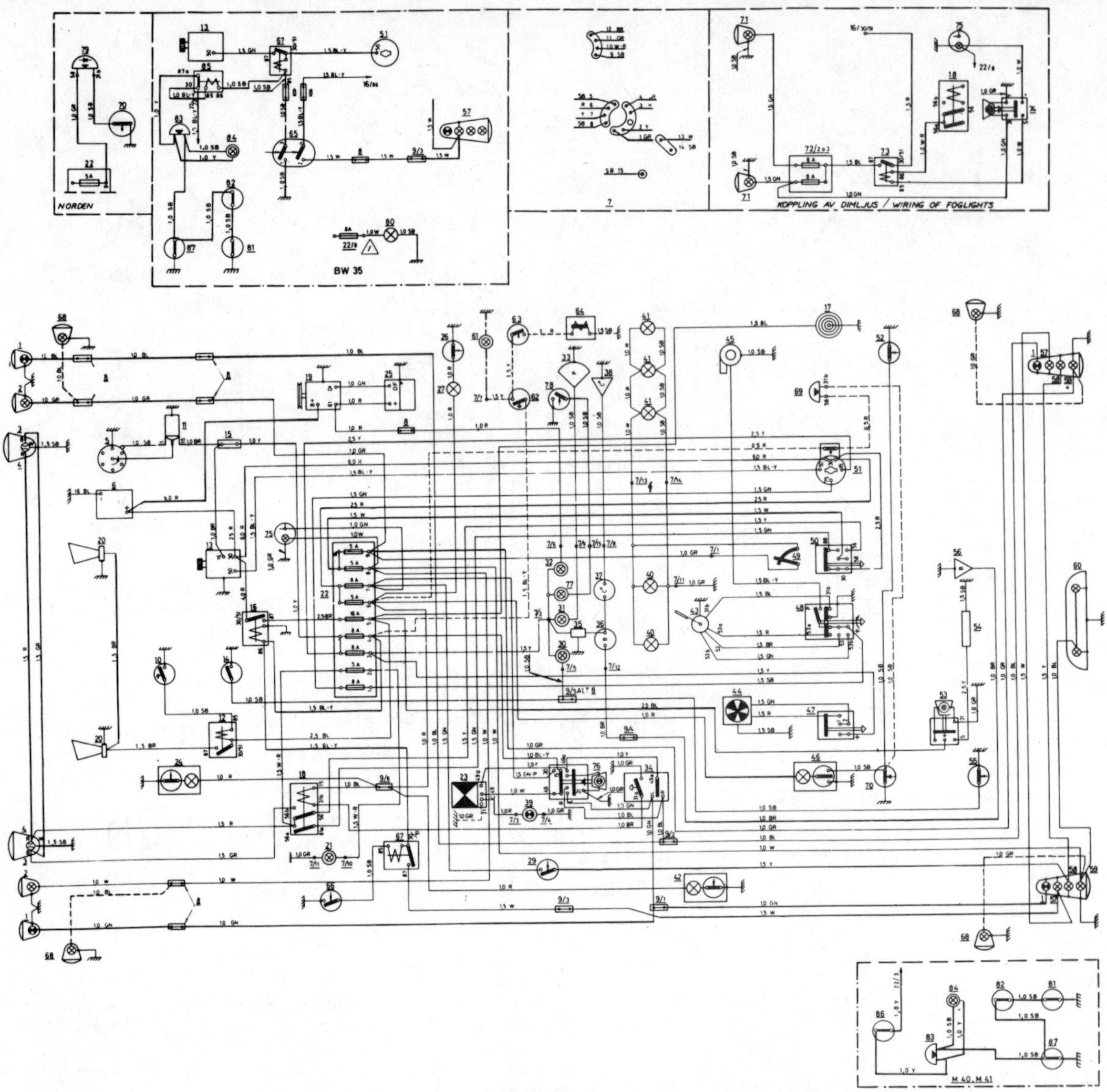

FIG 14:3 Wiring diagram for Volvo 164 (1971-72), carburetter engine

Key to Fig 14:3 1 Direction indicator flashers 2 Parking lights 3 Headlight dipped beams 4 Headlight main beams 5 Distributor firing order 6 Battery 7 Connection at instrument 8 Connector 9 Part of 6-pole connection unit 10 Horn ring 11 Ignition coil 12 Relay for horn 13 Starter motor 14 Brake warning switch 15 Resistor 16 Main relay, ignition switch 17 Cigarette lighter 18 Dip relay for main and dipped beams and headlight flasher 19 Alternator 20 Horn 21 Warning lamp for main beams 22 Fusebox 23 Flasher unit 24 Engine compartment light 25 Charging regulator 26 Contact, glove compartment light 27 Glove compartment light 29 Brake contact 30 Brake warning lamp 31 Oil pressure warning lamp 32 Battery charging warning lmap 33 Oil pressure switch 34 Switch for direction indicator and headlight flashers 35 Voltage stabilizer 36 Fuel gauge 37 Temperature gauge 38 Temperature gauge sensor 39 Flashers, warning lamp 40 Instrument panel light 41 Heater control light 42 Luggage compartment light 43 Windshield wipers 44 Heater 45 Windshield washer 46 Interior lamp 47 Switch for heater 48 Switch for windshield wipers and washer 49 Rheostat, instrument panel light 50 Light switch 51 Ignition switch 52 Door switch 53 Switch, electric heated rear window 54 Electric heated rear window 55 Switch for parking brake control 56 Fuel gauge tank unit 57 Reverse lights 58 Brake stoplights 59 Tail lights 60 License plate light 61 Overdrive warning lamp 62 Switch for overdrive 63 Switch, overdrive on gearbox 64 Solenoid for overdrive 65 Contact on transmission BW.35 66 Contact for reverse lights (M.400 and M.410 only) 67 Relay for reverse lights on M.400, M.410 and starter relay on BW.35 68 Side marker lights 69 Warning buzzer, ignition key 70 Door switch on driving side 71 Foglights 72 Fusebox for foglights 73 Relay for foglights 74 Switch for foglights 75 Clock 76 Switch for emergency warning flashers 77 Choke warning lamp 78 Choke contact 79 Warning buzzer, lights 80 Shift positions light, automatic ransmission 81 Contact, seat buckle passenger 82 Contact, passenger seat 83 Warning buzzer, safety belts 84 Warning lamp, safety belts 85 Relay, safety belts 86 Contact, gearbox M.41 87 Contact, seat buckle driver

Key to Cable Colour Code: **GN-R**=Green-red **SB**=Black **W**=White **Y**=Yellow **GN**=Green **GR**=Grey **BL**=Blue **R**=Red **BR**=Brown **BL-Y**=Blue-yellow **W-R**=White-red

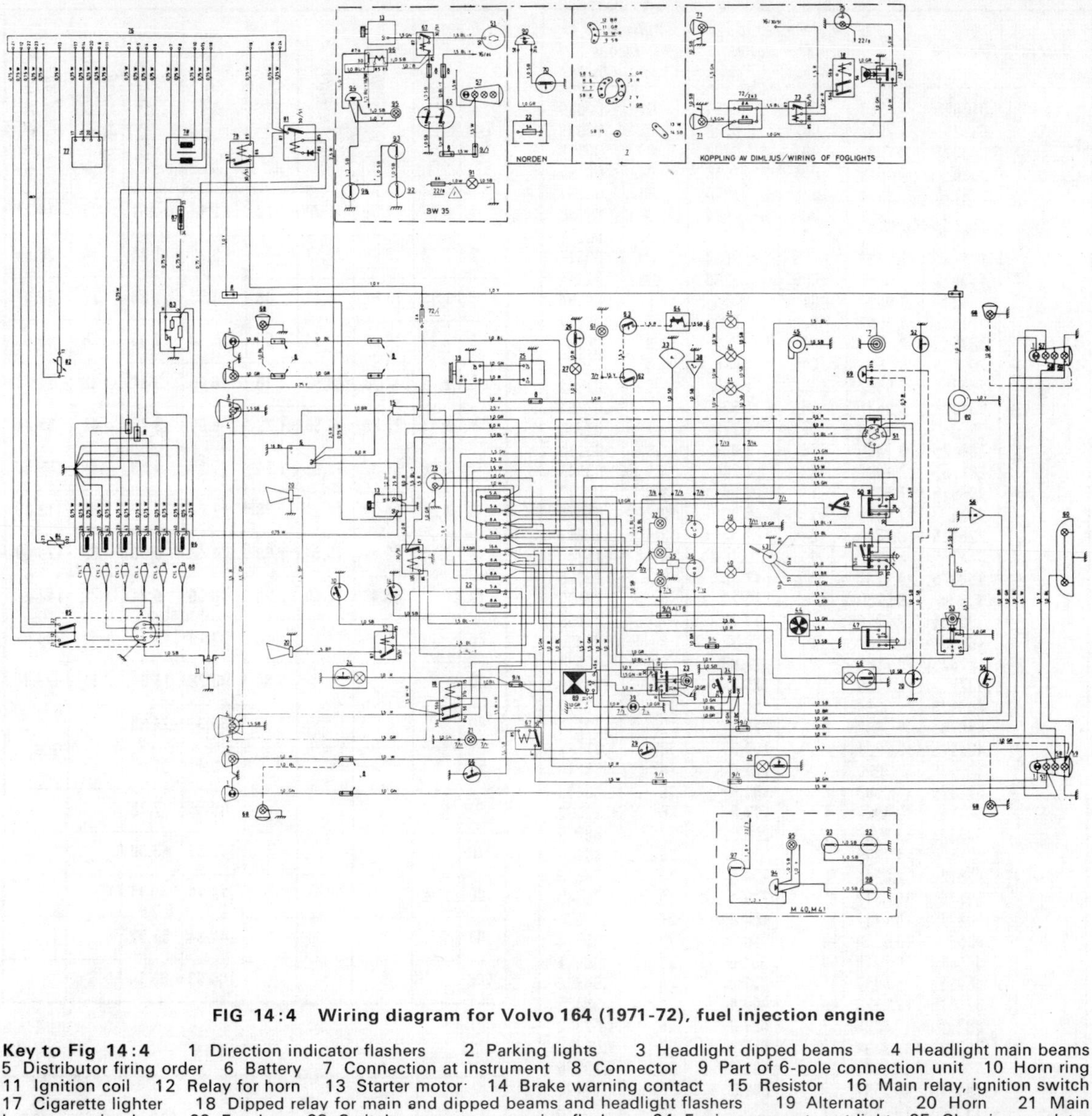

FIG 14:4 Wiring diagram for Volvo 164 (1971-72), fuel injection engine

Key to Fig 14:4 1 Direction indicator flashers 2 Parking lights 3 Headlight dipped beams 4 Headlight main beams 5 Distributor firing order 6 Battery 7 Connection at instrument 8 Connector 9 Part of 6-pole connection unit 10 Horn ring 11 Ignition coil 12 Relay for horn 13 Starter motor 14 Brake warning contact 15 Resistor 16 Main relay, ignition switch 17 Cigarette lighter 18 Dipped relay for main and dipped beams and headlight flashers 19 Alternator 20 Horn 21 Main beams warning lamp 22 Fusebox 23 Switch, emergency warning flashers 24 Engine compartment light 25 Charging regulator 26 Switch, glove locker light 27 Glove light 29 Brake contact 30 Brake warning lamp 31 Oil pressure warning lamp 32 Battery charging warning lamp 33 Oil pressure sensor 34 Switch for direction indicator and headlight flashers 35 Voltage stabilizer 36 Fuel gauge 37 Temperature gauge 38 Temperature gauge sensor 39 Flashers warning lamp 40 Instrument panel light 41 Heater control light 42 Luggage compartment light 43 Windshield wipers 44 Heater 45 Windshield washer 46 Interior light 47 Switch for heater 48 Switch for windshield wipers and washer 49 Instrument panel light rheostat 50 Light switch 51 Ignition switch 52 Door contact 53 Switch, electric heated rear window 54 Electric heated rear window 55 Contact for parking brake warning lamp 56 Fuel gauge tank unit 57 Reversing lights 58 Brake stoplights 59 Tail lights 60 License plate light 61 Overdrive warning lamp 62 Switch for overdrive 63 Switch for overdrive on gearbox 64 Solenoid for overdrive 65 Contact on automatic transmission BW.35 66 Contact for reversing lights (M.400 and M.410 only) 67 Relay for reversing lights on M.400, M.410 and starter relay on BW.35 68 Side marker lights 69 Warning buzzer, ignition key 70 Door contact on driving seat side 71 Foglights 72 Fusebox 73 Relay for foglights 74 Switch for foglights 75 Clock 76 Electronic control unit 77 Throttle valve switch 78 Pressure sensor 79 Relay for fuel pump 80 Fuel pump 81 Main relay for fuel injection 82 Temperature sensor 1 83 Thermal timer contact 84 Temperature sensor 2 85 Triggering contacts 86 Injection valves 87 Cold start valve 88 Spark plugs 89 Flasher unit 90 Warning buzzer, lights 91 Shift positions, light 92 Contact, seat buckle, passenger 93 Contact, passenger seat 94 Warning buzzer, safety belts 95 Warning lamp, safety belts 96 Relay, safety belts 97 Contact, gearbox M.41 98 Contact, seat buckle, driver

Key to Cable Colour Code: **SB**=Black **W**=White **Y**=Yellow **GN**=Green **GR**=Grey **BL**=Blue **R**=Red **BR**=Brown **BL-Y**=Blue-yellow **R-W**=Red-white

Inches	Decimals	Millimetres	Inches to Millimetres: Inches	Inches to Millimetres: mm	Millimetres to Inches: mm	Millimetres to Inches: Inches
1/64	.015625	.3969	.001	.0254	.01	.00039
1/32	.03125	.7937	.002	.0508	.02	.00079
3/64	.046875	1.1906	.003	.0762	.03	.00118
1/16	.0625	1.5875	.004	.1016	.04	.00157
5/64	.078125	1.9844	.005	.1270	.05	.00197
3/32	.09375	2.3812	.006	.1524	.06	.00236
7/64	.109375	2.7781	.007	.1778	.07	.00276
1/8	.125	3.1750	.008	.2032	.08	.00315
9/64	.140625	3.5719	.009	.2286	.09	.00354
5/32	.15625	3.9687	.01	.254	.1	.00394
11/64	.171875	4.3656	.02	.508	.2	.00787
3/16	.1875	4.7625	.03	.762	.3	.01181
13/64	.203125	5·1594	.04	1.016	.4	.01575
7/32	.21875	5.5562	.05	1.270	.5	.01969
15/64	.234375	5.9531	.06	1.524	.6	.02362
1/4	.25	6.3500	.07	1.778	.7	.02756
17/64	.265625	6.7469	.08	2.032	.8	.03150
9/32	.28125	7.1437	.09	2.286	.9	.03543
19/64	.296875	7.5406	.1	2.54	1	.03937
5/16	.3125	7.9375	.2	5.08	2	.07874
21/64	.328125	8.3344	.3	7.62	3	.11811
11/32	.34375	8.7312	.4	10.16	4	.15748
23/64	.359375	9.1281	.5	12.70	5	.19685
3/8	.375	9.5250	.6	15.24	6	.23622
25/64	.390625	9.9219	.7	17.78	7	.27559
13/32	.40625	10.3187	.8	20.32	8	.31496
27/64	.421875	10.7156	.9	22.86	9	.35433
7/16	.4375	11.1125	1	25.4	10	.39370
29/64	.453125	11.5094	2	50.8	11	.43307
15/32	.46875	11.9062	3	76.2	12	.47244
31/64	.484375	12.3031	4	101.6	13	.51181
1/2	.5	12.7000	5	127.0	14	.55118
33/64	.515625	13.0969	6	152.4	15	.59055
17/32	.53125	13.4937	7	177.8	16	.62992
35/64	.546875	13.8906	8	203.2	17	.66929
9/16	.5625	14.2875	9	228.6	18	.70866
37/64	.578125	14.6844	10	254.0	19	.74803
19/32	.59375	15.0812	11	279.4	20	.78740
39/64	.609375	15.4781	12	304.8	21	.82677
5/8	.625	15.8750	13	330.2	22	.86614
41/64	.640625	16.2719	14	355.6	23	.90551
21/32	.65625	16.6687	15	381.0	24	.94488
43/64	.671875	17.0656	16	406.4	25	.98425
11/16	.6875	17.4625	17	431.8	26	1.02362
45/64	.703125	17.8594	18	457.2	27	1.06299
23/32	.71875	18.2562	19	482.6	28	1.10236
47/64	.734375	18.6531	20	508.0	29	1.14173
3/4	.75	19.0500	21	533.4	30	1.18110
49/64	.765625	19.4469	22	558.8	31	1.22047
25/32	.78125	19.8437	23	584.2	32	1.25984
51/64	.796875	20.2406	24	609.6	33	1.29921
13/16	.8125	20.6375	25	635.0	34	1.33858
53/64	.828125	21.0344	26	660.4	35	1.37795
27/32	.84375	21.4312	27	685.8	36	1.41732
55/64	.859375	21.8281	28	711.2	37	1.4567
7/8	.875	22.2250	29	736.6	38	1.4961
57/64	.890625	22.6219	30	762.0	39	1.5354
29/32	.90625	23.0187	31	787.4	40	1.5748
59/64	.921875	23.4156	32	812.8	41	1.6142
15/16	.9375	23.8125	33	838.2	42	1.6535
61/64	.953125	24.2094	34	863.6	43	1.6929
31/32	.96875	24.6062	35	889.0	44	1.7323
63/64	.984375	25.0031	36	914.4	45	1.7717

UNITS	Pints to Litres	Gallons to Litres	Litres to Pints	Litres to Gallons	Miles to Kilometres	Kilometres to Miles	Lbs. per sq. In. to Kg. per sq. Cm.	Kg. per sq. Cm. to Lbs. per sq. In.
1	.57	4.55	1.76	.22	1.61	.62	.07	14.22
2	1.14	9.09	3.52	.44	3.22	1.24	.14	28.50
3	1.70	13.64	5.28	.66	4.83	1.86	.21	42.67
4	2.27	18.18	7.04	.88	6.44	2.49	.28	56.89
5	2.84	22.73	8.80	1.10	8.05	3.11	.35	71.12
6	3.41	27.28	10.56	1.32	9.66	3.73	.42	85.34
7	3.98	31.82	12.32	1.54	11.27	4.35	.49	99.56
8	4.55	36.37	14.08	1.76	12.88	4.97	.56	113.79
9		40.91	15.84	1.98	14.48	5.59	.63	128.00
10		45.46	17.60	2.20	16.09	6.21	.70	142.23
20				4.40	32.19	12.43	1.41	284.47
30				6.60	48.28	18.64	2.11	426.70
40				8.80	64.37	24.85		
50					80,47	31.07		
60					96.56	37.28		
70					112.65	43.50		
80					128.75	49.71		
90					144.84	55.92		
100					160.93	62.14		

UNITS	Lb ft to kgm	Kgm to lb ft	UNITS	Lb ft to kgm	Kgm to lb ft
1	.138	7.233	7	.967	50.631
2	.276	14.466	8	1.106	57.864
3	.414	21.699	9	1.244	65.097
4	.553	28.932	10	1.382	72.330
5	.691	36.165	20	2.765	144.660
6	.829	43.398	30	4.147	216.990

HINTS ON MAINTENANCE AND OVERHAUL

There are few things more rewarding than the restoration of a vehicle's original peak of efficiency and smooth performance.

The following notes are intended to help the owner to reach that state of perfection. Providing that he possesses the basic manual skills he should have no difficulty in performing most of the operations detailed in this manual. It must be stressed, however, that where recommended in the manual, highly-skilled operations ought to be entrusted to experts, who have the necessary equipment, to carry out the work satisfactorily.

Quality of workmanship:

The hazardous driving conditions on the roads to-day demand that vehicles should be as nearly perfect, mechanically, as possible. It is therefore most important that amateur work be carried out with care, bearing in mind the often inadequate working conditions, and also the inferior tools which may have to be used. It is easy to counsel perfection in all things, and we recognize that it may be setting an impossibly high standard. We do, however, suggest that every care should be taken to ensure that a vehicle is as safe to take on the road as it is humanly possible to make it.

Safe working conditions:

Even though a vehicle may be stationary, it is still potentially dangerous if certain sensible precautions are not taken when working on it while it is supported on jacks or blocks. It is indeed preferable not to use jacks alone, but to supplement them with carefully placed blocks, so that there will be plenty of support if the car rolls off the jacks during a strenuous manoeuvre. Axle stands are an excellent way of providing a rigid base which is not readily disturbed. Piles of bricks are a dangerous substitute. Be careful not to get under heavy loads on lifting tackle, the load could fall. It is preferable not to work alone when lifting an engine, or when working underneath a vehicle which is supported well off the ground. To be trapped, particularly under the vehicle, may have unpleasant results if help is not quickly forthcoming. Make some provision, however humble, to deal with fires. Always disconnect a battery if there is a likelihood of electrical shorts. These may start a fire if there is leaking fuel about. This applies particularly to leads which can carry a heavy current, like those in the starter circuit. While on the subject of electricity, we must also stress the danger of using equipment which is run off the mains and which has no earth or has faulty wiring or connections. So many workshops have damp floors, and electrical shocks are of such a nature that it is sometimes impossible to let go of a live lead or piece of equipment due to the muscular spasms which take place.

Work demanding special care:

This involves the servicing of braking, steering and suspension systems. On the road, failure of the braking system may be disastrous. Make quite sure that there can be no possibility of failure through the bursting of rusty brake pipes or rotten hoses, nor to a sudden loss of pressure due to defective seals or valves.

Problems:

The chief problems which may face an operator are:

1 External dirt.
2 Difficulty in undoing tight fixings
3 Dismantling unfamiliar mechanisms.
4 Deciding in what respect parts are defective.
5 Confusion about the correct order for reassembly.
6 Adjusting running clearances.
7 Road testing.
8 Final tuning.

Practical suggestion to solve the problems:

1 Preliminary cleaning of large parts—engines, transmissions, steering, suspensions, etc.,—should be carried out before removal from the car. Where road dirt and mud alone are present, wash clean with a high-pressure water jet, brushing to remove stubborn adhesions, and allow to drain and dry. Where oil or grease is also present, wash down with a proprietary compound (Gunk, Teepol etc.,) applying with a stiff brush—an old paint brush is suitable—into all crevices. Cover the distributor and ignition coils with a polythene bag and then apply a strong water jet to clear the loosened deposits. Allow to drain and dry. The assemblies will then be sufficiently clean to remove and transfer to the bench for the next stage.

On the bench, further cleaning can be carried out, first wiping the parts as free as possible from grease with old newspaper. Avoid using rag or cotton waste which can leave clogging fibres behind. Any remaining grease can be removed with a brush dipped in paraffin. If necessary, traces of paraffin can be removed by carbon tetrachloride. Avoid using paraffin or petrol in large quantities for cleaning in enclosed areas, such as garages, on account of the high fire risk.

When all exteriors have been cleaned, and not before, dismantling can be commenced. This ensures that dirt will not enter into interiors and orifices revealed by dismantling. In the next phases, where components have to be cleaned, use carbon tetrachloride in preference to petrol and keep the containers covered except when in use. After the components have been cleaned, plug small holes with tapered hard wood plugs cut to size and blank off larger orifices with grease-proof paper and masking tape. Do not use soft wood plugs or matchsticks as they may break.

2 It is not advisable to hammer on the end of a screw thread, but if it must be done, first screw on a nut to protect the thread, and use a lead hammer. This applies particularly to the removal of tapered cotters. Nuts and bolts seem to 'grow' together, especially in exhaust systems. If penetrating oil does not work, try the judicious application of heat, but be careful of starting a fire. Asbestos sheet or cloth is useful to isolate heat.

Tight bushes or pieces of tail-pipe rusted into a silencer can be removed by splitting them with an open-ended hacksaw. Tight screws can sometimes be started by a tap from a hammer on the end of a suitable screwdriver. Many tight fittings will yield to the judicious use of a hammer, but it must be a soft-faced hammer if damage is to be avoided, use a heavy block on the opposite side to absorb shock. Any parts of the steering system which have been damaged should be renewed, as attempts to repair them may lead to cracking and subsequent failure, and steering ball joints should be disconnected using a recommended tool to prevent damage.

3 If often happens that an owner is baffled when trying to dismantle an unfamiliar piece of equipment. So many modern devices are pressed together or assembled by spinning-over flanges, that they must be sawn apart. The intention is that the whole assembly must be renewed. However, parts which appear to be in one piece to the naked eye, may reveal close-fitting joint lines when inspected with a magnifying glass, and, this may provide the necessary clue to dismantling. Left-handed screw threads are used where rotational forces would tend to unscrew a right handed screw thread.

Be very careful when dismantling mechanisms which may come apart suddenly. Work in an enclosed space where the parts will be contained, and drape a piece of cloth over the device if springs are likely to fly in all directions. Mark everything which might be reassembled in the wrong position, scratched symbols may be used on unstressed parts, or a sequence of tiny dots from a centre punch can be useful. Stressed parts should never be scratched or centre-popped as this may lead to cracking under working conditions. Store parts which look alike in the correct order for reassembly. Never rely upon memory to assist in the assembly of complicated mechanisms, especially when they will be dismantled for a long time, but make notes, and drawings to supplement the diagrams in the manual, and put labels on detached wires. Rust stains may indicate unlubricated wear. This can sometimes be seen round the outside edge of a bearing cup in a universal joint. Look for bright rubbing marks on parts which normally should not make heavy contact. These might prove that something is bent or running out of truth. For example, there might be bright marks on one side of a piston, at the top near the ring grooves, and others at the bottom of the skirt on the other side. This could well be the clue to a bent connecting rod. Suspected cracks can be proved by heating the component in a light oil to approximately 100°C, removing, drying off, and dusting with french chalk, if a crack is present the oil retained in the crack will stain the french chalk.

4 In determining wear, and the degree, against the permissible limits set in the manual, accurate measurement can only be achieved by the use of a micrometer. In many cases, the wear is given to the fourth place of decimals; that is in ten-thousandths of an inch. This can be read by the vernier scale on the barrel of a good micrometer. Bore diameters are more difficult to determine. If, however, the matching shaft is accurately measured, the degree of play in the bore can be felt as a guide to its suitability. In other cases, the shank of a twist drill of known diameter is a handy check.

Many methods have been devised for determining the clearance between bearing surfaces. To-day the best and simplest is by the use of Plastigage, obtainable from most garages. A thin plastic thread is laid between the two surfaces and the bearing is tightened, flattening the thread. On removal, the width of the thread is compared with a scale supplied with the thread and the clearance is read off directly. Sometimes joint faces leak persistently, even after gasket renewal. The fault will then be traceable to distortion, dirt or burrs. Studs which are screwed into soft metal frequently raise burrs at the point of entry. A quick cure for this is to chamfer the edge of the hole in the part which fits over the stud.

5 **Always check a replacement part with the original one before it is fitted.**

If parts are not marked, and the order for reassembly is not known, a little detective work will help. Look for marks which are due to wear to see if they can be mated. Joint faces may not be identical due to manufacturing errors, and parts which overlap may be stained, giving a clue to the correct position. Most fixings leave identifying marks especially if they were painted over on assembly. It is then easier to decide whether a nut, for instance, has a plain, a spring, or a shakeproof washer under it. All running surfaces become 'bedded' together after long spells of work and tiny imperfections on one part will be found to have left corresponding marks on the other. This is particularly true of shafts and bearings and even a score on a cylinder wall will show on the piston.

6 Checking end float or rocker clearances by feeler gauge may not always give accurate results because of wear. For instance, the rocker tip which bears on a valve stem may be deeply pitted, in which case the feeler will simply be bridging a depression. Thrust washers may also wear depressions in opposing faces to make accurate measurement difficult. End float is then easier to check by using a dial gauge. It is common practice to adjust end play in bearing assemblies, like front hubs with taper rollers, by doing up the axle nut until the hub becomes stiff to turn and then backing it off a little. Do not use this method with ballbearing hubs as the assembly is often preloaded by tightening the axle nut to its fullest extent. If the splitpin hole will not line up, file the base of the nut a little.

Steering assemblies often wear in the straight-ahead position. If any part is adjusted, make sure that it remains free when moved from lock to lock. Do not be surprised if an assembly like a steering gearbox, which is known to be carefully adjusted outside the car, becomes stiff when it is bolted in place. This will be due to distortion of the case by the pull of the mounting bolts, particularly if the mounting points are not all touching together. This problem may be met in other equipment and is cured by careful attention to the alignment of mounting points.

When a spanner is stamped with a size and A/F it means that the dimension is the width between the jaws and has no connection with ANF, which is the designation for the American National Fine thread. Coarse threads like Whitworth are rarely used on cars to-day except for studs which screw into soft aluminium or cast iron. For this reason it might be found that the top end of a cylinder head stud has a fine thread and the lower end a coarse thread to screw into the cylinder block. If the car has mainly UNF threads then it is likely that any coarse threads will be UNC, which are not the same as Whitworth. Small sizes have the same number of threads in Whitworth and UNC, but in the $\frac{1}{2}$ inch size for example, there are twelve threads to the inch in the former and thirteen in the latter.

7 After a major overhaul, particularly if a great deal of work has been done on the braking, steering and suspension systems, it is advisable to approach the problem of testing with care. If the braking system has been overhauled, apply heavy pressure to the brake pedal and get a second operator to check every possible source of leakage. The brakes may work extremely well, but a leak could cause complete failure after a few miles.

Do not fit the hub caps until every wheel nut has been checked for tightness, and make sure the tyre pressures are correct. Check the levels of coolant, lubricants and hydraulic fluids. Being satisfied that all is well, take the car on the road and test the brakes at once. Check the steering and the action of the handbrake. Do all this at moderate speeds on quiet roads, and make sure there is no other vehicle behind you when you try a rapid stop.

Finally, remember that many parts settle down after a time, so check for tightness of all fixings after the car has been on the road for a hundred miles or so.

8 It is useless to tune an engine which has not reached its normal running temperature. In the same way, the tune of an engine which is stiff after a rebore will be different when the engine is again running free. Remember too, that rocker clearances on pushrod operated valve gear will change when the cylinder head nuts are tightened after an initial period of running with a new head gasket.

Trouble may not always be due to what seems the obvious cause. Ignition, carburation and mechanical condition are interdependent and spitting back through the carburetter, which might be attributed to a weak mixture, can be caused by a sticking inlet valve.

For one final hint on tuning, never adjust more than one thing at a time or it will be impossible to tell which adjustment produced the desired result.

GLOSSARY OF TERMS

Allen key	Cranked wrench of hexagonal section for use with socket head screws.
Alternator	Electrical generator producing alternating current. Rectified to direct current for battery charging.
Ambient temperature	Surrounding atmospheric temperature.
Annulus	Used in engineering to indicate the outer ring gear of an epicyclic gear train.
Armature	The shaft carrying the windings, which rotates in the magnetic field of a generator or starter motor. That part of a solenoid or relay which is activated by the magnetic field.
Axial	In line with, or pertaining to, an axis.
Backlash	Play in meshing gears.
Balance lever	A bar where force applied at the centre is equally divided between connections at the ends.
Banjo axle	Axle casing with large diameter housing for the crownwheel and differential.
Bendix pinion	A self-engaging and self-disengaging drive on a starter motor shaft.
Bevel pinion	A conical shaped gearwheel, designed to mesh with a similar gear with an axis usually at 90 deg. to its own.
bhp	Brake horse power, measured on a dynamometer.
bmep	Brake mean effective pressure. Average pressure on a piston during the working stroke.
Brake cylinder	Cylinder with hydraulically operated piston(s) acting on brake shoes or pad(s).
Brake regulator	Control valve fitted in hydraulic braking system which limits brake pressure to rear brakes during heavy braking to prevent rear wheel locking.
Camber	Angle at which a wheel is tilted from the vertical.
Capacitor	Modern term for an electrical condenser. Part of distributor assembly, connected across contact breaker points, acts as an interference suppressor.
Castellated	Top face of a nut, slotted across the flats, to take a locking splitpin.
Castor	Angle at which the kingpin or swivel pin is tilted when viewed from the side.
cc	Cubic centimetres. Engine capacity is arrived at by multiplying the area of the bore in sq cm by the stroke in cm by the number of cylinders.
Clevis	U-shaped forked connector used with a clevis pin, usually at handbrake connections.
Collet	A type of collar, usually split and located in a groove in a shaft, and held in place by a retainer. The arrangement used to retain the spring(s) on a valve stem in most cases.
Commutator	Rotating segmented current distributor between armature windings and brushes in generator or motor.
Compression	The ratio, or quantitative relation, of the total volume (piston at bottom of stroke) to the unswept volume (piston at top of stroke) in an engine cylinder.
Condenser	See capacitor.
Core plug	Plug for blanking off a manufacturing hole in a casting.
Crownwheel	Large bevel gear in rear axle, driven by a bevel pinion attached to the propeller shaft. Sometimes called a 'ring gear'.
'C'-spanner	Like a 'C' with a handle. For use on screwed collars without flats, but with slots or holes.
Damper	Modern term for shock-absorber, used in vehicle suspension systems to damp out spring oscillations.
Depression	The lowering of atmospheric pressure as in the inlet manifold and carburetter.
Dowel	Close tolerance pin, peg, tube, or bolt, which accurately locates mating parts.
Drag link	Rod connecting steering box drop arm (pitman arm) to nearest front wheel steering arm in certain types of steering systems.
Dry liner	Thinwall tube pressed into cylinder bore
Dry sump	Lubrication system where all oil is scavenged from the sump, and returned to a separate tank.
Dynamo	See Generator.
Electrode	Terminal, part of an electrical component, such as the points or 'Electrodes' of a sparking plug.
Electrolyte	In lead-acid car batteries a solution of sulphuric acid and distilled water.
End float	The axial movement between associated parts, end play.
EP	Extreme pressure. In lubricants, special grades for heavily loaded bearing surfaces, such as gear teeth in a gearbox, or crownwheel and pinion in a rear axle.

Fade Of brakes. Reduced efficiency due to overheating.

Field coils Windings on the polepieces of motors and generators.

Fillets Narrow finishing strips usually applied to interior bodywork.

First motion shaft Input shaft from clutch to gear-box.

Fullflow filter Filters in which all the oil is pumped to the engine. If the element becomes clogged, a bypass valve operates to pass unfiltered oil to the engine.

FWD Front wheel drive.

Gear pump Two meshing gears in a close fitting casing. Oil is carried from the inlet round the outside of both gears in the spaces between the gear teeth and casing to the outlet, the meshing gear teeth prevent oil passing back to the inlet, and the oil is forced through the outlet port.

Generator Modern term for 'Dynamo'. When rotated produces electrical current.

Grommet A ring of protective or sealing material. Can be used to protect pipes or leads passing through bulkheads.

Grubscrew Fully threaded headless screw with screwdriver slot. Used for locking, or alignment purposes.

Gudgeon pin Shaft which connects a piston to its connecting rod. Sometimes called wrist pin', or 'piston pin'.

Halfshaft One of a pair transmitting drive from the differential.

Helical In spiral form. The teeth of helical gears are cut at a spiral angle to the side faces of the gearwheel.

Hot spot Hot area that assists vapourisation of fuel on its way to cylinders. Often provided by close contact between inlet and exhaust manifolds.

HT High Tension. Applied to electrical current produced by the ignition coil for the sparking plugs.

Hydrometer A device for checking specific gravity of liquids. Used to check specific gravity of electrolyte.

Hypoid bevel gears A form of bevel gear used in the rear axle drive gears. The bevel pinion meshes below the centre line of the crownwheel, giving a lower propeller shaft line.

Idler A device for passing on movement. A free running gear between driving and driven gears. A lever transmitting track rod movement to a side rod in steering gear.

Impeller A centrifugal pumping element. Used in water pumps to stimulate flow.

Journals Those parts of a shaft that are in contact with the bearings.

Kingpin The main vertical pin which carries the front wheel spindle, and permits steering movement. May be called 'steering pin' or 'swivel pin'.

Layshaft The shaft which carries the laygear in the gearbox. The laygear is driven by the first motion shaft and drives the third motion shaft according to the gear selected. Sometimes called the 'countershaft' or 'second motion shaft.'

lb ft A measure of twist or torque. A pull of 10 lb at a radius of 1 ft is a torque of 10 lb ft.

lb/sq in Pounds per square inch.

Little-end The small, or piston end of a connecting rod. Sometimes called the 'small-end'.

LT Low Tension. The current output from the battery.

Mandrel Accurately manufactured bar or rod used for test or centring purposes.

Manifold A pipe, duct, or chamber, with several branches.

Needle rollers Bearing rollers with a length many times their diameter.

Oil bath Reservoir which lubricates parts by immersion. In air filters, a separate oil supply for wetting a wire mesh element to hold the dust.

Oil wetted In air filters, a wire mesh element lightly oiled to trap and hold airborne dust.

Overlap Period during which inlet and exhaust valves are open together.

Panhard rod Bar connected between fixed point on chassis and another on axle to control sideways movement.

Pawl Pivoted catch which engages in the teeth of a ratchet to permit movement in one direction only.

Peg spanner Tool with pegs, or pins, to engage in holes or slots in the part to be turned.

Pendant pedals Pedals with levers that are pivoted at the top end.

Phillips screwdriver A cross-point screwdriver for use with the cross-slotted heads of Phillips screws.

Pinion A small gear, usually in relation to another gear.

Piston-type damper Shock absorber in which damping is controlled by a piston working in a closed oil-filled cylinder.

Preloading Preset static pressure on ball or roller bearings not due to working loads.

Radial Radiating from a centre, like the spokes of a wheel.

Radius rod Pivoted arm confining movement of a part to an arc of fixed radius.

Ratchet Toothed wheel or rack which can move in one direction only, movement in the other being prevented by a pawl.

Ring gear A gear tooth ring attached to outer periphery of flywheel. Starter pinion engages with it during starting.

Runout Amount by which rotating part is out of true.

Semi-floating axle Outer end of rear axle halfshaft is carried on bearing inside axle casing. Wheel hub is secured to end of shaft.

Servo A hydraulic or pneumatic system for assisting, or, augmenting a physical effort. See 'Vacuum Servo'.

Setscrew One which is threaded for the full length of the shank.

Shackle A coupling link, used in the form of two parallel pins connected by side plates to secure the end of the master suspension spring and absorb the effects of deflection.

Shell bearing Thinwalled steel shell lined with anti-friction metal. Usually semi-circular and used in pairs for main and big-end bearings.

Shock absorber See 'Damper'.

Silentbloc Rubber bush bonded to inner and outer metal sleeves.

Socket-head screw Screw with hexagonal socket for an Allen key.

Solenoid A coil of wire creating a magnetic field when electric current passes through it. Used with a soft iron core to operate contacts or a mechanical device.

Spur gear A gear with teeth cut axially across the periphery.

Stub axle Short axle fixed at one end only.

Tachometer An instrument for accurate measurement of rotating speed. Usually indicates in revolutions per minute.

TDC Top Dead Centre. The highest point reached by a piston in a cylinder, with the crank and connecting rod in line.

Thermostat Automatic device for regulating temperature. Used in vehicle coolant systems to open a valve which restricts circulation at low temperature.

Third motion shaft Output shaft of gearbox.

Threequarter floating axle Outer end of rear axle halfshaft flanged and bolted to wheel hub, which runs on bearing mounted on outside of axle casing. Vehicle weight is not carried by the axle shaft.

Thrust bearing or washer Used to reduce friction in rotating parts subject to axial loads.

Torque Turning or twisting effort. See 'lb ft'.

Track rod The bar(s) across the vehicle which connect the steering arms and maintain the front wheels in their correct alignment.

UJ Universal joint. A coupling between shafts which permits angular movement.

UNF Unified National Fine screw thread.

Vacuum servo Device used in brake system, using difference between atmospheric pressure and inlet manifold depression to operate a piston which acts to augment brake pressure as required. See 'Servo'.

Venturi A restriction or 'choke' in a tube, as in a carburetter, used to increase velocity to obtain a reduction in pressure.

Vernier A sliding scale for obtaining fractional readings of the graduations of an adjacent scale.

Welch plug A domed thin metal disc which is partially flattened to lock in a recess. Used to plug core holes in castings.

Wet liner Removable cylinder barrel, sealed against coolant leakage, where the coolant is in direct contact with the outer surface.

Wet sump A reservoir attached to the crankcase to hold the lubricating oil.

INDEX

THE AUTOBOOK SERIES OF WORKSHOP MANUALS

Alfa Romeo Giulia 1962 on

Aston Martin 1921-58

Audi 100 1969 on

(Austin, Morris etc.) 1100 Mk. 1 1962-67

(Austin, Morris etc.) 1100 Mk. 2, 1300 Mk. 1, 2, America 1968 on

Austin A30, A35, A40 Farina

Austin A55 Mk. 2, A60 1958-69

Austin A99, A110 1959-68

Austin J4 1960 on

Austin Maxi 1969 on

Austin, Morris 1800 1964 on

BMC 3 (Austin A50, A55 Mk. 1 Morris Oxford 2, 3 1954-59)

Austin Healey 100/6, 3000 1956-68

(Austin Healey, MG) Sprite, Midget 1958 on

BMW 1600 1964 on

BMW 1800 1964-68

BMW 2000, 2002 1966 on

Chrysler Valiant Straight Six 1966-70

Citroen DS 19, ID 19 1955-66

Citroen ID 19, DS 19, 20, 21 1966-70

Datsun 1200 1970 on

Datsun 1300, 1600 1968 on

Datsun 240Z Sport 1970 on

De Dion Bouton 1899-1907

Fiat 124 1966 on

Fiat 124 Sport 1966 on

Fiat 125 1967 on

Fiat 500 1957-69

Fiat 600, 600D 1955-69

Fiat 850 1964 on

Fiat 1100 1957-69

Fiat 1300, 1500 1961-67

Ford Anglia Prefect 100E 1953-62

Ford Anglia 105E, Prefect 107E 1959-67

Ford Capri 1300, 1600 1968 on

Ford Capri 2000 GT, 3000 GT 1969 on

Ford Classic, Capri 1961-64

Ford Consul, Zephyr, Zodiac, 1, 2 1950-62

Ford Corsair Straight Four 1963-65

Ford Corsair V4 1965-68

Ford Corsair V4 1969 on

Ford Cortina 1962-66

Ford Cortina 1967-68

Ford Cortina 1969-70

Ford Cortina Mk. 3 1970 on

Ford Escort 1967 on

Ford Falcon V8 1964-69

Ford Thames 10, 12, 15 cwt 1957-65

Ford Transit 1965-72

Ford Zephyr Zodiac Mk. 3 1962-66

Ford Zephyr V4, V6, Zodiac 1966 on

Hillman Avenger 1970 on

Hillman Hunter 1966 on

Hillman Imp 1963-68

Hillman Imp 1969 on

Hillman Minx 1 to 5 1956-65

Hillman Minx 1965-67

Hillman Minx 1966-70

Hillman Super Minx 1961-65

Holden Straight Six 1948-66

Holden Straight Six 1966 on

Jaguar XK120, 140, 150, Mk. 7, 8, 9 1948-61

Jaguar 2.4, 3.4, 3.8 Mk. 1, 2 1955-69

Jaguar 'E' Type 1961-69

Jaguar 'S' Type 420 1963-68

Jaguar XJ6 1968 on

Jowett Javelin Jupiter 1947-53

Landrover 1, 2 1948-61

Landrover 2, 2a 1959-71

Mercedes-Benz 190b, 190c 200 1959-68

Mercedes-Benz 220 1959-65

Mercedes-Benz 220/8 1968 on

Mercedes-Benz 230 1963-68

Mercedes-Benz 250 1965-67

Mercedes-Benz 250/8 1968 on

Mercedes-Benz 280/8 1968 on

MG TA to TF 1936-55

MGA MGB 1955-68

MG MGB 1969 on

Mini 1959 on

Mini Cooper 1961 on

Morgan 1936-69

Morris Marina 1971 on

Morris Minor 2, 1000 1952-71

Morris Oxford 5, 6 1959-71

NSU 1000 1963 on

NSU Prinz 1 to 4 1957 on

Opel Ascona, Manta 1970 on

Opel G.T. 1900 1968-72

Opel Kadett, Olympia 993cc, 1078cc 1962 on

Opel Kadett, Olympia 1492, 1698, 1897cc 1967 on

Opel Rekord C 1966 on

Peugeot 204 1965-72

Peugeot 404 1960-69

Peugeot 504 1968-70

Porsche 356a, 356b, 356c 1957-65

Porsche 911 1964-69

Porsche 912 1965-69

Reliant Regal 1962-70

Renault R4, R4L, 4 1961 on

Renault 6 1968 on

Renault 8, 10, 1100 1962 on

Renault 12 1969-71

Renault R16 1965 on

Renault Dauphine Floride 1957-67

Renault Caravelle 1962-68

Rover 60 to 110 1953-64

Rover 2000 1963 on

Rover 3 Litre 1958-67

Rover 3500, 3500S 1968 on

Saab 95, 96, Sport 1960-68

Saab 99 1969 on

Saab V4 1966 on

Simca 1000 1961 on

Simca 1100 1967 on

Simca 1300, 1301, 1500, 1501 1963 on

Skoda One (440, 445, 450) 1957-69

Sunbeam Rapier Alpine 1955-65

Toyota Corolla 1100 1967 on

Toyota Corona 1500 Mk. 1 1965-70

Toyota Corona 1900 Mk. 2 1969 on

Triumph TR2, TR3, TR3A 1952-62

Triumph TR4, TR4A 1961-67

Triumph TR5, TR250, TR6 1967 on

Triumph 1300, 1500 1965 on

Triumph 2000 Mk. 1, 2.5 PI Mk. 1 1963-69

Triumph 2000 Mk. 2, 2.5 PI Mk. 2 1969 on

Triumph Herald 1959-68

Triumph Herald 1969-71

Triumph Spitfire Vitesse 1962-68

Triumph Spitfire Mk. 3 1969-70

Triumph GT6, Vitesse 2 Litre 1969 on

Vauxhall Velox, Cresta 1957-69

Vauxhall Victor 1, 2, FB 1957-64

Vauxhall Victor 101 1964-67

Vauxhall Victor FD 1600, 2000 1967 on

Vauxhall Viva HA 1963-66

Vauxhall Viva HB 1966-70

Vauxhall Viva, HC Firenza 1971 on

Vauxhall Victor 3300, Ventura 1968 on

Volkswagen Beetle 1954-67

Volkswagen Beetle 1968 on

Volkswagen 1500 1961-66

Volkswagen 1600 Fastback 1965 on

Volkswagen Transporter 1954-67

Volkswagen Transporter 1968 on

Volvo P120 1961-70

Volvo P140 1966 on

Volvo 1800 1961 on